AMERICAN
SOLDIERS OVERSEAS

Recent Titles in
Perspectives on the Twentieth Century

AMERICAN SOLDIERS OVERSEAS

The Global Military Presence

ANNI P. BAKER

Perspectives on the Twentieth Century

Edward R. Beauchamp, Series Adviser

Westport, Connecticut
London

Library of Congress Cataloging-in-Publication Data

Baker, Anni P.
  American soldiers overseas : the global military presence / Anni P. Baker.
    p. cm.—(Perspectives on the twentieth century, ISSN 1538–9626)
  Includes bibliographical references and index.
  ISBN 0–275–97354–9 (alk. paper)
    1. Military bases, American—Foreign countries. 2. United States—Armed
  Forces—Foreign countries. I. Title. II. Series.
  UA26.A2B35   2004
  306.2'7—dc22   2004050864

British Library Cataloguing in Publication Data is available.

Library of Congress Catalog Card Number: 2004050864
ISBN: 0–275–97354–9
ISSN: 1538–9626

First published in 2004

Praeger Publishers, 88 Post Road West, Westport, CT 06881
An imprint of Greenwood Publishing Group, Inc.
www.praeger.com

Printed in the United States of America

The paper used in this book complies with the
Permanent Paper Standard issued by the National
Information Standards Organization (Z39.48–1984).

10 9 8 7 6 5 4 3 2 1

Contents

★ ★ ★ ★ ★

Series Foreword

Whoever first coined the phrase, "When the siècle hit the fin," described the twentieth century perfectly! The past century was arguably a century of intellectual, physical, and emotional violence unparalleled in world history. As Haynes Johnson of the *Washington Post* has pointed out in his *The Best of Times* (2001), "since the first century, 149 million people have died in major wars; 111 million of those deaths occurred in the twentieth century. War deaths per population soared from 3.2 deaths per 1,000 in the sixteenth century to 44.4 per 1,000 in the twentieth."[1] Giving parameters to the twentieth century, however, is no easy task. Did it begin in 1900 or 1901? Was it, in historian Eric Hobsbawm's words, a "short twentieth century" that did not begin until 1917 and ended in 1991?[2] Or was it more accurately the "long twentieth century," as Giovanni Arrighi argued in *The Long Twentieth Century: Money, Power, and the Origins of Our Times?*[3] Strong cases can be made for all of these constructs and it is each reader's prerogative to come to his or her own conclusion.

Whatever the conclusion, however, there is a short list of people, events, and intellectual currents found in the period between the nineteenth and twenty-first centuries that is, indeed, impressive in scope. There is little doubt that the hopes represented by the Paris Exhibition of 1900 represented the mood of the time—a time of optimism, even utopian expectations, in much of the so-called civilized world (which was the only world that counted in those days). Many saw the fruits of the Industrial Revolution, the application of science and technology to everyday life, as having the potential to greatly enhance life, at least in the West.

In addition to the theme of progress, the power of nationalism in conflicts—not only over territory, but also economic advantage and intellectual dominance—came to characterize the past century. It was truly a century of war, from the "little" wars of the Balkans and colonial conflicts of the early 1900s to the "Great" War of 1914–1918 that resulted in unprecedented conflict during the remainder of the century.

Every century has its "great" as well as "infamous" individuals, most often men, although that too would begin to change as the century drew to a close. Great political figures such as Lenin, Trotsky, Stalin, Hitler, Mussolini, Churchill, the two Roosevelts, de Gaulle, Adenauer, Mahatma Gandhi, Mao Tse-tung, Ho Chi Minh, and others were joined in the last part of the century by tough, competent women like Golda Meir, Indira Gandhi, Margaret Thatcher, and scores of others who took the reins of power for the first time.

A quick listing of some major events of the century includes World War I, the Russian Revolution, the rise of fascism, the Great Depression of the 1930s, the abdication of Edward VIII, Pearl Harbor and World War II, the unleashing of atomic bombs on Hiroshima and Nagasaki, the long Indochina War, the Cold War, the rise of nationalism (with an increase in nation states from about fifty to almost two hundred), the establishment of Israel, the triumph of the free market, an increasingly strident battle between religious fanaticism and secular preferences, and on and on. At the same time that these events occurred, there was a great creative flourishing of mass entertainment (especially television and the Internet), not to mention important literary, dramatic, cinematic, and musical contributions of all kinds.

These elements incorporate some of the subject matter of this new series focusing on "Perspectives on the Twentieth Century," which strives to illuminate the past century. The editor actively seeks out manuscripts that deal with virtually any subject and with any part of our planet, bringing a better understanding of the twentieth century to readers. He is especially interested in subjects on "small" as well as "large" events and trends, including the role of sports in various societies, the impact of popular music on the social fabric, the contribution of film studies to our understanding of the twentieth century, and so on. The success of this series is largely dependent on the creativity and imagination of its authors.

Edward R. Beauchamp

★ ★ ★ ★ ★

Introduction

In the awful days after the attacks in New York and Washington on September 11, 2001, the American public demanded some explanation for the stunning catastrophe. What did "we" do to arouse such anger, people asked. Why do "they" hate us? Political commentators offered a variety of responses, but Americans quickly realized that answers were not easy or obvious. Several years later, in the wake of rising anti-American sentiment across the globe, scholars and pundits continue to debate the issue.

Among the immediate, specific catalysts for the attack, however, was the American military presence in Saudi Arabia, a foreign incursion that many Muslims resented, even hated. Most Americans now know that since the Gulf War of 1991, about 5,000 United States Air Force and Army personnel have been stationed in the desert nation, rotating in and out for three-month tours. The Americans have had no contact with the civilian population and no discernible economic effect on the wealthy nation. Yet their presence has aroused rage, because Saudi Arabia, home to the holy cities of Mecca and Medina, is sacred land to devout Muslims.

That the U.S. military presence in an allied nation inspired violence from a few fanatical opponents may have surprised some people in the West. It shouldn't have. Opposition to the U.S. forces in Saudi Arabia began as soon as troops started mobilizing for the first Gulf War, and protests turned deadly after the end of the conflict. In November 1995 and June 1996, bombs ripped through American military installations in Riyadh and Dharan, killing a total of twenty-six people. And opponents promised more to come; the leader of one anti-American group said that if the Americans remained in the country, they would "pay the price . . . 20, 30, 100, 200, 1,000 dead."

For that matter, violent opposition to U.S. military installations overseas has not been restricted to the Middle East. During the late 1980s, Communist groups resisting the bases in the Philippines killed half a dozen Americans in targeted assassinations. Earlier still, leftist terrorists in West Germany attacked American bases and personnel, successfully detonating bombs at the U.S. Army, Europe (USAREUR) headquarters in Heidelberg in 1972, and in 1985 at the huge Rhine–Main Air Force base near Frankfurt.

The destructive fury of Islamic fundamentalists, Communist nationalists and left-wing terror groups represents only the most extreme reaction to the U.S. armed forces overseas. But American bases and personnel stationed in other nations have always evoked some sort of response from their host societies, whether open-armed welcome, mild curiosity, indifference, or outright hostility.

And there have been many, many host societies. During the six decades since the end of the Second World War, the U.S. forces have created a web of installations all over the world, from Saudi Arabia to Puerto Rico, from Okinawa to Iceland. In virtually all cases, the personnel at overseas installations have interacted with the local population in some way; military–civilian contact is almost everywhere more extensive than has been the case in Saudi Arabia. It is inevitable that a population of foreign military personnel, bringing relative wealth, a tradition of unabashed, even stubborn American pride, and, not least, masses of high-tech weaponry will have an impact on any host society in which it is placed.

The purpose of this study is to examine the social, economic, and political impact of the post–1945 U.S. military presence around the world. As a work of history, it focuses primarily on the Cold War era, a period that ended in 1989 with the fall of the Berlin Wall and the transformation, albeit patchy and incomplete, of the Soviet sphere from communism to democracy. But the "New World Order" that optimists predicted has in fact brought new crises necessitating a continued, even expanded, American military presence around the globe. Therefore, rather than end with the drawdown of U.S. bases in Europe in the early 1990s, we will examine the enduring U.S. military presence overseas, and plans for the future.

To those who spent a period of their lives—a few months, a few years or longer—on a military base in Japan or Germany, the history of the American military presence overseas might be interesting in a personal sense, connecting individual experience with larger events. An examination of the impact of the U.S. forces on their host nations is, however, more than just an antiquarian curiosity. As the United States moves forward as a global power, with all the suspicion and controversy that role entails, past experience can provide important lessons and models.

Before suggesting what might be learned from the past 60 years, a few observations about Cold War–era basing are in order. First of all, the American military presence during those decades was characterized by immensity. Many overseas bases were home to huge numbers of troops, civilians, and family members; 10,000, 20,000, even 30,000 Americans could be found tucked away on the outskirts of a little European or Asian town. Numerically speaking, the majority of installations were tiny—radar and communications stations in Greenland or Norway, for example—but better-known and more significant were the "Little Americas" that sprang up around the world.

The second observation follows from the first: Cold War–era bases were, as it happened, relatively permanent. The period from the early 1960s to the end of the Cold War is sometimes called the "garrison era," and the term is quite apt, implying solidity and permanence. Most bases were established at the end of the Second World War or the early 1950s and remained in place until the early 1990s or later. There are several interesting and important exceptions, where the host nation demanded the withdrawal of U.S. troops: Morocco, Libya, and France during the Cold War, and the Philippines and Panama at the Cold War's end; but generally the bases became part of the local scenery. Political and economic uncertainty plagued the bases over the years, of course, causing difficulties and inconvenience. For example, local employees avoided accepting jobs with the U.S. forces when they suspected the bases might disappear a few years later. In the end, however, most installations stayed, and their relative permanence had long-ranging effects on both the U.S. forces and the host communities.

The third observation is, perhaps, the least intuitive but most important of all. During the Cold War era, most personnel were stationed in affluent, industrialized nations: Europe, mostly West Germany, or in Northeast Asia, primarily Japan and South Korea.[1] Although in the early years Germany and Japan, devastated by military defeat and occupation, could hardly have been considered rich, they soon recovered their former economic strength. South Korea, too, was not initially a wealthy nation, but by the 1980s it had gained a place in the first world. Contrary to common belief, impoverished host nations like Panama and the Philippines were the exceptions, not the rule. Furthermore, most of the nations hosting U.S. installations enjoyed relative political stability and the rule of law. Analysts have argued about whether political and economic stability was the result of the American presence or in spite of it, but the fact that most large Cold War bases were located in relatively stable, wealthy nations is undeniable.

One last factor to keep in mind is that the threat faced by Cold War forces—the Soviet Union (for many years China was assumed to march in lock step with its Communist neighbor)—appears, especially in retrospect, to have been a stable nation unlikely to initiate a suicidal nuclear war with the United States. While the superpowers could and did field huge military forces, collect vast numbers of nuclear weapons, and support a seemingly endless series of proxy wars, neither nation, it is now fairly clear, had any intention of deliberately attacking the other in the absence of a massive provocation. Perhaps the American policy of military containment worked, or perhaps the leaders of the Soviet Union were more interested in maintaining power than promoting world revolution. Maybe stability came from a combination of these and other factors. But the result was a balance of power between two nations with a mutual interest in the status quo. Moreover, the U.S. forces in Europe and Asia understood their mission to be that of defending the freedom not only of the United States but of their host nations. Personnel in West Germany, for example, believed that they were protecting Germans from Soviet attack, and troops in Japan believed they stood between the Japanese and Communist China.

Compare this profile of the "typical" Cold War base—a huge, permanent garrison in an industrialized nation, directed at a stable and predictable threat—with the military installation of the future, according to the most likely scenario. First, the new base will not be a "Little America" but rather a smaller, camp-like "Forward Operating Base" (FOB) or an even more primitive "Forward Operating Location" (FOL), where limited numbers of troops will be deployed for 6 months to a year, without their families. Second, the plan calls for flexible action and short duration, so soldiers will live in tents, not dormitories, and there will be few of the amenities common to Cold War-era bases. While in reality many of the new bases are likely to stay for years or decades, planners do not expect to put down deep roots in the host communities.

Third, future basing sites will be located in some of the poorest, most conflicted areas of the world, areas where economic and political systems are fragile and rudimentary, where culture and social norms are very different from those with which Americans are familiar. And the threat is no longer the lumbering Soviet Union, but a dynamic, vicious global terrorism independent of the control of any state, and based on religious fanaticism which is not, at least at this time, particularly concerned with traditional power politics. U.S. troops deployed to the rough, boot camp-like FOBs or FOLs will not be defending the local population against attack but will be using the installation itself for incursions into hostile areas. The Cold War sense of shared defense has diminished if not entirely disappeared.

The U.S. overseas base of the future, we can safely conclude, seems to have little in common with the garrison town of the past. If we accept the likelihood that future military deployments overseas will probably be very unlike those of the past, what can the Cold War experience teach us, really? If we remain with the four points of comparison used above, some lessons do emerge. First of all, host nation reactions to "Little Americas"—both

positive and negative—suggest that smaller is better. A less prominent profile diminishes inconvenience and resentment, perceptions of national
humiliation, and widespread resistance. On the other hand, smaller bases
are not without drawbacks. Opposition can crystallize around a small
presence as well as a large one, Saudi Arabia being the best example of this
possibility. And a small, shadowy presence does not have the same opportunity to develop a positive public face through constructive participation
in host society traditions and culture, as occurred, for example, in West
Germany in the 1950s.

Second, past history indicates that "temporary" deployments have a
way of becoming permanent, or at least extended in time, and a small,
temporary deployment that outstays its welcome is at least as problematic
as a large one understood by all to be permanent. Host communities will
expect economic benefits from any military presence, while hoping that
negative effects like environmental damage and cultural upheaval will be
minimal. A "temporary" deployment that ushers in no economic growth
but does bring inconvenience and danger will be doubly unpopular. Even
when a military presence is expected to be temporary, measures must be
taken to work with the host community; past experience can help determine the best ways to handle minor problems before they spiral out of
control.

Third, the shift from bases in wealthy industrial areas to impoverished
ones will require careful handling, especially in the struggle against an
adversary motivated largely by cultural and religious impulses, as is the
case with Islamicist terror groups. During the Cold War era, the relative
affluence and stability of most host nations, particularly in Europe, served
to mitigate the pernicious social and cultural effects of the presence of
large numbers of young, unattached men. However, in host nations where
there has been a more noticeable economic imbalance between American
military and host civilian, the negative effects on host societies have been
appalling. This holds true for postwar Germany and Japan, as well as less-
developed areas like the Philippines, Panama, and even South Korea and
Okinawa several decades ago, case studies which are discussed in detail in
the following chapters. Although only a fraction of U.S. military personnel
were stationed in less-developed areas during the Cold War, a disproportionate amount of military–civilian conflict occurred as a result of their
impact on the host societies. Whether poor but conservative communities
in the Middle East and Central Asia will tolerate the brothels, bars, and
cultural blending that characterized less-developed Cold War–era host
communities is not positively known, but we can safely assume that such
developments would be explosive. The military must not slacken its ongoing and increasingly sophisticated efforts to minimize its negative impact
on host societies, especially those which, because of their poverty or traditional culture, are particularly vulnerable.

Finally, the markedly different type of threat faced by the military forces of the future will make the experience of troops deployed overseas quite different from that of the past. The training, drilling, and preparation may be somewhat similar, of course. But off-duty time will not be. Rather than touring historic sites in Japan, drinking wine with German friends, or sunning on a beach in Panama, the soldier of the future will be confined to the base to avoid confrontation with civilians of uncertain loyalty. The troops of the future, on a more intense and permanent war footing, will have less interaction with their hosts, and what interaction takes place will be characterized by caution, even suspicion. Past experience, however, indicates that careful and well-conceived efforts to reach out to the host community can pay off even in the most tense situations. Civil affairs activities should not be dismissed as sideshows, but should be considered as essential to force readiness as having the right equipment or supplies.

It is fair to say, then, that although there will be many differences between Cold War garrisons and the overseas bases of the future, an analysis of America's history as a global military presence will provide valuable guidelines for moving forward, as well as illuminating where we have been. And it is quite a story. The U.S. armed forces had a surprisingly large impact, both positive and negative, on host nation affairs, including but not limited to the making and breaking of presidents and prime ministers, the development of national (and nationalistic) protest movements, the creation, shaping, and distortion of communities, the revitalization of economically depressed areas, environmental damage through maneuvers and training, introduction of the English language and American culture, and even, tragically, the growth of exploitative sex industries.

It is also important to note that circumstances in host communities have affected the military subculture as well. In a few cases, for example, the host community has become much wealthier than its American guests, isolating them in impoverished "ghettos" and dangerously diminishing troop morale and discipline while draining U.S. military budgets. Conversely, when the streets and neighborhoods outside the bases have been allowed to become seedy and rundown, their ugliness depresses civilians and military personnel alike. While a supportive atmosphere from the civilian community can boost morale, in some areas popular hostility toward the military has circumscribed the freedom of personnel to travel safely, even short distances from base. Host community support for the American forces, or lack thereof, has been a significant influence on the quality of life on overseas installations.

This book is not meant to be an exhaustive examination of every American military presence in the world. Many bases are not mentioned here, perhaps unfairly. It is neither an index of the specific military installations in the regions discussed, nor an account of American military strategy. Rather, it focuses on a number of important military communities that illustrate various elements of the overseas military dilemma. Bases in West Germany, Panama, Okinawa, the Philippines, and South Korea receive their own chapters. In addition, the Cold War overseas presence is placed in the context of the larger military history of the United States.

We begin with a brief examination of the armed forces in the United States from the founding of the nation until the Second World War. Although it is often said that the young nation kept its armed forces out of "foreign entanglements" as recommended by George Washington, in fact the U.S. armed forces intervened quite frequently in affairs outside the United States, and the experiences of "overseas" duty—whether in Indian Territory, Panama, or the Philippines—set the stage for further involvement. America's first major military (peacetime) presence in Europe was after the First World War during the Allied occupation of the Rhineland. The army took on this task reluctantly, and withdrew as soon as possible. By the early twentieth century, the United States had emerged as an economic power, but the desire or sense of obligation to "police the world" certainly had not yet become an element of the U.S. worldview.

The second and third chapters detail the next and more lasting "entanglement" in Europe and Asia, resulting from the Second World War and the longer occupation of Germany and Japan. At the war's conclusion, the United States enjoyed a virtual monopoly on effective world power, other nations having been decimated by the conflict. Gradually, as Cold War tensions deepened, American leaders assumed responsibility for defending the non-communist world. In order to "contain" communism, the United States created a system of military bases all over the world, adding extensive housing areas in which military personnel and their families could live almost as if they had never left home.

The fourth chapter explores the challenges the U.S. forces experienced as they settled into their new role. Problems included pressure from political allies and economic competitors, such as the reconstructed Japan and West Germany, as well as political opposition to the U.S. presence from newly independent colonies who wanted nothing to do with the West. Other problems arose as the United States became more deeply involved in the divisive war in Vietnam. The war damaged America's reputation, spawning antiwar protest movements across the world, and tore apart the U.S. military itself as veterans returned with anger, bitterness, and deep cynicism about the military establishment.

The next five chapters analyze the U.S. military presence in individual nations. Chapter 5 picks up the story at the end of the Vietnam era, examining the crisis in the U.S. Army in West Germany and the measures taken to revitalize that institution in the 1980s. The armed services enjoyed much support from the anti-communist Reagan administration in Washington, but at the same time the U.S. Army and Air Force in West Germany endured a large popular protest movement against nuclear missile deployment, much hostility from younger Europeans, and even, as noted previously, sporadic acts of anti-military terrorism. The example of the U.S. forces in Germany demonstrates the importance of maintaining a defense consensus among host nation populations. If the people do not see the need for defense measures, their patience is taxed by any sign of the military presence, whether in the form of maneuvers, missiles, or merely the sight of uniformed personnel.

Chapter 6 looks at Panama and the notorious Canal Zone, where U.S. military personnel and civilians lived in an old-fashioned colonial relationship with the host society. Operating under the jurisdiction of the United States, the Canal Zone gravely offended the national pride of Panama. Intense public pressure finally forced the United States to turn the Canal over to the Panamanians and withdraw its military presence there, a presence that had long been considered essential to America's strategic posture in the Western hemisphere. Panama is one of several cases where vestiges of nineteenth-century-style imperialism have come back to haunt the U.S. forces in their relations with host nations. Renegotiating agreements and treaties to reflect an equal relationship between host and guest and preserve the host's dignity and sovereignty is essential to maintaining an overseas military presence in the long term.

Chapter 7 deals with the history of the U.S. forces in the Philippines, where the unpopularity of President Ferdinand Marcos intermingled with opposition to the U.S. presence. During the 1980s the U.S. forces became more closely identified with the Marcos regime, and the corrupt and power-hungry dictator looked like an American puppet to many opponents. Unrest in the Philippines was exacerbated by a huge and grotesque sex trade catering largely to Americans, which horrified and humiliated the Philippine populace. The history of the U.S. forces in the Philippines provides an excellent example of the lethal combination of a past colonial relationship, gross economic disparity, and ill-considered support for a brutal and unpopular ruler solely because he stood on the side of the United States in the war on communism.

Chapter 8 examines the huge complex of military installations in Okinawa, an island south of Japan, which since 1945 has served, in effect, as an American military reservation. Sporadic protests erupted over the years, but real fury over the U.S. presence exploded in 1995 with the brutal kidnapping and rape of a twelve-year-old girl by three American servicemen. The anger that swept the island did not originate with the rape; rather, the crime was the last straw (albeit a particularly heinous one) for the Okinawans. They raged not only at the Americans, but at their fellow citizens on other islands. For decades they had shouldered most of the burden of the U.S. military presence for all of Japan, but politicians on the mainland, not eager to spread the bases more evenly, had tacitly allowed the Americans free rein on the distant southern island. The case of Okinawa illustrates how an extensive military presence often pits the interests of local host community and larger nation against each other, as the desires of unwilling hosts are sacrificed to larger security interests.

Chapter 9 explores the bases in the Republic of Korea (ROK) and especially the peculiar subculture of "camp followers" around the bases. While areas outside military bases, even in the United States, tend to attract prostitution, one scholar has suggested that in Korea the industry was sanctioned by the Korean government, which wished to keep the U.S. Army in the country as protection from its dangerous neighbor to the north but also wanted to shield the general population from "contamination" by American soldiers. In the early years of the U.S. presence, therefore, the ROK government brought low-status Korean women and girls into the towns around military bases to serve as prostitutes. In recent years, as Korea has become more affluent, women from poorer nations like the Philippines and Russia have been trafficked in to work at the bars and brothels near U.S. bases. For their part, many U.S. soldiers have found the slumlike conditions of the camptowns degrading and dehumanizing, and a yearlong tour in Korea has persuaded many a soldier to leave the military for a civilian career. Meanwhile, relations between the U.S. forces and the Koreans have been steadily disintegrating, and only in the past year have the Americans taken serious steps to improve them. The example of South Korea shows that neglecting relations with host communities and allowing a bad public image to develop and persist can have devastating consequences.

The final chapter of the book examines the future of the U.S. presence overseas in light of current threats. On one hand, a reformed and updated force presence throughout the world, able to respond immediately to events as they happen, would seem to be in the interests of the United States and its allies. On the other hand, however, the plan to step up military activity and establish bases in new host nations is proving to be wildly unpopular in the Islamic world, among America's traditional allies, and even among many in the United States. If transformation is to be successful, planners must take seriously the legitimate concerns of critics and make a convincing case for new force postures.

Do the many mistakes made by the U.S. forces overseas suggest that the entire enterprise has been a mistake? Such a view is probably shortsighted. For all the problems the American forces have created or exacerbated in some areas, in others they have brought benefits as well—social, economic, political. And, although it is beyond the scope of this study, any final judgment on the American forces overseas must also include an assessment of the importance of the military mission. For those who believe the American military presence overseas to be entirely unnecessary, any inconvenience or abuse, however minor, will be viewed as unjustified. To those who believe an American military presence overseas is the only thing keeping the enemy from destroying the free world, the disturbing degradation that sometimes develops alongside a military base may be a small price to pay for safety. To those between these two extremes (the majority of readers, presumably) the equation is complicated and difficult.

Ultimately, the reader must decide whether the wide-ranging effects of the U.S. military overseas have been a fair price to pay—and many millions have paid it—for the protection and security provided by the U.S. armed forces during the Cold War and after. Moreover, the reader must consider whether the lessons of the global American forces presence have been learned, and learned properly, by those who are directing a new phase of this presence.

1

The Development
of the U.S. Armed Forces

INTRODUCTION

From the onset of the European presence in the New World, military force, or the threat of its use, characterized interaction between European and Native societies, as well as among the various European groups themselves. From their arrival in the early sixteenth century, the Spanish and Portuguese used military violence to enslave Native Americans. In the 1750s, British armies fought their ancient enemies, the French, in the New World, while the British navy went to war against pirates and Spanish sea vessels in the waters of the Caribbean. During the American Revolution, rebel armies and British regular forces battled over the political future of the colonies.

However, while the use of military violence was accepted as necessary and normal by almost all inhabitants of the New World (with the significant exception of pacifist groups such as the Quakers), the creation of traditional state-organized military forces in the European settlements met with fierce opposition. When the United States came into existence, these disputes did not evaporate; on the contrary, they grew stronger and more potent. Citizens and political leaders debated several issues: first, should the military forces of the new nation be comprised of citizen armies—militias— or should a professional standing army constitute the main body of the military? How large a military did the new nation really need? And, most importantly, what purpose would the military serve? Would American forces be used to quell domestic disturbances, to police the frontier, to interfere in European affairs? The founders' fundamental reluctance to imitate models of European warfare bestowed on the U.S. military an ambivalence in governmental support, societal status and mission, lasting until the middle of the twentieth century.

An examination of the development of the U.S. armed forces from the Revolution to America's entry into World War II clearly illustrates this dilemma. Though lawmakers and the public cherished the ideal of a citizen militia, the army had become a permanent professional force by the end of the War of 1812, putting to rest the debate over a citizen versus a standing army. However, after every armed conflict, including the First World War, the federal government drastically slashed military manpower and appropriations; the ghost of the citizen army, called up in conflict and quickly disbanded in peacetime, still held sway. Throughout the nineteenth and early twentieth centuries, moreover, the status of soldiers in the army and navy remained low, reflected in the poor career prospects and generally dreadful living conditions endured by enlisted men and their officers.

At the same time, the mission of the armed services changed more dramatically. Throughout U.S. history the military has been regarded as a purely defensive instrument, but in fact both the army and navy played essential roles in expanding the power and the scope of the nation. The army "conquered the West" by forcing Native Americans onto reservations, while the navy intervened numerous times in the affairs of Latin American nations. At the end of the century, the nation became a full-fledged imperialist power with colonies in the Caribbean and the Pacific, subdued and maintained by the U.S. Army, Navy, and Marine Corps. The armed forces did not become a permanent global force until the 1940s, but in spite of traditional suspicion among the American public, they maintained a presence beyond the nation's borders from the early years of the republic.

CITIZENS VERSUS MERCENARIES

The question of volunteer versus standing army was of particular importance to the founders of the United States. The "citizen soldier" appeared to many to be a uniquely American phenomenon—a civilian who would leave his trade or career to fight for his country in time of war, a tradition fertilized by the existence of militias dating from the first years of European colonization. In the colonial period, militias acted as training vehicles, supply networks, and recruiting stations for volunteers,[1] and occasionally fought a battle or two. The tradition of a volunteer army called together only in time of need was held dear by many Americans. One nineteenth-century admirer, General John A. Logan, who served in the Civil War, described the citizen soldier as "a free man, fighting for home, family, country, and the government of which he is a factor. . . . His whole training from childhood . . . has given him a character of independence, of self-reliance, of quick action, and ready command of expedients."[2] Logan viewed the citizen soldier, or volunteer, as superior to the soldier "whose services had either been purchased by some sort of pecuniary recompense, or secured by the iron hand of compulsion"—that is, professional mercenaries or conscripted troops, both of whom filled the ranks of traditional military forces in Europe.

While Logan and others admired the concept of the citizen soldier, many military men, including George Washington, leader of the rebel forces during the Revolutionary War, despised colonial volunteers as amateurish and undisciplined, and distrusted them in times of emergency. During the French and Indian War of 1756–1763, conventional wisdom among British army officers held the militia to be little more than a mob, and likely to run away from real danger.[3]

On the other hand, most of the founders of the nation, including Washington, recognized that the colonists had good reason for their suspicion of professional standing armies.[4] These, as the colonists knew well, served not only a foreign policy function, but also as a monarch's repressive tool against the people. "It is a very improbable supposition, that any people can remain free, with a strong military power in the very heart of their country . . ." wrote Samuel Adams in 1768.[5] Moreover, the professional standing army generated a culture and ethos distinct from that of civilians; history was rife with examples of standing armies abusing and exploiting the populace they were charged to protect, whether at the monarch's behest or not. Finally, many in the colonies opposed the establishment of a strong central government, and a professional military force embodied that undesirable possibility.

When the Revolutionary War broke out, the troops fighting on the American side were organized into two military institutions: the first was the citizen militia, the second the standing ground and naval forces of the Continental Congress. The militia, contrary to expectations, acquitted itself well, at times fighting as regular troops in battle against the British, but more commonly acting as a guerilla force, conducting sabotage or performing other support functions. The Continental army itself resembled nothing so much as the trained British regular army it was fighting against, and performed well in its encounters with the British. The professional naval forces did not enjoy the success of the army—by 1780 the British navy had captured most of the ships and men of the American fleet. The French navy came to the rescue in 1781, thwarting a British attempt to rescue the land forces of General Cornwallis. The two sides signed the Treaty of Paris on September 3, 1783.

Although the new nation appreciated the efforts of the Continental army and navy, it could not afford to maintain a large peacetime force, even had it so desired. On June 2, 1784, the war safely over, Congress virtually disbanded the Continental army. In 1785, the last frigate of the Continental navy was auctioned off for $26,000.[6]

THE U.S. ARMY IN THE NINETEENTH CENTURY

The need for a land-based military force, however, did not disappear with the end of the Revolution. The traditional state-based militias that survived were reformed and upgraded in 1792 with the Uniform Militia Act.[7] They did not suffice to meet the needs of the new nation, however, especially in the Northwest frontier in Ohio, where settlers demanded protection from Indian attacks. George Washington, now president, asked for and received Congressional funds to form the Legion of the United States in 1792 as a professional army to fight Native Americans in Ohio, replacing citizen militias, which had been disastrously ineffective in early battles.[8] The Legion, a standing force of 5,000 men, did in fact have great success on the frontier. Although the Legion was abolished and replaced by a tiny standing army in 1796, it is fair to regard it as the first incarnation of the permanent standing army that exists today.

The fortunes of the small army waxed and waned with changing relations between the United States and revolutionary France. It was expanded in 1812 in response to the onset of war with Britain, a war that originated in a British blockade of American shipping. The army's role was to relieve the blockade by capturing Canada; unfortunately, its effort was, in the words of one military historian, "a demoralizing tale of poor strategy and weak leadership."[9]

In 1815, after the end of the war, the government significantly reformed the army. It received an authorization of 12,000 men, and a centralized command with a General Staff and a General of the Army was created. In subsequent years the numbers of troops decreased, but the centralized nature of the institution did not change. In spite of continued misgivings about the long-term effects of creating a professional standing force, the U.S. Army was firmly planted in American soil.

As the nation expanded, the army became the advance agent in the territorial expansion of the United States.[10] From 1815 until the "closing of the frontier" in 1890, army forts dotted the frontier in a loose barrier running north to south. The army still had to make do with small numbers of officers and men, though, no matter how far the frontier stretched. Authorized numbers remained at around 10,000 officers and men until the Civil War.[11]

In the decades before the Civil War, from 1815 to the mid-1840s, the main task of the army was to enforce the Indian Removal Policy, an unofficial plan that became a formal program in 1830. The idea was to move the Indians to the west of the Mississippi, opening up traditional Indian land to white settlement. The government hoped the tribes would leave voluntarily, or with enticements, but President Andrew Jackson authorized force if they refused to cooperate. The army spent several decades enforcing this policy under difficult conditions. The Seminole Wars lasted for decades, subsiding briefly then flaring again with new attempts by the Indians to resist eviction. At the end of this long, brutal series of battles, the Seminoles and other groups had been forced off their traditional lands and sent West.

The Mexican–American War of 1846–1847 expanded the territory of the United States, for better or worse, to include California, New Mexico, Arizona, Nevada, Utah, and Texas. The war enormously increased the territory for which the army was responsible; by 1857 the army operated 138 posts in the western territories. Nevertheless, Congress authorized fewer than 18,000 troops to staff them.[12]

The Civil War, of course, brought hundreds of thousands of men into the armed services on both sides. Far from being the short, romantic battle many had expected, the war dragged on for four years, involving total mobilization of combatants and civilians. Both North and South relied on recruitment of volunteers to fight the war, and the Regular Army of the Union, an institution distinct from the state-based volunteer units, did not expand significantly during the conflict. The Confederacy established a Regular Army, but it was a negligible factor in the war. Many of the volunteers on both sides had been involved in militias and thus were already partially trained. So many men signed up that the two belligerent governments had difficulty equipping and supplying them.

The history of the Civil War has been told elsewhere, and is beyond the scope of this brief survey. Suffice it to say that at the end of four years of brutal fighting, 620,000 Americans lay dead from battle or disease, while 475,000 were wounded.[13] After the Civil War, the armed forces of the victorious Union side drastically reduced its size, while the volunteer forces of the Confederacy were disbanded. Six months after the end of hostilities, 800,000 of 1 million men in the Union volunteer forces had demobilized.[14] A year later, only 11,000 men remained.[15]

At the end of the war, the army occupied the South in an attempt to prevent the former Confederacy from re-establishing white supremacy and autonomous or independent local government. In 1867 the South was divided into five military districts in which the army exercised martial law powers. These were intended to protect the republican governments that had been set up by the victorious North, but unrepentant white southerners established the Ku Klux Klan, a terrorist organization, or rather, a web of local terrorist groups, to intimidate local governments and newly freed slaves. The only institution capable of taming the KKK was the army, but with its small numbers, it could do little. Civilian authorities in the South, moreover, sympathetic to or even actively involved in the KKK, did much to hinder the attempts of the army to suppress the movement. Unsupported by the federal government, the army lost the mandate to protect changes brought by the Civil War, and black southerners became enmeshed in a sharecropping system hardly different from that which had existed before.

During the last half of the nineteenth century, the army pursued what are often called the "Indian Wars." Even during the Civil War volunteer troops had fought groups of Native American warriors, pushing them farther and farther west. After the end of the conflict, homesteading, discoveries of gold and silver, and the development of transcontinental railroads opened the West to white exploration and settlement. The government abandoned its promise to the Indians that the West would remain their territory and began a new program of forcing the Indians onto reservations, usually on less desirable land that whites did not want. The Indians naturally objected to this plan, and resisted their forcible resettlement; the army, however, carried out the distasteful policy.

The army was, in a way, trapped between the various interest groups of white society and the resistance of the Native Americans. Prospectors and homesteaders called for the extermination of the Indians and pressed the army toward ever more brutal methods. Humanitarians and missionaries wanted not extermination, but "civilization"—conversion to Christianity, education, and acculturation to white ways. Both attitudes were anathema to the Indians, who wished to be left alone. The conflict continued, becoming increasingly ugly. By 1890, the Indians had been almost entirely forced onto reservations, and the army no longer needed the large number of forts that spread across the West. In 1891 about one quarter of the forts of 1889 had been abandoned.[16]

Another role performed by the army in the final quarter of the nineteenth century was that of policing strikes. It was first called in to take on this assignment in 1877, when citizen militias, renamed the National Guard after the Civil War, proved unreliable, at times siding with the strikers, in other instances going overboard in repressing them. Eventually the National Guard became more adept at this task, and by the 1890s put down strikes much more frequently than the Regular Army.

In 1898, with the Spanish–American War, the U.S. Army entered the era of overseas imperialism. While not at its best during the war with the Spanish over Cuba—"within measurable distance of a military disaster," Teddy Roosevelt called the army's performance at Santiago[17]—the army managed, with the invaluable aid of the Cubans and the U.S. Navy, to defeat the Spanish forces, already weakened by several years of Cuban rebellion. The defeat of Spain presented the United States with a protectorate over Cuba and annexation of Puerto Rico. The U.S. also annexed Spain's colonies in the South Pacific—the Philippines, a sprawling island archipelago much influenced by Spanish culture, and the island of Guam.

The acquisition of territories outside continental North America marked a new phase in U.S. expansion.

THE U.S. NAVY IN THE NINETEENTH CENTURY

The creation of the U.S. Navy in 1796, while small and inexpensive by modern standards, generated a great deal of debate throughout the country. The navy enjoyed the support of the Federalists, who viewed it as the kernel of future U.S. power, as well as that of New England shipping concerns and coastal communities in the South dependent on international trade. Political leadership in the interior states, on the other hand, opposed it, claiming that it benefited only coastal businesses, and would lead the nation into war.[18]

The navy did in fact play a role in the wars of the French Revolutionary era, and particularly in the Napoleonic Wars. In 1803 Napoleon declared war on Britain, and both sides began to attack neutral U.S. shipping. After a protracted debate pitting the two sides—coastal shipping interests and settlers in the interior—against each other, the United States fought against Britain in the War of 1812. This conflict ended with the Treaty of Ghent on Christmas Eve 1814 and removed the United States from European affairs until the next century.

From then on, as the economic power of the United States expanded, the navy expanded as well, patrolling the seas of the world in protection of U.S. shipping interests. As early as the first half of the century, navy squadrons monitored the Mediterranean, the Pacific, Brazil and the South Atlantic, East India, the West Indies, and Africa. With the help and protection of the navy, American exports grew from $20 million in 1790 to $334 million in 1860.[19]

The navy participated in the Mexican–American War through its blockade of the Mexican coast and by maintaining shipping lanes for American transit. It achieved a stunningly successful amphibious landing near Veracruz in 1847, in which not a single sailor was killed, largely because there was no Mexican defense of the area.[20] When white settlement reached as far as the coast of California, the navy protected American commerce in the Pacific. Sometimes this "protection" was more aggressive than defensive. In 1854, Commodore Matthew Perry approached Tokyo Bay in Japan and compelled the Japanese to open their nation, until then firmly isolationist, to American commerce. Similar "gunboat diplomacy" forced Korea, known as the "Hermit Kingdom," to accept foreign trade and influence.

During the Civil War the navy was split in two—many of its largest bases in the South, such as Pensacola and Charleston, were taken by the rebels, and others were destroyed by the Unionists rather than allowed to fall into Confederate hands. The U.S. Navy played a vital role in the Civil War, blockading the South and preventing it from selling its cotton and buying war materiel. While Confederate Secretary of the Navy Stephen R. Mallory did manage to create a respectable fleet for the South, the North, with its numerous shipyards and venerable maritime traditions, maintained its supremacy.

After the Civil War, most of the personnel of the Union navy were demobilized, and most Union ships decommissioned. Refusing to turn decisively to steam, the navy continued to insist that its ships be primarily wind-powered. Engines and boilers were small or nonexistent, and captains were discouraged from using steam—if they used too much coal, they were required to pay for it themselves.[21] By 1880, the navy consisted of forty-eight obsolete vessels, the laughingstock of other naval powers.[22]

In 1882 Congress authorized a modest modernization plan, so modest, in fact, that no funds were available for the development of new vessels. A year later, however, Congress released $1.3 million for the construction of four steel ships, three cruisers, and a dispatch vessel[23]—the inception of the modern navy. But its mission remained unchanged from the pre–Civil War era: protecting American trade and keeping shipping lanes open for the private commercial fleets that cruised the globe selling American goods.

During the early 1890s, this somewhat casual attitude changed. Secretary of the Navy Benjamin F. Tracy began to advocate a completely different naval concept: a Great Power navy based on battleships, not light cruisers. Initially, he asked for a total of 100 modern warships. He did not achieve his lofty goal, but during the 1890s Congress did authorize the production of nine battleships.[24] The transformation of the navy was due in large part to the writings of Commander Alfred Thayer Mahan, who published a collection of his lectures on naval theory and strategy entitled *The Influence of Sea Power Upon History, 1660–1783,* in which he argued that the United States could and should become a sea power similar to Great Britain in the eighteenth century. The construction of a powerful fleet would achieve this goal, and Mahan's ideas became the rationale for naval expansion at the end of the century.

The effort seemed to bear fruit when victory in the Spanish–American War, primarily through the efforts of the navy and its amphibious arm, the U.S. Marine Corps, brought the United States new overseas territories. The navy was needed now more than ever to police the seas surrounding the new lands. In addition to Cuba, Puerto Rico, Guam, and the Philippines, all former Spanish colonies, the U.S. annexed Wake Island, Hawaii, and Samoa to serve as naval stations for fleets in the South Pacific. Navalists—those who advocated a "Great Navy"—stressed the importance of the navy in the new American empire. Of course, navy officers advocated expansion not merely because it served American interests, but because it served the interests of the institution that claimed their own allegiance and identity—the U.S. Navy itself.[25]

THE ARMED FORCES AS A SUBCULTURE

Life in the military, whether in the army or navy, officer or enlisted, was always quite distinct from civilian life—a fact bemoaned by those suspicious of a standing military and celebrated by those who dismissed the "softness" of the civilian world. This was true in peacetime as well as war. Most obviously, the exercise of discipline was an unalterable fact of military culture. Samuel Adams noted that "the maxims and rules of the army, [sic] are essentially different from the genius of a free people, and the laws of a free government. Soldiers are used to obey the absolute commands of their superiors . . ."[26] On these grounds, Adams and others argued for a small citizen army rather than a professional one, which, they feared, would bring the values and habits of absolutism and coercion into civilian life. In the end the citizen army did not become the main instrument of military force in the United States; but fortunately, as the tradition of a standing army and navy unfolded in the first years of the new nation's existence, neither officers nor enlisted men became the militaristic martinets Adams had feared. On the contrary, they tended to be decidedly amateur—generally of low quality, poorly trained, and often unfit for any other profession. After 1815, attempts to establish a professional officers' corps created the beginnings of a military subculture among both enlisted and officers. In order to examine the evolution of a distinct military society, officers and enlisted personnel must be discussed separately, as rank distinguished the lives of military personnel from one another almost as much as military service distinguished the soldier from the civilian.

OFFICERS

One of the most important military developments of the nineteenth century was the growth of a professional commissioned officers' corps. The accidental officers of the early Republic could do little more than bend to the whims of Federalists and Republicans vying for power—at times the military enjoyed financial and moral support; at other times it received almost nothing. As educated professionals with a clear and relatively unified set of values, however, officers were better able to articulate the role of the armed forces in American society and politics.

The first step in creating a professional officer's corps was the founding of the Military Academy at West Point in 1802, a measure George Washington had long advocated. For training naval officers, the Naval Academy at Annapolis, Maryland was established in 1845. Both academies contributed to the standardization and training of the officer corps, an increasing necessity in the nineteenth century as technology changed and military skills became more complex.

The existence of the military academies generated controversy in a nation with a deep suspicion of standing armies and hereditary classes. They were indeed designed to create career officers with a national consciousness, rather than state or regional loyalty. Appointments to the academies were assigned in part on the basis of home state; in the early nineteenth century, the majority of army cadets came from the larger and better educated population of the North, but in 1843 Congress legislated that cadets be selected from each state.[27] Informal regional frictions within the academies endured, especially in the years leading up to the Civil War, but overall the cohesiveness of the academies provided an important boost to a nation that had not yet fully gelled.[28] In 1819, military authorities set the minimum age of entrance to West Point at 14, rising to 16 in 1840. Up to two-thirds of cadets left the academies before finishing, sometimes due to academic deficiency, but in most cases because of an inability to adjust to the harsh discipline. All the graduates of West Point earned degrees in engineering, and after 1817 virtually all army officers had graduated from the academy.[29]

With a few notable exceptions, the army officer corps remained the province of white men, although some black officers fought during the Civil War and served in the peacetime army. During the war, almost 100 black officers served with temporary commissions, but during the second half of the nineteenth century, only eight black officers received commissions after completing their training and education at West Point. The first black cadet entered in 1870 but ran afoul of the command when he tried to counter the racism of the corps. He was dismissed after failing a class in 1874.[30] The lives of black cadets and officers were socially isolated, filled with subtle and not so subtle snubs and affronts, constant reminders that race was a more important factor than any merit gained by hard work, brilliance, or character. After Charles Young graduated from West Point in 1889, no other black cadet graduated until 1936. The Naval Academy did not even admit black candidates until 1945.[31]

Even after the harsh discipline of the service academy, life for military officers was not easy. Assignments to isolated posts or on ships could be lonely and boring, and among the most common diversions for officers were drinking and dueling. Dueling was so frequent in the navy that two-thirds as many naval officers died in duels as were killed in battle between 1798 and the outbreak of the Civil War.[32] After naval hero Stephen Decatur was killed in a duel in 1820, higher ranking officers no longer dueled, but entry-level officers, known as midshipmen, continued the practice. Only in 1857 did the navy begin to punish dueling by dismissal.[33] Likewise, dueling became common in the army, although the Articles of War of 1806 and the General Orders of 1814 outlawed it.[34] Because the American navy was patterned after the Royal Navy, its officer culture was particularly aristocratic and it took many customs and attitudes from that ancient British institution. On ship, the captain of a vessel was an absolute monarch, accustomed to being obeyed in every order.[35] Army officers, while possessing considerable authority over their men, never exercised the degree of control of the naval officer.

Army officers usually served at distant posts, away from the comforts of civilization, exposed to danger and, too often, roasting or freezing in harsh climates. Before the Civil War, for example, many officers served in the endless battles against the Seminoles in Florida, where about 14 percent of Regular Army personnel died of disease.[36] After the Mexican–American War, officers were even more likely to be stationed at small, isolated posts. In most cases, garrisons comprised less than 100 people, soldiers and family members included.

The most imperative task on frontier posts was to keep white settlers and Indians apart. Most officers viewed the settlers as the biggest problem on the frontier because they demanded to be allowed to exploit the Indians as they saw fit, and frequently sued officers in court when they were prevented from doing so. When an officer found himself in court, moreover, he faced judges and juries made up of settlers, who were distinctly unsympathetic to his point of view.[37] In fact, some officers sympathized with the Indians rather than the settlers, because the settlers were usually the instigators of problems and the bane of existence to Indian and army officer alike.

After the Civil War, the settling of the frontier proceeded apace, and by the late 1880s was all but finished. This led to one of the greatest transformations in army life thus far, as the traditional role of the army officer as policeman of the frontier faded into the past. Military officers began to enjoy higher social status, and their fixed pay became more attractive in the long deflationary years after 1873.[38]

Through almost the entire nineteenth century, one of the biggest problems among military officers was the lack of promotion opportunities. In an estimate presented to the Secretary of War in 1836, a graduate of that year's West Point class, for example, would spend eight years as a second lieutenant, ten years as a first lieutenant, and twenty years as a captain. He would not reach colonel until his fifty-eighth year of service.[39] Similar statistics applied to the navy. Officers were promoted within their units rather than taking positions throughout the service. Too often, the only way to advance in rank was to fill the shoes of a colleague who had died, usually from some disease or old age. The system encouraged men to stay in their regiments for life, developing a regimental identity and loyalty typical of European armies. To make matters worse, there was no retirement plan for officers. Many men stayed in service long past the age when they could perform their duties, simply because they could not afford to retire. Because of this, many talented officers resigned their commissions after only a few years of service, especially when they could expect more success in civilian life. Qualified engineers in civilian employ, for example, could earn several times the pay of an army officer.

The Civil War temporarily changed this pattern of stagnation, enabling many officers to rise dramatically through the ranks to reach colonel or even general within a few years. But in the long run, the war exacerbated the slow pace of promotion. Many Civil War veterans continued on in service for decades, having drawn from the war such a vital part of their identities and values. In 1895, for example, an astounding 271 captains and lieutenants were Civil War veterans, and nine generals from the Civil War remained on active duty.[40]

In 1882 Congress finally established a retirement system, with mandatory retirement at 64 and optional retirement after forty years of service. Still, in 1885 one-third of the officers in the army were between 41 and 50 years old—another twenty years would pass before this large Civil War cohort would progress through the system.[41] Even so, it was a sign of improvement that by the 1870s over three-fourths of the graduates of West Point made the army their careers.[42]

While the army officers of the nineteenth century shivered the years away in windy outposts on the northern plains or contended with the oppressive heat of the deserts of the southwest, naval officers could choose from a wider variety of assignments, including many that were safe and enjoyable. During the decades before the outbreak of the Civil War, for example, the Mediterranean Squadron's role involved stops at the port cities of Southern Europe and North Africa, and officers assigned to that unit generally fit in plenty of sightseeing and glittering social life.[43] But not all assignments were easy and safe. In the first decades of the nineteenth century, the navy ferreted out pirates, first along the Barbary Coast of North Africa, and then in the Caribbean. This was dangerous work, not least because yellow fever decimated crews and officers. Another role of the navy was to protect commerce along the coast of South America and in Asia, particularly China. A third assignment, one that, shamefully, American vessels conducted with little enthusiasm or competence, was to patrol the African coast on the lookout for slavers. The British also attempted to stamp out the slave trade, and in 1842 the British and Americans signed a treaty pledging to put their efforts to this worthy cause. But the Americans lagged far behind; between 1845 and 1850, for example, the British freed about 27,000 Africans, while the Americans had liberated only about 1,000.[44] Most officers did in fact wish to eliminate the slave trade, but they commanded neither the funding nor the support of American courts, which, when cases came to trial, often set accused slavers free without punishment.

ENLISTED MEN

If the life of the nineteenth-century military officer could be difficult, the life of the enlisted man must be described as barbaric. Military life for the common soldier or sailor was harsh, monotonous, and physically arduous. Most enlisted men came from the lowest-ranking groups in society, especially immigrants and laborers. Thus, they were regarded with scorn and suspicion by the middle-class civilian public. Moreover, the very act of joining the armed services condemned a man in the eyes of his peers, given the strong aversion to the military typical of Americans of all classes.[45] One naval officer described his crew as "persons who are disqualified by their vices from employment on shore—thieves, gamblers, drunkards, play actors, circus riders. Many of them escaped civil punishment by enlisting."[46] Enlisted men were thought by many civilians to be either desperate, unable to obtain or hold a job, or the kind of refuse who could not fit in to civilian life and would tolerate the draconian discipline and harsh conditions of the military.

It is not surprising, then, that the army and navy alike always had trouble recruiting enough enlisted personnel. To meet military standards, recruits had to be white, male, meet height and weight requirements, and speak English—although this last was usually ignored. Regiments themselves carried out recruiting, as did a General Recruiting Service established in 1825.[47] The largest percentage of recruits came from the North, where large numbers of lower-class whites and immigrants lived and worked. In the South, where African American slaves performed most of the manual labor, there were fewer white working-class men, so relatively small numbers of recruits hailed from below the Mason-Dixon line.[48] The pre–Civil War military ranks were filled with German and Irish immigrants from the northern cities; in the army, foreign-born soldiers constituted up to two-thirds of enlisted men before the Civil War, and about half the sailors in the navy had been born outside the United States.[49] Many of these men did not know English, but they learned the necessary vocabulary quickly enough, or they suffered for it.

Officers enforced discipline strictly. While the army had abolished corporal punishment in 1812, it continued to be used frequently in the navy. Flogging or lashing with a cat-of-nine tails—a whip of nine cords, each with a lead pellet or knot at the end—was authorized and common. Regulations specifically prohibited flogging with a wire whip or a cat-of-nine tails that had been soaked in salt water,[50] but for minor offenses sailors received whippings by a thick rope called a colt.[51]

The treatment of sailors became so intolerable that during the decades before the Civil War progressive elements of the civilian public took an active interest in reform. Humanitarian organizations like the American Seamen's Friend Society, dedicated to improving living conditions in the navy, flourished alongside abolitionist groups.[52] The campaign to outlaw flogging in the navy gained steam in the 1840s, with public opinion decidedly in favor of ending the practice. Older officers worried that discipline would erode and argued that the men preferred it because only troublemakers suffered the lash,[53] but Congress finally authorized a ban in 1850.

Even when sailors had been freed from the threat of corporal punishment, their lives were not easy. Food rations carried along on voyages remained a perennial nightmare. Charles Nordhoff, a journalist, described the provisions during his navy service: "I have seen drinking water pumped out of our tanks, into a butt on deck, which smelt so abominably as to make any approach to it utterly impossible, ere it had stood in the open air an hour or two and I have seen a biscuit literally crawl off the mess cloth . . ."[54] Diseases of malnutrition had been endemic to naval forces for centuries; "Limey," the nickname for British sailors, came from the limes the sailors ate to ward off scurvy, or lack of Vitamin C, which rotted teeth and caused bleeding and joint pain.

Army soldiers enjoyed somewhat better food, but at a high cost. Generally, on the isolated posts of the army, men had to grow much of their own provisions and raise their own livestock, chores that consumed most of the men's time. In times of relative peace, enlisted men in the army performed a great deal of manual labor—building forts, growing crops, caring for livestock, cutting wood for fuel, maintaining roads, and other projects. It was hard, boring work, the very labor that they had often joined the army to escape, and desertion was a common response. In 1830, for example, approximately 20 percent of enlisted men deserted before their time of service was finished.[55]

Sailors could not desert as easily as soldiers because they were confined to cramped, uncomfortable ships, but their desire to escape was often just as great, and desertion was a common problem when ships put into port. To make matters worse, during most of the naval conflicts of the nineteenth century, ships enforced blockades rather than engaged in active combat. Blockading was tedious and uncomfortable, and hurt recruitment; in the Mexican–American War, while the army signed up more than its share of adventure-seeking volunteers, the navy struggled to reach authorized manpower.[56] Waiting out endless blockades, sailors sweltered under the hot sun in summer, drinking fetid water and subsisting on rancid rations, and huddled in unheated quarters belowdecks in winter.

Aside from actually deserting, the main method of escape for the enlisted man was through alcoholic drink, and intoxication was such a problem among the military—among officers as well as enlisted personnel—that the temperance movement of the late nineteenth century evolved in large part as a reaction against it. Neither soldiers nor sailors found much difficulty in procuring liquor, no matter what rules officers might lay down. In fact, alcohol received official sanction with the notorious grog ration.

Many reformers blamed the daily grog ration—cups of whiskey mixed with water—for encouraging a bestial atmosphere among the men. The army abolished the grog ration in 1830, but the navy doled out two cups of grog each day to its sailors until the Civil War.[57]

WOMEN AND FAMILIES

Women had an important place in the successful function of the military, especially the army. Whether as wives or mistresses, domestic workers, nurses, or more usually in some combination of tasks, women performed much essential work for the men on active duty. Until the end of the nineteenth century, however, the armed forces did not make any official provision for wives of soldiers or officers. Those who accompanied their husbands from post to post did so at their own cost, and, while officers' wives could make do in officers' quarters, most enlisted wives lived outside the posts.

As in civilian society, deep class and racial distinctions in the ranks divided women associated with the military. Whatever their status, their lives involved hardship and many challenges, but it would be an error to view them as victims of exploitation or oppression. Especially on army posts in the West, women were too rare to be taken for granted, and they were highly valued by the men among whom they lived.

Officers' wives were usually, but not always, white middle-class "ladies" and were the center of social life on frontier posts. Officers treated them with the chivalry typical of the Victorian period, exaggerated by the knowledge that the women could have chosen easier lives in the civilian world. Many a young woman fell in love with a uniform at a West Point ball, only to be whisked off to the frontier only days after the wedding, expected to keep house in a tent or a dugout cut into the banks of a stream. Officers' wives were often the products of a military upbringing themselves; multigenerational traditions of service developed in military families among both men and women. But other women had had no contact with the military before they married into the institution. In any case, they were expected to make the best of any situation, and most officers' wives learned to identify with the armed forces as closely as their husbands did.

Enlisted wives were viewed as belonging to an entirely different social class, and when, in letters or journals, officers' wives counted the number of women at a post or camp, they usually ignored the wives of soldiers. The army, however, authorized a limited number of women, usually spouses of enlisted men, to work as laundresses for the regiments, for which they received rations and pay. Enlisted wives also worked as domestic servants for officers' families (as did enlisted men), and many enterprising enlisted wives on isolated posts operated lucrative small businesses—cooking or baking, tailoring, or midwifery. Enlisted wives often came to the military from the east, employed as nurses or maids of officers' families. When they arrived at a post with their employers, they were immediately deluged by offers of marriage from soldiers and noncommissioned officers, and few remained in their jobs for long. The exceptions to this rule were African American women; race barriers prevented them from marrying enlisted men, except men from the all-black 9th and 10th Cavalry or 24th and 25th Infantry units.

Unmarried men and those unaccompanied by their wives often took mistresses or common-law wives. Many, if not most, of these women were nonwhite; white women, even those known to be professional prostitutes, could easily find relative financial security with a soldier husband. On the frontier, Indian and Mexican women provided sexual and other services to enlisted men and officers, and later, in Southeast Asia, Filipina women took similar roles. It is difficult to know the extent of the practice. General George Custer, whose exaggerated romantic attachment to his wife Libby is well documented, was rumored to have had a beautiful Cheyenne mistress named Mo-nah-se-tah; it is probable that other officers without wives had mistresses as well. Among enlisted personnel, the existence of mistresses was acknowledged even by officers' wives. One famous case, that of Mrs. Nash, was told by officers' wives in letters and memoirs. Mrs. Nash, a talented and energetic Mexican woman, was never actually married to the several soldier "husbands" she lived with, but she was known as a skilled midwife and healer to the families she worked for. It was not until Mrs. Nash passed away that it was discovered that she was a man. One of her "husbands" confessed that he knew of the deception, but Mrs. Nash's housekeeping skills were such that he did not mind. Her final "husband," however, humiliated by the episode, committed suicide.

In any case, commanders did not attempt to regulate or stamp out these relations, only interfering when a woman caused trouble on the post or was discovered to suffer from venereal disease. At that point, she would be expelled from the camp and forbidden entrance. Expulsion could have serious repercussions; when Mattie Merritt, a black servant, was accused of theft and expelled from Fort Cummings, New Mexico, the black soldiers stationed at the fort became so angry they threatened the white officers responsible with violence. The incident reveals not only simmering racial tensions in the segregated forces, but also the centrality of the presence of women for both officers and enlisted men.

THE U.S. FORCES AT THE BEGINNING
OF THE TWENTIETH CENTURY

By the eve of World War I, the U.S. forces had changed significantly from the days when the founders of the nation debated whether to establish a standing army or to rely on citizen volunteers in time of need.

The Spanish–American War in 1898 made the U.S. Navy the most important branch of the armed services because it connected the new American
empire, patrolling the seas of the world, protecting U.S. commerce, and
sometimes opening new markets like Japan, Korea, and China.

The navy also protected the territorial integrity of the United States with
its fleet of battleships. Because of its fortunate geographic location, the
United States did not have much to worry about from land invasions, but
naval threats from Japan, Germany, and Great Britain grew more worri-
some at the beginning of the twentieth century. More importantly, the
United States viewed itself as the primary power in the western hemisphere,
and therefore any significant penetration of the region by a European or
Asian power was considered a threat. Thus, the navy grew from an
authorized strength of 16,000 men in 1899 to 60,000 in 1916, with an
increase in combat vessels from thirty-six to seventy-seven during the same
period.[58] The navy also joined the Anglo–German arms race, with fourteen
Dreadnought battleships by 1914.

Unlike the navy, growing in importance, the army at the turn of the century still suffered from post-frontier malaise. It lacked a clear, focused mission after its use as a land constabulary in the West ended. In spite of this
official lacuna, the army busied itself in the years after the destruction of
the Spanish empire, intervening or threatening to intervene in Cuba,
Panama, Nicaragua, Mexico, and the Philippines. These interventions suggested that a modernized standing army would become an important factor in U.S. foreign policy, but they also distracted attention from the
wholesale reform the army desperately needed. Secretary of War Elihu
Root (1899–1904) began this process with significant changes during his
tenure, including the creation of a Prussian-style General Staff and the
beginnings of a reformed militia.[59] Technology also advanced at a rapid
pace, and the army adopted the use of airplanes, automobiles, telegraphs
and telephones, and machine guns, among other innovations.

But during the first decade of the twentieth century, the fundamental
principle of the U.S. forces remained as it had been for a century—to avoid
involvement with European military conflicts and to protect American
interests, whether those included commercial shipping, colonial holdings,
neighboring nations, or the borders of the United States. For most of these
tasks, the navy seemed to be better suited than the land-based army.

WORLD WAR I

When World War I began in 1914, most Americans saw little wisdom in
being drawn into a conflict that seemed to have nothing to do with the
United States. The nation did not view itself as part of the European world,
and it watched European politics with distaste and incomprehension. But
the German navy's use of submarine warfare put American shipping and

American lives in danger. The sinking of the Lusitania in 1915 brought America to the brink of war; at the last minute, though, President Woodrow Wilson resisted, declaring that "there is such a thing as a man too proud to fight." The Germans, too, backed away from war with the United States and agreed in April 1916 to halt attacks on neutral shipping. Wilson was re-elected in 1916 with the slogan, "He kept us out of war."

Barely two months after his victory, however, Wilson faced one of the biggest challenges of his political career. In January 1917, the Germans resurrected their strategy of submarine warfare, this time "unrestricted." All ships, combatant or neutral, sailing in the waters around Europe were considered targets. More American ships came under attack, and in March Wilson declared war on Germany.

In retrospect, historians may judge the American entrance into the conflict to be the death knell for Germany's war effort, but at the time it did not appear particularly threatening. The U.S. Army, which would make the greatest American contribution to the war effort, was simply unprepared for a war of the type being fought on the fields of northern France. Units of the Regular Army were scattered in small overseas bases in the Philippines, China, Puerto Rico, Alaska, and the Panama Canal Zone, and military strategy concentrated on policing the American empire rather than commanding millions of men, using the most advanced weaponry, in trench warfare.

American involvement in World War I proved to be an important step on the way to the development of the modern global U.S. military that is the subject of this study. It was the first time that the nation became involved in what appeared to be another traditional conflict in Europe, with no direct threat to American soil. As noted above, however, American economic and political interests now spread far beyond the geographically contiguous borders of the continental United States, and the nation could no longer pretend to be a bystander in world affairs. American involvement in the war exposed huge numbers of citizen soldiers to the rigors and benefits—and there were benefits for those who made it out alive—of military service overseas, and conversely, introduced the European populace to the "Doughboy." Large American military populations brought in their wake tensions and misunderstandings, as well as friendship and advantages for both sides, that have influenced politics and societies throughout the world. The sight of American soldiers strolling down streets in overseas garrison towns has become commonplace, but it was a portentious novelty in 1917.

The government instituted a draft in May 1917, and soon thousands of American men were entering the pipeline that would take them to the killing fields of Europe. A total of 24 million men registered for the draft, of which 4.8 million served (many of them voluntary enlistees). The draftees came from all walks of life, some recent European immigrants, others unable to find Europe on a map. Draftees spoke fifty-one different languages[60] and were armed with only their enthusiasm and their confidence in the superiority of the United States.

Their first stop involved a brief period of basic training in stateside camps. Given the large numbers of soldiers involved, the war effort entailed changes in the customary camp regime. New training centers were established across the country, many in the Northeast. Although the centers did their best, training was cursory and equipment was inadequate, to say the least, especially in the early months when the camps themselves had not been completed.

A new type of military brought changes in the role and position of the soldier in civilian society, both at home and abroad. The soldiers going off to fight in Europe did not appear to be the dregs of society that professional soldiers often had seemed, but rather brave and innocent hometown boys who needed to be protected from vice, one of the notorious accompaniments of traditional military service in the eyes of the civilian public. The army made efforts to shield the new citizen soldiers from the dangers of gambling, drinking, and sex—training bases in the United States were chosen for a number of reasons, but one important qualification was that the surrounding community be relatively free of such temptations.[61] Inevitably, of course, the presence of hordes of recruits attracted camp followers, and the men, freed from the mores and restrictions of home, took the opportunity to experiment. The Commission on Training Camp Activities (CTCA) did what it could, closing down brothels, rounding up suspected prostitutes, and going after store owners who sold alcohol to soldiers, an illegal commercial activity.[62] It wasn't easy. The classic school bus song "100 Bottles of Beer on the Wall" dates from this era, attesting to the preoccupations of soldiers. However, although the soldiers did their best to flout prohibitions, army efforts to protect the soldiers from vice paid off such that the VD rate remained very low for soldiers stationed in the United States.[63]

The doughboys arriving in France were at best half-prepared to fight in a modern war, and surely not at all prepared for the horrors they would witness. General John J. Pershing, commander of the AEF, knew this and insisted that the soldiers receive several months of hard training before they were sent to the trenches. Practice and drill took place in the rural area of Lourrain, near Gondrecourt. The training period in France proved to be an eye-opening experience for the doughboys and local French peasants. Even the most personal habits came under scrutiny. The Americans, most of whom had never been far from home, cringed at the French habit of bathing only once a week or so, while the French scoffed at the American need to scrub down after a day's work. The Americans introduced teeth-brushing to the French, as well as gum-chewing, a habit later generations of Americans would make famous throughout the world.

Interaction between soldiers and civilians brought major divergences of opinion between American and French military leaders. One of these was on the question of sexual contact and VD. Divergent hygiene standards among soldiers and French peasants did not discourage soldiers from pursuing French women, and naive soldiers were amazed at the relatively free ways of the French. The U.S. Army tried to control this contact in order to prevent VD. Pershing and other commanders in the States considered venereal disease to be more than an irritating health problem among soldiers. They viewed VD as a serious moral and public health threat, assigning much more importance to the problem than did military forces in Europe or elsewhere. American mothers, they suggested, did not want to send their sons to war just to have them return home with "social diseases." But attitudes in France were quite different. Prostitution was legal and an accepted element of the social fabric, and partly as a result, the VD rate among American soldiers rose precipitously. For Pershing, reducing the disease rates became a priority, but the French suggestion to set up brothels for the use of American soldiers was hastily rejected. The army tried to stem the increase of infection by withholding a portion of each soldier's pay, then declaring the brothels off-limits and posting military police to enforce the rule. French authorities objected to the stringency of American rules, insisting that they put "decent" French women and girls at risk of assault by desperate soldiers, particularly African Americans. The army refused the French request to import black prostitutes and continued the battle against VD, insisting to the skeptical French that it was a matter of hygiene rather than morals. The effort, while far from perfect, worked well enough that by September 1918 there was only one case per thousand.[64]

Black soldiers played an important and often underestimated role in the American war effort. Most worked in supply and transportation, the stevedores wearing old blue uniforms from the 1860s. Four black infantry units—the 369th, 370th, 371st, 371st—served in Europe, but white congressmen from the South objected to their fighting alongside white soldiers, so they were transferred to French command. The French, who had been fighting and dying in the trenches alongside colonial troops from Senegal, Morocco, and Vietnam, accepted them gladly.[65] About 367,710 black soldiers served in the army; the navy, a more traditionally white branch of service, counted only 5,328. About 90 percent of black servicemembers were conscripted.[66] Native American soldiers also played an important role in the war effort, mostly in infantry units. They earned a reputation as fierce warriors, partly a result of longstanding stereotypes, partly based on their documented record of bravery in combat. The Germans held to these stereotypes as much as any group, and German authorities suppressed any news that German forces faced Native American troops for reasons of morale.[67]

After the Armistice of 1918, Wilson argued for the creation of a League of Nations; he believed that greater U.S. involvement with the rest of the world would prevent future wars. As it turned out, Wilson was ahead of his time in many ways. Opinion in the United States ran against Wilson's tendency toward engagement and in favor of renewed isolationism, the policy that had governed American relations with Europe for more than 100 years. No one argued that the United States should take responsibility for maintaining world peace. The demobilization of veterans proceeded apace: By June 1919, only eight months after the end of the war, 2.6 million enlisted men and 128,000 officers had returned to civilian life.[68] By 1927 the strength of the Regular Army stood at 118,750.[69]

However, the U.S. Army did not abandon Europe completely, at least not right away. Instead, it shouldered a new burden when it joined the armed forces of France and Great Britain to take part in the military occupation of the Rhineland.

The U.S. Third Army, a unit created on November 7, 1918, initially took over occupation duties in the Rhineland. Its mission involved "following the retreating German troops and enforcing the terms of the armistice," and it included a troop strength of 200,000.[70] In General Order No. 218 (G.O. 218), the headquarters of the American Expeditionary Forces explained the Third Army's purpose: "You have come not as despoilers or oppressors, but simply as the instruments of a strong, free government whose purposes towards the people of Germany are beneficent. During our occupation the civil population is under the special safeguard of the faith and honor of the American army."[71] After the Third Army was deactivated in June 1919, the remaining small garrison of American forces—fewer than 10,000 men—stayed on until February 1923 as the American Forces in Germany (AFG).[72] General Henry Allen commanded the AFG in a semi-circle zone around its headquarters in the medieval Rhine city of Koblenz.

The American occupation of the Rhineland can be judged successful in some important ways. U.S. troops gained the trust of many German citizens, who perceived them as kinder and more generous than the other allies. Secondly, the American forces worked together with their allies for an extended period of time—much longer than they had cooperated over the war effort itself. And finally, many American soldiers formed close ties with Germany and German families—by 1920, one-tenth of the American command had married German women.[73] After a visit to review the AFG in 1921, one congressman asserted that "service in Europe tends to broaden the men, teaches them new languages, and manners, and provides them with work and amusement that will be of great value in the later years of their lives."[74] This rosy picture may have been an exaggeration, but there was a kernel of truth in it.

Taken as a whole, however, the occupation of the Rhineland was a failure. Most obviously, it did not achieve its stated aim of maintaining a demilitarized buffer zone between Germany and France, and in fact the Allied occupation continued to serve as a major rallying-point for German nationalists of all stripes, including Adolf Hitler. The occupation also brought sharp focus on the divergent, even opposing attitudes of Americans and their European allies. The Americans, not having fought the war as long, and not having been subjected to the high level of dehumanizing war propaganda that existed in other nations, thought rather well of their former foes. The French, on the other hand, viewed the Germans as unregenerate militarists, and remained pessimistic for the future, while the British were distracted by other troubles in their sprawling empire. As one historian puts it, "French anxiety, British disinterest, American naiveté, German fear and hope" combined to make the occupation a difficult and disillusioning one for the American forces.[75]

It started out with promise. The introduction to a report by Colonel I. L. Hunt, summarizing the successes and failures of the Third Army's tenure, illustrates well the worthy intentions of the American occupiers: ". . . a quarter of a million men of a new race from overseas began their march down the valley of the Moselle to the Rhine. . . . For a century and a half the men of this new race had been shaping in the new world an idea based upon the immutable principle that all men are created equal and are endowed by their Creator with certain inalienable rights, among which are life, liberty and the pursuit of happiness."[76] The Hunt report is an essential document for students of the history of the U.S. forces overseas. Hunt wisely recommended that in any future military occupation, the U.S. forces learn from the mistakes made in the Rhineland and take a more sensitive and respectful attitude toward the occupied people. Some scholars have suggested that the failures and difficulties of the military occupation after World War II could have been prevented or minimized if military planners had followed Hunt's advice more closely than they did. But, as will become clear, many of the mistakes of the first occupation, if indeed they can be classified as such, were repeated in the second.

One of Hunt's objects of criticism was the "anti-fraternization order." According to this Third Army directive, personnel should "limit their personal relations [with Germans] to an attitude of "courteous tolerance."[77] The order, while intended to maintain discipline, drew resentment from the Germans who saw it as a sign that the Americans viewed themselves as superior. The first anti-fraternization order lasted only nine months and was a dismal failure, due in large part to the necessities of troop billeting. While officers lived in private rooms, enlisted men were sent to reside with German families in homes where there was usually only one heated room—the kitchen. The family, and, of necessity, the soldiers, would sit in the kitchen after supper in order to keep warm, and a family-like intimacy was impossible to avoid. Hunt condemned the pointless anti-fraternization rule, noting that ". . . by preventing open association with the civil population, it precluded [U.S. soldiers'] acquirement of the broadening influences which usually are obtained from residence in a foreign land . . ." But, he added philosophically, "the Government took the viewpoint that the forces had been sent into Germany to insure the fruits of a hard-earned victory, not for their personal pleasure or profit."[78]

Hunt took issue with other laws, which, he said, were almost designed to be broken frequently. In particular, he noted three types of regulations that absorbed most of the time and energy of occupation law enforcement: travel pass laws, sanitation and hygiene laws, and alcohol restrictions. The travel pass laws ordered that any civilian traveling anywhere, even a short routine trip, had to have a specially issued pass for that one trip. This caused considerable hardship and aggravation, and villagers often simply ignored the rule. Second, the Americans required that the German villages conform to American standards of hygiene and sanitation, most notably insisting that they remove manure piles from their yards. The manure piles, while providing excellent breeding grounds for flies, also provided fertilizer for the fields, and the farmers did not want to give them up. A total of 918 infractions of the sanitation laws had to do with manure, according to Hunt. And finally, the Americans, influenced by the temperance movement in the United States, limited the sale of beer and wine and outlawed the sale of schnapps or other hard liquor to Germans as well as Americans. Because alcohol played a large role in German social traditions and culture, these rules were frequently broken, by both Germans and Americans. Reviewing the most common infractions coming to the attention of the AFG, Hunt concluded that rules that "upset the people's scheme of life" were especially troublesome. He advised that "it is wise to study the national habits and customs of an occupied country before issuing orders, and that, when issued, those orders should be so framed as to avoid interference with national habits and customs as far as possible."[79] This bit of wisdom was perhaps Hunt's most enduring contribution to history, but unfortunately it was too often ignored as the American forces became involved with world affairs in later decades.

What was the impact of this first European occupation? According to American sources, the U.S. troops, small in number though they were, had a lasting and beneficial influence on the civilian population. Few signs of the occupation remained after it ended, however, and it is doubtful that most Germans were affected in any way by the American presence. French rule had a more significant impact, bringing severe hardship to the Germans. Ironically, the American forces came to sympathize with their former enemies more than their erstwhile allies. The French, or so it seemed to Americans, were vindictive and cruel to the Germans, and most French soldiers came from the lowest classes of French society; they appeared poor and unattractive even to the French.[80] The Americans found that one of their more unexpected tasks involved mediation between the harsh demands of the French and the needs of the German civilian population. In his memoirs, Henry Allen noted the irony: "Little did one imagine, when we came to the Rhine as a direct result of the war to collaborate with our "associates" under Armistice conditions, that we should in the end be serving in a way as a moderator for our recent enemy against her traditional enemy, our traditional friend."[81]

The Americans were not always loved by the Germans, however. Unused to the effects of strong drink, inebriated soldiers made nuisances of themselves and became a source of crime and vandalism. Women who fraternized with Americans found themselves harassed and "blacklisted" and had trouble meeting prospective German husbands. During the first months of the occupation, considerable tension between Americans and Germans made cooperation difficult, although early tensions abated somewhat over time.[82]

This first occupation experience, positive and negative, presaged the later American presence in Europe. Taken altogether, the men stationed in Germany during the early 1920s, like those of the 1940s, 1950s, or 1960s, enjoyed their stays and did not wish to return home; some, in fact, had enlisted specifically to serve in Germany. Troop reductions continued, however, until in the summer of 1922 when only 1,700 American troops remained in Germany.[83] Civilians at home wanted the men back, tending to assume, if they thought about it at all, that the men suffered from homesickness and poor conditions, or that they were being corrupted by European ways.[84] Moreover, growing isolationism called for a removal of the troops and withdrawal from European affairs. By early 1923, President Warren Harding succumbed to pressure to recall the troops in Europe. The occupation of the Ruhr region by France and Belgium in January 1923 persuaded the Americans to pull out rather than participate in an occupation they thought was unjust. On February 19, 1923, Henry Allen left the fortress of Ehrenbreitstein in Koblenz, and the first U.S. occupation of European territory was over.

2

World War II and the Occupation Years

INTRODUCTION

American involvement in the Second World War transformed most aspects of American politics, economic life, culture, and society, including the armed forces. Although the aftermath of the Spanish–American War and World War I expanded the scope of the American forces, first in Southeast Asia and then in Europe, World War II turned the U.S. armed forces into a truly global military presence. Whether deployed as defenders, occupiers, peacekeepers, or combatants, after 1941 the U.S. military came to represent American power throughout the world. Moreover, the war transformed the role of the armed services in American society, giving weight to the notion of military service as a patriotic duty and reinforcing the image of the U.S. soldier, sailor, or airman as the young man or woman from home. Military service became respectable, and with the generous benefits given to veterans of the war, it served as a means of upward mobility for millions.

The most immediate and obvious impact of U.S. troops during the war came during combat against the Germans, Japanese, and Italians. The numerous battles of World War II and the combat behavior of U.S. troops have been described in countless monographs, novels, and films, and, while fascinating, are not the focus of this study. The non-combat experience of U.S. soldiers overseas during and immediately after the war, however, set the stage for the era of the global U.S. forces.

Between 1941 and 1945, millions of American servicemen and women left their civilian homes and occupations and served in dozens of nations, from Brazil to Ireland, from New Zealand to North Africa. Many personnel served not in combat, but as support for troops in battle; millions more waited to join the fight. The social, cultural, and economic effects of this "friendly invasion" were almost everywhere deep and long-lasting. American money in the service of the Allied war effort swept away traditional economies, bringing new jobs and new possibilities along with tensions and growing pains. Soldiers exported new cultural practices, from chewing gum to dance steps to novel ways of treating women. Thousands of intercultural marriages and even more thousands of babies are just two of the better-known legacies of the GIs. The wartime presence even changed the landscape and geography of previously isolated areas as the U.S. Army Corps of Engineers constructed roads, docks, and landing strips for military use, which later reverted to civilian control.

At the war's end, the U.S. occupation of Germany, Japan, and other nations prolonged the extensive American presence overseas. The question of what to do with the Axis nations, particularly Germany and Japan, which had unleashed horrific suffering on the world in the name of national–racial superiority, vexed Allied leaders. Should the belligerent states be punished, even destroyed? Or should they be rebuilt and their populations educated to join the family of democratic nations? At first the Americans tried to enforce a punitive policy toward the civilian population, but they eventually settled on a course of reconstruction to be carried out by U.S. troops remaining in Germany and Japan as military government authorities.

The GIs, it must be admitted, were not perfect guests in their temporary homes. The economic disparity between the well-supplied soldiers and the impoverished civilians exacerbated the already wide gulf between victor and vanquished. Soldiers indulged in black-market trading of canned food, military supplies, and especially cigarettes, greatly to their own benefit and at the expense of desperate civilians. American personnel also became famous for their bawdy behavior, including drunkenness, street fighting, and harassment and exploitation of women. Discipline problems, while perhaps understandable in the first postwar days when feelings ran high and the manners of combat were still fresh, continued shamefully for years, endangering the well-meaning efforts of those trying to spread democratic values.

SLOUCHING TOWARD WAR

In the years after the brief American occupation of the Koblenz area, the United States reverted to an isolationist policy, avoiding involvement in European and world affairs, rejecting membership in the League of

Nations, and cutting funds for the military. The Great Depression exacerbated this trend, and even veterans of the First World War found themselves literally out in the cold as promised benefits disappeared. In 1932 a demonstration of unemployed veterans on the Mall in Washington DC—the "Bonus March"—was fired upon by police and two marchers were killed. By 1933, the U.S. Army was tiny—smaller than Portugal's.[1]

Traditional mistrust of military service resurfaced in the postwar years. Civilians once again tended to view enlisted men in the peacetime army as one of society's more disreputable subcultures, accustomed to the regimented and harsh barracks atmosphere and unsuited for family life. The old expression "If the army wanted soldiers to have families, it would have issued them" was never more true than during this period. Instances of judges giving offenders a choice between jail and the army, although probably exaggerated, did occur in the 1930s.[2] Altogether, the army had never been so ill-prepared or suffered from such low status as it did in the 1920s and 30s.[3]

However, ominous developments in Europe in the 1930s did not go unnoticed by American policymakers. While a vociferous isolationist faction led by Charles Lindbergh and the group America First lobbied for nonintervention, more prescient minds including Senator Claude Pepper and President Franklin Delano Roosevelt understood well the double threat of Japanese expansion and Nazi aggression. After Hitler invaded Poland in 1939, the U.S. Army and Navy began a hasty buildup. In September the U.S. forces numbered only 334,000, but over the next two years the number of troops rose to 1.8 million.[4] The Selective Service System—the draft—aided the development of the armed forces tremendously. Initiated in September 1940 after a huge fight with the isolationists, it eventually encompassed one-sixth of American males, and brought in 10 million of a total 16 million men and women "GIs"—the term came into use in 1941[5]—to serve in the armed forces between 1941 and 1945.[6] Draftees spread unevenly through the services; until 1942, the Navy and Marines filled their ranks with volunteers, while the Army Air Force (AAF), the most glamorous of the branches of services, turned away applicants throughout the war. Draftees were most likely to find themselves in the infantry, although those with useful skills were sometimes directed to branches where those skills would be used—of course, a running joke in the draft army pointed to the experienced chef repairing trucks while the mechanic was assigned to the kitchen.

The influx of tens of thousands of mostly, it must be admitted, unenthusiastic civilians had an enormous and lasting impact on the tradition-bound institutions of the armed forces, especially the army. The draconian discipline of enlisted men, the attention to spit and polish, tended to go by the wayside with civilians who were on the one hand not as focussed on military detail,[7] and on the other, perhaps less in need of it than enlisted men of an earlier age. Regular career soldiers, especially non-commissioned officers, or sergeants, condemned the "civilianization" of the army as ushering in softness and laxity. For their part, draftees saw army life as alien and uninteresting. Moreover, beginning in the late nineteenth century, the professional army had become more and more "southern" in culture and demography. As conscription spread through the army, a geographical and cultural divide between draftees from Northeastern cities and career NCOs from small towns in the South developed.[8] Education, class, and culture all played a role in making the army experience a difficult and unpleasant one for many. Surveys showed that higher levels of education corresponded with increasing dissatisfaction with army life,[9] but the letters, diaries, and memoirs of personnel reveal that many former civilians from all backgrounds and walks of life had difficulty adjusting to the rigors and boredom of the training camp. Still, they learned to cope, and in time a subculture of the civilian soldier developed, with its jokes, jargon, and, in cartoonist Bill Maudlin, semiofficial chronicler.

The vast majority of active duty personnel were male, but women played an important role in the war effort. Aside from the millions of civilian women who took jobs in armament factories, served as civilian nurses and office workers, and ran volunteer efforts on the home front, women served in the armed forces as well. Each branch had a separate corps for women, giving rise to acronyms that passed into common vocabulary in the 1940s—the Women's Army Corps (WAC), the Women Accepted for Volunteer Emergency Services (WAVES) of the Navy, the Coast Guard SPARs. Even the Marine Corps allowed women to serve, although not in a separately named branch. While women were not permitted to serve in combat, they performed valuable and dangerous work both in the United States and overseas. In 1942, female nurses were among the first POWs of the war, captured by the Japanese in the Philippines and forced, along with their male comrades, to endure the notorious Bataan Death March.

African American soldiers served in large numbers during World War II. Their services, in fact, led directly to the postwar civil rights movement, as black soldiers saw their white colleagues rewarded for their service while they went unrecognized. African Americans, too, were usually barred from combat, assigned to segregated units in construction, transportation, and supply. They made up about 10 percent of U.S. personnel during the war.[10]

The sudden and rapid growth of the armed forces affected families at home, labor markets and schools, and the men themselves. As during the First World War, the militarization of society also affected the towns and cities located near training camps, which experienced burgeoning growth as the numbers of trainees exploded. The host communities, called "impact areas" by the army, pre-dated the training camps in some cases, while others grew up in response to the needs of the camps. During the prewar buildup, military/civilian relations frayed under the pressure of social and cultural problems brought by huge numbers of soldiers. In the abstract the civilian population supported its men and women in uniform, but closer up, neighbors distrusted the troops, often with good reason, and tried to restrict their access to off-base areas. Large installations such as Fort Bragg in Fayetteville, North Carolina, or the Navy base at Norfolk, Virginia, concluded agreements with local communities to keep the enlisted men in certain parts of town where businesses catered to them.[11] The new soldiers, for their part, felt that the civilian population treated them badly and resented the suspicion and disdain. It was true that servicemen in stateside camps caused innumerable drunken brawls, sexual assaults, and other misbehavior, as had occurred during World War I. Separated from the restricting influences of home, family, and neighbors and set in an atmosphere of coarse barracks culture with hundreds of other unaccompanied men, it was not surprising that "GI towns" sprang up around virtually every training camp.[12] To a large extent, this had always been true, an aspect of military life that contributed to the poor image of the army. For that matter, it was true to a greater or lesser extent of armies everywhere. But with the enormous number of draftees pouring in, elements of army life that had been previously hidden or ignored by all but those most directly affected by them received greater attention. To an even greater extent than during the First World War, the American public began to worry about alcohol abuse, prostitution, and venereal disease affecting their sons in uniform. In response, the army, using its earlier experience, conducted a huge campaign against VD, which helped to keep stateside disease rates low.

With the growth of the armed forces, soldiers, sailors, and marines became increasingly visible to the civilian public in ways not seen in America before or after the war. (The visibility of U.S. men and women in uniform continued in the many regions of the world where American personnel were and still are stationed, as described in the following chapters.) Uniformed troops on leave traveled from camp to their homes or to nearby cities using busses and trains; the sight of groups of sailors on shore leave in New York City was so common as to become a cliché; convoys and chartered trains moved troops from camp to port, where they shipped out. All these sights became normal elements of life during the war. No one could blame young men and women for traveling on leave or on assignment, and they were required to wear their uniforms in transit. When a young man arrived home in uniform, proud relatives and friends admired his new look. But at the same time military authorities fielded complaints about troops taking up space on public transportation and about the inconvenience of military convoys on public streets;[13] civilians needed an adjustment period as well.

GIs OVERSEAS DURING WORLD WAR II

The U.S. officially entered the war when Japan attacked the naval station at Pearl Harbor, Hawaii, on December 7, 1941. Some kind of Japanese attack against American installations had been expected, although it appears that no one had anticipated Pearl Harbor—rather, the Philippines was believed to be a likely target, and commanders created uneven plans for defense of those islands. The Philippines was indeed attacked by air nine hours after Pearl Harbor, and several weeks later a ground invasion pushed back the U.S. and Philippine forces to the Bataan peninsula (see Chapter 7). The Japanese attacked Guam on December 10 and Wake Island on December 11, where 500 Marines repulsed the initial invasion and held the island until a second, successful invasion on December 23.[14] Meanwhile, Germany declared war against the United States a few days after Pearl Harbor, and America found itself in a two-front war.

With the American entrance into the conflict, the great machinery of the U.S. war effort began to swing into gear, slowly and inefficiently to be sure, but with the vast power of American industry and agricultural might behind it. American personnel were deployed throughout the world—to the Canadian Northwest, Iceland and Greenland, Panama, Brazil, the Caribbean, to the island archipelagos of the South Pacific, Australia and New Guinea, to India and Burma, to North Africa, Kenya, the Middle East, and to Great Britain.[15] Small forces of army, navy and Marine Corps personnel had been stationed in American territories and colonies before the war, but the first contingent of U.S. troops to be sent overseas after hostilities commenced was a naval convoy of about 4,600[16] that had been en route to Hawaii on December 7. It was quickly renamed Task Force South Pacific and ordered to Brisbane, Australia, where it set up shop in a local hotel.[17] Australia would see thousands of Americans pass through in the next four years as the Japanese advance threatened the continent. As many as 1 million American troops would be stationed for some period in Australia during the Second World War (although some historians see this as an overly generous estimate).[18] In any case, at the height of the war effort, as much as 5 percent of Australia's population was American. The GIs joined the battle almost immediately; throughout 1942 they fought to push the Japanese advance back from the islands directly north of Australia.[19]

One of the first concerns of military planners was the defense of the United States itself. The attack on Pearl Harbor proved that the Japanese would not shrink from bold action. In retrospect it is fairly clear that the Japanese never posed a serious threat to the mainland, but this was certainly not clear at the time. One of the more regrettable acts during the war was the internment of thousands of Japanese and Americans of Japanese ancestry who were viewed as a potential "Fifth Column" on the West Coast. The fact that Hawaiians of Japanese ancestry served with distinction in the U.S. forces only highlights the irrationality of the internment. A more logical defense measure positioned troops to the far Northwest, in Canada and Alaska, where they built highways to connect the region to the main arteries of the United States. The army also reinforced units already in Panama, where commanders feared an attack on the Panama Canal. None of these forces ever saw combat, and defense of the mainland turned out to be a tiny sideshow compared with the major fronts overseas.

In Europe, the majority of U.S. troops went to Great Britain, where, from 1942 on, hundreds of thousands of allied troops prepared for an amphibious assault on occupied Europe. By the eve of the Normandy landing, about 1.7 million Americans had been deployed to the British Isles.[20] Most GIs stationed in Europe did not go into battle until 1944; many of them, therefore, had lived in Britain for more than two years, training and waiting. Before actual combat, in some cases long before combat, Americans "invaded" Allied countries, from which armies of Americans, Canadians, British, Australians, New Zealanders, and others would launch invasions or counterattacks against the Axis enemies.

What was this "friendly invasion" like for the civilians who experienced it? Perhaps the most noticeable aspect of the American presence in other nations, the one most commented on by observers from all regions, was its immense wealth. For the hard-pressed British, the Americans enjoyed what seemed to be an almost sumptuous life, with plenty of fresh food, fuel, clothing, and entertainment. Having been supplied with products and services unavailable to civilians, they then imposed sometimes intolerable burdens on the general supply of food, drink, fuel, tobacco, alcohol, and other goods available on the civilian economy, because they could easily afford what were luxuries to their Allies. In Australia, for example, GIs drank their generous rations of milk with gusto, then bought expensive shakes at milk bars, leaving little left over for civilians.[21]

Throughout the world, American supply lines were the envy of friends and enemies. The American "tooth to tail" ratio—the number of combat troops to support staff—stood at around one to three, which was higher than any other major army fighting the war—although not nearly as high as it is today, at approximately one to eleven. This ratio was probably unavoidable, given the 3,000-mile-long supply line to Europe and the 6,000 miles to the South Pacific.[22] In addition, supplies brought from the United States took pressure off the host economies, which in most cases could hardly feed and clothe their own civilian populations. Not that the Americans always brought all their supplies with them; in Australia, GIs received uniforms and full rations, which included meat, fresh eggs, coffee, and carbohydrates, from the Australians.[23] They found the mutton that was a staple of the Australian diet hard to take, however, and some GIs said that the food they received was that which had been rejected by the Australian troops.[24]

Still, many a British or Australian soldier would have found it incredible that the Americans complained of their rations or their general standard of living. It was all relative, of course, and the Americans were living in foreign countries, adjusting to unfamiliar ways. But by any measure, for virtually any product, the American ration was more generous than any other. Some examples bordered on the absurd: the British toilet paper ration was three sheets a day, while the American ration gave each GI twenty-two and a half sheets.[25] The level of waste was correspondingly high—according to one chronicler of the American presence in Britain, it was said with only slight exaggeration that the scrapings from one American mess hall meal could feed a British family for a month.[26]

The Americans were paid more than other Allied soldiers as well—in the case of the British, more than four times more.[27] The higher pay of the Americans in Australia sparked resentment, particularly as Australian soldiers, with their own pay more generous than that of British soldiers, had enjoyed acting the role of wealthy cousins while stationed in Britain. Throughout the world, local civilians working for the armed forces were paid generously, a discrepancy even more noticeable in areas of the world poorer than Britain or Australia. In New Guinea, for example, American pay scales were so much higher than local wages that native New Guineans refused to work for the Australian authorities, who paid thirty-five cents and two plugs of tobacco per week. Local people also made good money washing clothes, shining shoes, or cleaning for the Americans. In Australia, women could earn twenty pounds a week doing laundry, more than many positions requiring special skills or education.[28]

The Post Exchange (PX) system spread along with the GIs—soldiers could buy in the PX items not supplied to them by the army, although in fact just about everything was. By the end of the war the PX was the largest retail system in the United States and the world.[29] The American soldiers, as the rhyme had it, were "overfed, overpaid, oversexed and over here."

The effects of this relative wealth were widespread, as might be imagined, and exacerbated the second most remarked upon characteristic of the Americans: their enthusiasm for meeting young women. In this they played an unfair game with their competitors. The very health and vigor of the Americans contrasted with the poverty, pallidness, and exhaustion of British men, suffering for several years from nightly bombing attacks and meager food rations. The Australians, who by and large did not suffer such privations, still held up poorly, according to some, when contrasted with the GIs. The Americans, it was often remarked, seemed more comfortable spending time with women and girls, while the Australians, like the British and Irish, tended to rely more on male friends for companionship outside of sex.

The GIs' success in their sexual conquests during the war years was famous, or notorious, throughout Britain and Australia. In Britain, it gave rise to many vulgar jokes and puns: "Look before you jeep or you'll be Yanked in maternity"[30] or "Have you heard about the new utility knickers? One Yank and they're off!"[31] Not all women thought it exciting or glamorous to be seen with Americans. Many women attached social stigma to associating with GIs, and concerned mothers forbade their daughters from "ruining" themselves. Still, a huge number of women did date Americans, and many formed more lasting attachments. Although accurate numbers are hard to come by, it appears that between 70,000 and 80,000 British women and about 12,000 Australians married U.S. soldiers at the end of the war.[32]

The sexual conquest described above, more or less voluntary on both sides, was most noticeable in the white, English-speaking nations of Australia and Great Britain. In some very remote areas, like Northwest Canada, there was less sexual activity than might be expected due to cultural isolation, exhausting work, and the small numbers of women available.[33] Likewise, in many of the Pacific islands, the venereal disease rate never became out of control, suggesting relatively low rates of sexual activity.

Generally speaking, however, military authorities battled to reduce extremely high rates of VD wherever the GIs went, ranging from fifty cases per thousand to five hundred cases per thousand. This situation existed, simply speaking, because GIs very frequently patronized brothels and street prostitutes. Women in Britain, Ireland, and Australia who became intimate with American soldiers tended to see themselves in emotional relationships motivated by personal preference, and while some were motivated by material considerations, most white, English-speaking women associating with GIs could be called prostitutes only in an unfairly broad sense of the word. In other parts of the world, however, women interacting with GIs most definitely worked in the commercial sex trade, usually in brothels and sometimes as streetwalkers. Some had been employed in the sex industry before the war began; a tragically large number of others, however, had been coerced or forced into sexual labor by recruiters promising young women and girls employment as waitresses, maids, and the like.

Records describing the War Department's efforts to stem the VD rate implicitly and explicitly discuss the issue of organized prostitution, tolerated by or even assisted by military authorities in each region. According to recent research by Yuki Tanaka, a Japanese scholar studying the issue of Asian "comfort women" used by the Japanese and Allied forces during and after the war, in 1942 and 1943 the U.S. Army battled dangerously high rates of VD in a variety of locales, including the Middle East, India, Africa, and the Caribbean.[34] Some measures taken by military authorities included, in order of severity: handing out condoms and chemical prophylactic kits (microbicide creams and wipes to be applied after sex) at prophylactic stations in red-light districts; tracking down the sexual contacts of soldiers with VD and treating them; mandating use of prophylactic kits, enforced by medics stationed outside brothels; placing certain brothels off-limits and controlling others by requiring sex workers to be checked and treated for VD; and conniving with local authorities to set up brothels reserved for U.S. forces, with the workers strictly monitored and supervised.

Although official military policy prohibited the use of brothels by soldiers and officers (military police raided and shut down brothels near camps in the United States), commanders overseas generally did not attempt to eradicate the industry, and often argued for unorthodox measures in the fight against VD, such as quasi-ownership or management of brothels by the military. Military authorities took such steps secretively, well aware of the public outcry that would ensue should the news reach the home front. But the military steadfastly believed that their soldiers were not to blame for the problem. One military investigator cited by Tanaka explained that VD rates are affected by "the characteristics of the people among whom soldiers are stationed. Their morals and customs, and especially the physical attractiveness of the native women have a direct bearing upon the desire of soldiers to associate with them . . . ."[35] Commanders saw VD as the fault of the women, not the soldiers. The view that seductive and wily foreign women ensnared naïve soldiers remained a closely held belief in the armed forces throughout the twentieth century and probably earlier.

Drinking was a pastime that went along with sexual activity, often preceding it or following it. In Britain, it was not uncommon for thirsty GIs to "drink a pub dry"—an event much resented by local miners, farmers, and factory workers who arrived later after long working days.[36] In areas such as Canada's northwest, where alcoholism was an endemic problem, GI binge drinking aggravated already existing problems in local communities.[37] Drinking and the problems associated with it would become an increasing scourge after the war ended, but during the war years, military discipline, hard work, and shortages mitigated the tendency somewhat.

Given the financial strength and sexual success of American soldiers, as well as the confident belief among many GIs that U.S. troops had come to pull the world's chestnuts out of the fire, it will come as no surprise that the Americans gained a reputation for their arrogance and braggadocio. Australians, accustomed to coming to the aid of their mother country, chafed at the notion that they now needed help, and in later years sometimes claimed that they could have defended themselves alone.[38] The British, who had perhaps a more realistic attitude toward world affairs as a result of their longer involvement, found the casual self-confidence of the Americans baffling and sometimes frustrating. At the same time, the "can-do" spirit of the Americans brought a much-needed jolt of energy to the dispirited allies.

Because of the shared English language, many American soldiers were initially under the illusion that Britain and Australia were very much like the United States, but they soon came up against the reality that these were foreign nations with their own very different histories and cultures. In spite of a common tongue, mutual misunderstandings around language and behavior abounded,[39] from different terms for the same item to the treatment of women. Likewise, many young people in Britain and Australia had grown up with Hollywood movies showing them "what Americans were like," leading to extremely unrealistic expectations, to say the least. In fact, the images of Americans created in Hollywood shaped the expectations of young and old, and many were bitterly disappointed when, inevitably, the Americans did not live up to the celluloid ideal.

Tensions between Australians and Americans festered as larger numbers of GIs arrived in the summer of 1942. The Americans' superior rations, arrogant behavior, and the threat of success with Australian women magnified poor management on the part of Australian and American commanders. Throughout the late summer and fall, numerous conflicts, fights, even minor riots erupted over slights and insults. On Thanksgiving Day, emotions reached the boiling point. Several MPs intercepted a drunken GI who refused their requests for his pass, and when the MPs began to beat him, his Australian drinking companions came to his aid against the MPs. The situation quickly grew out of control, with thousands of Australians and Americans duking it out in the streets. Many or most of the participants viewed it as a fight between two national groups, but some more perceptive witnesses called attention to the anti-authority aspect of what came to be known as "The Battle of Brisbane."[40] The fighting went on for several days, but even when it was over, the air had not cleared. Clashes and violence continued to flare up throughout the rest of 1942 and into 1943. Strict censorship around the issue, which allowed rumors to flourish and spread, merely inflamed tensions. Eventually the hostility simmered down as troops shipped out to the islands of the South Pacific, but the Battle of Brisbane and other riots revealed the fragility of relations between the Americans and their Australian hosts.

Another source of violence was the racial segregation of the U.S. military. In Australia, white attitudes toward the native Aboriginal people more or less mirrored white American attitudes toward African and Native Americans, and black American soldiers in Australia suffered the same discrimination in housing and recreation options that they suffered in the United States. In Britain, however, many people perceived the hypocrisy of fighting the anti-Semitic Nazi regime with racially segregated armed forces, and were troubled by the racism of Americans.[41] Officials in both nations viewed black troops as a potential source of trouble and tried to restrict the amount of contact between black soldiers and the white populace. Still, a recurring theme of the GI experience overseas, during and after the war, was the conflict of different racial attitudes. White GIs from the South recoiled at seeing white European women dancing with, dating, or even marrying black men, while many a European found a bad taste in his mouth from the casual but brutal racism of the American GI, who talked about freedom and democracy but denied it to his fellow citizens because of the color of their skin.

Ironically, given the levels of racism among many soldiers, American troops were associated for many people throughout the world with African American innovations, such as jazz music. Older, more conservative people disapproved of the sensual genre but young people flocked to hear it, and wherever the Americans stayed, a blues, jazz, or swing band would inevitably appear. Jitterbugging, too, was an American export controversial for the older set but popular among the young.

American racial attitudes irritated many Europeans, but for their part the Americans found the British class system to be puzzling. In the United States, "land of [white] opportunity," fundamental distinctions based on class, while they existed, were not insuperable, as many GIs could attest from their army experiences. Class barriers, less important to Americans, formed more permanent social boundaries in Britain. Another American complaint about the British was their "passivity"—some GIs felt that the British, while admirably stoic under the long months of German bomb attacks, should get up and move, take action, do something.[42]

In spite of the American citizen soldier's preference for action, he was not particularly scrupulous about military discipline and appearance. He had fundamentally not lost his civilian character. He slouched, put his hands in his pockets, and chewed gum; the unsoldierly image of the GI bemused those who could not reconcile a victorious army with this vision of slackness. Some were drawn to this casualness, while others found it repellent.[43] Gum chewing created perhaps the most lasting cliché of the American GI—chomping on wads of it, handing it out to children, spreading the habit throughout the world.

Given all these difficulties, misunderstandings, and plain bad behavior, it might be supposed that a worldwide negative reaction to the Americans would have erupted, but, in fact, it was not so, notwithstanding the real hostility of the Battle of Brisbane and other episodes. In spite of their many faults, or perhaps even because of them, it seemed impossible for most people to really hate the GI. In the beginning, the grateful British and Australians welcomed the Americans, cheering them and buying them drinks.[44] The genuine appreciation lasted even as the expressions of enthusiasm disappeared. Even after the welcome wore off and problems began to arise, relationships between the American troops and local populations were complex and nuanced. For every young man resentful at the GIs' relative affluence and romantic success, there were fellow soldiers who trusted and valued their Americans comrades in arms. For every girl who refused to sully her reputation for an American man, there were many young women, just as carefully brought up, who eagerly volunteered to serve as hostesses at respectable Red Cross dances, spending their free evenings with the attractive foreigners. For every elderly person offended by American vulgarity, another was charmed by the naïve friendliness and eagerness to please—or who remembered what it was like to be a young, lonely soldier heading off to the fields of northern France. Americans were not all alike, although the army did its best to make them so, both in their military service and their off-duty activities. The marriages between GIs and local women, the long and close friendships, the lasting ties between Americans and their hosts attest to the positive impact of many of America's citizen soldiers.

VICTORY IN EUROPE

On June 6, 1944, the Western Allies landed on the northern coast of France, in Normandy, spearheading a huge offensive to push the Germans out of the Western European lands they occupied and back to Germany, as the Soviets had done successfully in the East. The fighting was brutal and thousands of lives lost, but gradually the Allies established a beachhead and began to move out across France. The liberation of towns and villages in Northern Europe was something that neither liberator nor liberated ever forgot, even though the passage of time brought stresses and strains between the two. For the Americans, with little awareness of the tangled and tense history of Europe, this hard-won liberation was profoundly moving. Soldier–journalist Orval Faubus wrote, "If ever I have seen a sincerely happy and grateful people, it is these liberated French."[45] The French welcomed the liberators from whatever nation with the best food and wine, with hugs and kisses, singing and dancing. Fifty years later the Americans who liberated towns and villages in France still return on the anniversary of liberation to celebrate and remember those who died.

The first American troops arrived on German soil in October 1944, when they occupied the border city of Aachen. To the Aacheners, the Americans were liberators—the townspeople feted the GIs with food and wine and festivities just as the French had. The GIs accepted this hospitality gratefully. But to the people back home, photos and descriptions of American GIs cavorting with Germans scandalized those who thought of all Germans as enemies. The military authorities quickly decreed a halt to celebrations with Germans and instituted a clearly outlined policy of occupation. The Germans were to be treated as vanquished enemies, not as people liberated from the Nazis, and there was to be no "fraternization"— no unnecessary interaction with Germans.

The news of the "liberation" of Aachen, while causing an uproar in the United States, was not, of course, publicized in the Nazi-controlled press.

Germans in the western regions awaited the Americans and British with a mix of hope and fear. The hope was that the Americans and British would be just and merciful, and realize that many Germans had been victims of the Nazis just as the citizens of other nations had been. The fear was that the Allies would not agree with this view and would treat all Germans as co-offenders. As the days and weeks wore on, many Germans in the west consoled themselves with the thought that the Americans and British were certain to be kinder than the Russian soldiers in the east, who, accurate rumor had it, exacted revenge for the immeasurable suffering of their people.

As the slow, step-by-step pressure on the Germans proceeded—with a bloody halt in November–December 1944 during the last German counteroffensive, the Battle of the Bulge—the French continued to celebrate their freedom, and the Germans to worry over their future.

The Americans occupied Germany town by town. Generally, they met little or no resistance to their arrival, although in the first weeks and months the Americans feared a last fanatical resistance from so-called "Werewolf" organizations. For the most part, the Werewolf turned out to be a mirage. The raggedy Volkssturm, young boys and elderly men dispatched by Nazi holdouts to defend their towns, knew quite well that their few weapons, usually surplus materiel from the First World War and assorted antique hunting pieces, would not last against the well-equipped and professional Allied forces. In most cases, the Volkssturm members returned to their homes as soon as the local Nazi functionaries fled. The level-headedness of most Volkssturm spared all sides a good deal of grief, because the Allies were not willing to lose a single man on the mission to occupy Germany. In the case of even light resistance, the Allies brought out their heavy artillery and flattened the area.

When the Americans arrived in a town, the local officials remaining behind would raise a white flag as a signal of surrender, and the citizens of the town would hang bedsheets and tablecloths out their windows. The officials would turn the town over to the American officer in charge of the unit that had captured the area—depending on the size of the town, either a company or a battalion commander. The officer and his men would distribute copies of Gen. Dwignt D. Eisenhower's Proclamation No. 1 on placards and signposts, and also read through a loudspeaker in the town center. The order's famous first words were: "We come as conquerors, not as oppressors." It went on to say that every order from the commander must be obeyed immediately and without complaint, and it detailed an almost complete curfew, stringent travel restrictions, the confiscation of weapons and communications equipment (including cameras and carrier pigeons), and other limitations. The provisions in Proclamation No. 1 were sensible—after all, the war still continued—but they put a damper on the hopes of many anti-Nazi Germans that their people would be treated as victims of Nazism rather than co-conspirators.

After a day or two of rest, the combat unit would move on, turning over the occupied town to a unit of Military Government (MG), a branch of the army distinct from the combat organizations fighting the Germans. It had been created during the war upon the general realization that the Nazis could not be allowed to continue to rule Germany, and that the chaos they had unleashed could only be controlled through martial law. Preparations for military rule in Germany, through an institution known as Office of Military Government, United States (OMGUS), began around 1943 but never became a priority for the War Department. Although it was the ultimate administrative power in areas occupied by American force, OMGUS and its state and local branches remained understaffed and overworked, and as more towns came under its jurisdiction it faced intense and immediate problems. For one thing, the basic utility systems providing water, electricity, and fuel were often damaged or destroyed in areas that had been bombed; almost every large city had sustained at least partial damage, and some were just mounds of rubble. Secondly, security and order had to be established and maintained for the safety of the Germans, the thousands of newly released Displaced Persons (DPs), and the GIs themselves. The DPs constituted a tragic problem. Starved and brutalized for years, they not only took revenge on their German captors—and any Germans they came across—but they suffered from life-threatening health problems caused by the brutal confinement they had endured. Infectious diseases such as cholera and typhus loomed, and many DPs did damage to themselves though indiscriminate eating and drinking. Thousands of DPs died in the days after their release through overstress of their fragile systems. To prevent harm from coming to them, MG troops rounded up the local DPs and put them back in the very camps from which they had been so recently released. It was hardly an ideal solution.

The MG was also responsible for the safety and welfare of the U.S. forces in occupied towns. Primarily, they needed and wanted comfortable housing, which the MG provided through requisitions of German residences, one of the most notorious aspects of the occupation. In the "wild" requisition phase, immediately following the capture of a town, the GIs would simply approach a building—office, hotel, or private home—and demand that the occupants leave immediately. They were not allowed to take more than a few personal items, and they received no receipt for the building or its contents. In time, the requisition process would become regularized; occupants were given three hours to leave, an MG officer would inventory the contents of the building, and displaced residents would be compensated. Even so, the requisitions placed a difficult burden on occupants, who scrambled to find new places to stay.

When Germany surrendered in May 1945, the war in Europe officially ended. The fighting stopped, but a ruined continent had to be rebuilt and a decent social order re-established. For administrative purposes, Germany was divided into four zones, governed by the "Big Three"—the U.S., Great Britain, and the Soviet Union—and France, at the insistence of the irrepressible Charles de Gaulle. The idea was that the four nations, Roosevelt's "Four Policemen," would work together to rebuild Europe and provide collective security for the entire world, a sort of updated Concert of Europe of the Metternich era.

The "Four Policemen" disagreed on many major things, such as what kind of political and economic systems would be established in postwar Germany and other nations. However, they did agree on a few issues. Official policy toward Germany included the "Four Ds": denazification, demilitarization, decartelization, and democratization. Under denazification the Allies eliminated all vestiges of National Socialism from German life. GIs in the American Zone spent weeks prying swastikas from above municipal office doors and collecting Nazi flags, stamps, and other paraphernalia, some of the material making its way back to the United States as war souvenirs. Denazification also included the removal from office of all Nazi functionaries and the confiscation of the property of Nazi organizations, from the Gestapo and SS to the Hitler Youth. Demilitarization meant dismantling Germany's armed forces, rounding up German soldiers as POWs, and destroying heavy armaments. Decartelization involved breaking up the large centralized industries that had helped Hitler develop his war machine, and democratization meant "re-educating" the Germans—helping them unlearn the lessons and habits of authoritarianism and the totalitarian state.

On the local level, the MG did its best to fulfill the "Four Ds," especially denazification and democratization. At first denazification proved fairly popular among the German populace. There was no great outcry when Allied soldiers arrested Nazi leaders, who had been figures of scorn and resentment for years. When the troops came for the "small fry" though, discontent spread, and when, in September 1945, General Lucius Clay, commander of OMGUS, insisted that anyone who had been a member of the Nazi party was to be punished, denazification lost most of its remaining support. Many Germans had joined the party not out of conviction but convenience; these people, popular belief held, should not be treated like those who had enthusiastically supported the evil program of the Nazis.

Americans were also the most committed democratizers of the four powers. Through public education, the early establishment of local and state elections, and other efforts, the American leaders hoped to teach the Germans the ways of freedom and democracy. These were lofty goals, and the occupiers inevitably fell short of them. Historian Edward Peterson has concluded that the successful democratization of West Germany came about through MG's withdrawal from involvement in German life; the absence of interference and the resentment that would have been an inevitable consequence enabled the Germans to rebuild quickly.[46]

VICTORY IN JAPAN

Unlike the victory over Europe, for which credit must be given to a coalition of Allies, the war against Japan belonged almost entirely to the United States. Ironically, the United States was not Japan's main target. China fell first to Japanese aggression and paid mightily for its proximity to the island, as did Korea, the Philippines, Indonesia, Malaysia, and the peoples of Southeast Asia and the South Pacific islands. The United States, however, became the main fighting force against the Japanese, its industrial power turning out vast amounts of war materiel that the Japanese could not match. (Other Allies fought in the theater, such as Australia in New Guinea and the British and Chinese in Burma.) Churchill and Roosevelt had agreed that priority be given to defeating Hitler first, then the Allies would focus on the Japanese. But by 1944 the U.S. Army, Navy, and Marines moved closer, island by island, to an invasion of mainland Japan. As the U.S. Army under General Douglas MacArthur liberated the Philippines from Japanese rule, the Marines established landing strips close to Japan on the islands of Iwo Jima and Guam. After the war in Europe ended, American forces prepared for a final, massive assault on Japan. An invasion of the main islands would, planners estimated, cost hundreds of thousands of American and Japanese lives. The Battle of Okinawa, a horrifying bloodbath (see Chapter 8), afforded a frightening preview of what the U.S. forces could expect, or so military and political leaders believed.

The invasion of Japan was not to be. In the summer of 1945, scientists at Los Alamos developed the atomic bomb, a weapon of unparalleled destructive power. The Japanese populace was no stranger to death from the skies; the USAAF, headed by General Carl Spaatz and then General H. H. Arnold, used the new tactic of strategic bombing to destroy Japan's industrial capacity. By 1945 all major cities in Japan and most of the secondary cities had been extensively bombed; in one raid, Tokyo suffered 90 percent destruction, for example. But the A-bomb raised destructiveness to a new level, and it would leave radiation to poison life for years; it would do the damage of the raid on Tokyo with just one bomb. President Harry S. Truman, only a few months into his administration, made the difficult decision. The first atomic bomb fell from the Enola Gay on Hiroshima on August 6, 1945. The second destroyed Nagasaki on August 9. The Japanese formally surrendered on August 15.

As a result, Japan was not occupied village by village while the war continued, as Germany had been. Rather, a massive sea and airlift of American troops to the defeated nation brought occupation forces to the island in a relatively orderly fashion. Another major difference was that the government of Japan continued to exist, with the Emperor as titular head. Japanese militarists had been removed from office, but the occupiers did not take over the entire role of government as they had in Germany. There had been some discussion of whether the Emperor should be tried as a war criminal, but American leaders decided that by remaining in office he would provide leadership and stability through the difficult times ahead. Moreover, because the victory belonged primarily to the United States, Japan was not divided into zones as Germany had been.

Another difference was the role of General MacArthur. MacArthur was the commander of the U.S. Army in the Pacific, and he became the head of the Occupation forces in Japan—the Supreme Commander of the Allied Powers, or SCAP; the term became shorthand for the occupation authority in general. There were few other Allied troops involved; about 39,000 British Commonwealth Occupation Forces (BCOF) from Australia, New Zealand, India, and Great Britain supported the U.S. forces in Japan,[47] but the Chinese were fighting a civil war, and the Soviets refused to put their troops under American command.

MacArthur's rule was absolute. He held enormous, almost unfathomable power, and he was not afraid to use it. For better or worse, he also knew how to maintain a sense of godlike distance, which earned him the fear and respect of the Japanese people (and the Americans, for that matter) in the early postwar years.

The U.S. forces began arriving in Japan on August 30 in troop transport planes. By December 1945 430,000 had amassed in Japan.[48] JCS 1380 ordered the occupying forces to make far-ranging changes in Japanese political life and society and to go after the roots of militarism in Japanese tradition. One of SCAP's first actions was to prosecute those responsible for the war. Members of the Japanese forces who were convicted of war crimes were removed from office and punished, and, in some cases, executed. But SCAP went much further, democratizing society and especially the economic life of Japan. Although MacArthur is often seen with good reason as a conservative and was adopted as a hero by many right-wing organizations in the United States, he presided over reforms in Japan that were almost socialist: dismantling the zaibatsu, the large corporations that held economic power in Japan; encouraging unions, many of which became socialist or even communist; and instituting widespread land reform. Women received the right to vote, the new, American-created constitution gave equality to the sexes, and reformers tried to modernize elementary and secondary education to emphasize creative thinking rather than the rote learning that had been the tradition in Japan. Not all the reforms took root, of course, and many traditional institutions and habits regrew when the Americans left, but the seeds of change had been planted.

In both Germany and Japan, the civilian population had suffered during the war, and by the time peace came, they were demoralized and drained of energy. Both the Japanese and Nazi regimes had demanded the total allegiance and commitment of the people, which they had received, and at the end, the people, exhausted and numb, felt they had been betrayed by their leaders. As a result, almost no revanchist spirit emerged in either nation. In addition, in both nations the occupiers enjoyed positions of unique authority and power, while the defeated populace took roles as employees, servants, beggars, procurers—but never as equals. The Germans and Japanese both took to trading on the black market, working in the military sex trade, and begging for favors and food from the Americans. It seemed a hopeless situation. But in spite of mistakes and abuses, the American presence did take measures to help reconstruct the two nations.

THE GIS

Unfortunately, the behavior of the GIs hindered efforts to set a good example to the vanquished populations. At the close of hostilities, morale and discipline among the GIs on both fronts suffered a tremendous collapse. Authorities tried to ship GIs home as rapidly as possible, but air travel was not yet common, and the fleet of troop ships was not up to the task. Millions of Americans in Europe and Asia waited impatiently for passage home. Boredom turned to anger as the weeks became months, with no clear end in sight. By early 1946 GI protests in European and Asian cities exploded with thousands of soldiers demonstrating and rioting.

To make matters worse, even the lowliest private found himself in a position of immense power relative to the civilian population. The GIs became notorious for sexual misbehavior, drunkenness, fighting, and various types of crime.

In Germany, even after the war was over, the "no fraternization" rule continued to be in effect but was roundly ignored, at least in GI interactions with women. GIs continued to uphold their longstanding reputation as the most enthusiastic fraternizers of all the Allies, whistling and hooting at any woman they saw, and almost immediately traffic in sex began in earnest. Especially in defeated Germany, women looked to GIs for protection and even more crucially, food and supplies. Former GIs exchanged stories of women trading sexual favors for tins of corned beef, cigarettes, soap, or chocolate. Almost every German woman, it seemed, took on a kind of "amateur prostitution" in order to survive. In fact, the social fabric of Germany had so disintegrated that a woman refusing to take part in this informal trade was considered selfish in not providing for her family. Germany was most well-known for this but it was extremely common in other parts of war-ravaged Europe, in the liberated nations as well as in the former enemy states of Germany and Italy.

In Japan, the U.S. forces inherited the tradition of "comfort stations" or brothels run exclusively for the armed forces. The story of Korean, Philippine, and Chinese "comfort women" kidnapped and raped by the Japanese forces has come to light through the research of Korean and Japanese historians. What is less commonly known, however, is that in the first months of the

American Occupation of Japan, municipal officials in the towns and cities where U.S. troops were concentrated set up a similar system of brothels exclusively for the American forces. In Tokyo this system was called the Recreation and Amusement Association and at its peak counted more than 34 facilities, including bars, hotels, cabarets, and "comfort stations."[49] The system gained favor from high-ranking officials of the Japanese government, who worried about mass rapes by the U.S. troops—similar to those perpetuated by Japanese forces in Nanking, for example. Military commanders winked at the comfort stations while they wrestled with astronomical VD rates. The women working in military brothels had been recruited from the ranks of former prostitutes, dancers, and other entertainers, but many high school girls, women whose families had been killed in Hiroshima or Nagasaki, office workers, and women working for the Japanese government were recruited as well, sometimes through coercion or deception. The economic collapse of Japan was as dire as that of Germany, and women in comfort stations earned high salaries, but they serviced sometimes dozens of men each night and suffered lasting physical and psychological harm.

The Japanese government described the work as "patriotic" and said that the women stood on the front lines protecting other women from rape and assault. Americans in Japan had indeed committed a startling number of rapes when they first arrived, including two on the first day the U.S. forces touched ground in Japan. Evidence suggests that the rate of sexual assaults declined when the comfort stations were in their prime, but they also fostered a huge increase in the culture of prostitution in occupation Japan. By the time pressure from U.S. military chaplains forced SCAP to end the practice of "comfort stations" and a few months later to put all brothels and clubs off-limits, about 150,000 women worked as prostitutes. They had no other choice of employment, so they continued to work as streetwalkers, forcing the practice into public spaces. The VD rate among GIs continued to rise, and another wave of sexual violence followed the change in SCAP's approach to prostitution.[50] As the occupation wore on, a level of sexual exploitation similar to that in Germany developed. Americans purchased or coerced sex from Japanese women of all types, from professional streetwalkers to servants and maids working for American families in occupied Japan.

Some types of crime were not characteristic of the American GI. In contrast to the Soviet soldier, the GI in Germany did not tend to rape, although there was a rash of rapes in the spring of 1945—perhaps a response to the anger and shock GIs felt as they discovered the web of concentration camps throughout Germany. Japanese women suffered frequent rape by Americans, but not the vengeful, organized mass rape by the Soviets in Germany. GIs, however, tended to steal items of great value—jewelry, cash, antiques— that they shipped home. One of the most sensational cases involved the theft of the Hessian crown jewels by an American officer couple. Even at the beginning of the twenty-first century, almost 60 years after the end of the war, the recovery of stolen items continues. Stealing from Germans was endemic in the chaotic conditions of postwar Germany, and distinctions between requisitioning, exploitative bartering, and theft blurred. In Japan the Americans also collected Japanese valuables and souvenirs. Ceremonial swords, pistols, and Japanese war flags were among the highly desired trophies brought home by GIs in Japan. However, there has been no widespread recovery of looted Asian art on the scale of that from Europe.

In Germany, the Reichsmark quickly lost all value, and commercial activity moved to informal black markets, which sprang up in all cities and large towns. While the Americans did not create the black market, the American cigarette became the accepted currency. Soldiers seized the opportunity to trade PX items such as cigarettes, liquor, coffee, and chocolate for valuable items to ship home. In Japan, the currency never collapsed as it did in Germany, but American goods fetched a high price in black market trading.

Alcohol fueled much misbehavior among GIs. Drinking became one of the most difficult and problematic issues of the occupation. Drunken, obnoxious GIs harassed passersby, vandalized bars and restaurants, and generally created a negative image of the American soldier. Civilians resented the depredations of drunken soldiers, and commanders worried about a possible backlash against GI behavior. A common view was that expressed to a U.S. intelligence officer by a German worker: "The Ami is great, as long as he isn't drunk, because then he fights with anyone who gets in his way, just for the fun of fighting."[51] In France, too, the Americans had a reputation as belligerent drunks. Europeans were not unfamiliar with excessive alcohol intake, but many American soldiers, brought up in the more abstemious culture of the Bible belt, were unaccustomed to strong drink, and it showed.

In such an environment, it was not surprising that civilians both resented the Americans for their arrogance and looked to them as sources of supply. The liberated French remembered GIs as flaunting their wealth, wasting food, liquor and cigarettes with the assurance that more was available. On the other hand, a job with the Americans meant regular meals and the protection of the powerful. Throughout Europe and Asia, women lined up to take the washing and cleaning jobs that the Americans offered, and civilians crowded around the mess halls, waiting for scraps of food. Thefts of supplies from Army depots were common; GI guards often sympathetically turned their backs on pilfering, even handing over items themselves. For at least two years after the end of the war, the economies of American-occupied Germany and Japan depended in large part on black market bartering and the sex trade.

The crude Wild West atmosphere of the occupation strained relations with civilians and endangered the mission of reconstruction in the defeated nations. Exploitative economic relations sparked resentment, and an atmosphere of drunkenness, sexual excess, and casual violence did not impress the local population. It also put a strain on the structure of the military itself as commanders struggled with poor discipline bordering on insubordination. VD rates remained high, endangering the health of the men. By late 1945 SCAP and OMGUS decided, in conjunction with civilian leaders, to allow the spouses and children of military personnel to join them overseas. It was thought that the presence of families would calm the chaotic atmosphere and provide a sense of normalcy for the men. The decision was not an easy one to make, as leaders could not absolutely guarantee the safety of the families. Nevertheless, the first wives and children arrived in Germany and Japan in the spring and summer of 1946. While the problems of the occupation did not disappear overnight, commanders did see the presence of families gradually restrain the worst excesses, and "normalize" life in very abnormal circumstances.

3

★ ★ ★ ★ ★

The Creation of a Worldwide Basing System

INTRODUCTION

To a great extent, the Cold War began and ended as a non-war. The United States and the Soviet Union never faced each other directly on the battlefield, and the numerous instances of hostilities that marred the post-war era never escalated into a conflagration on the scale seen earlier in the century. Rather, both superpowers stationed huge numbers of troops outside their own borders, training and practicing, waiting for the day when the other side might make an offensive move. To achieve this defensive perimeter, the United States and its allies constructed an extensive—and expensive—system of bases ringing the USSR and its satellites. In some regions, authorities merely spruced up and reopened old World War II bases; in other cases entirely new systems evolved. In many areas, new construction was a desperately needed economic stimulus, but the new installations transformed isolated regions in ways not always for the better, though sometimes the host population successfully resisted the continued presence of the U.S. forces or limited their activities and influence. The power of the United States, however, overwhelmed most objections. It was a unique time, and not destined to last.

Along with the creation of the worldwide basing system of the Cold War, the military also developed an extensive network of facilities for the families of military personnel, signaling the permanence, or at least the long-term nature, of the system. The "Little Americas," as they were sometimes

called, included housing, shopping, schools, and recreation opportunities
for military families, imitation American towns in which the military
population could feel at home, whether in Tokyo, Libya, or Germany.
Military communities isolated Americans from their host communities to a
rather unfortunate extent, but they also freed up needed housing and office
stock, and, by keeping Americans among themselves, minimized some of
the negative effects of the American presence while allowing positive contact to develop. In the 1950s and early 1960s, relations between many
American military communities and their hosts beneficially influenced
both societies as interaction tended to be voluntary and positive. Particularly in Europe, where military personnel and host civilians shared a similar
culture, broadly speaking, these years were the golden age of "friendship"
activities, such as military band concerts, dances and balls, parades, and
festivals. Problems and controversies did not disappear; irritations from
aircraft noise and maneuver damage to rowdy troop behavior and anti-
American nationalism continued to occupy the time and energy of those
assigned to cultivate military–civilian relations. On the whole, however, as
host nation economies developed and the military became more family-
oriented, many of the problems of the occupation dwindled to relative
insignificance.

THE BEGINNING OF THE COLD WAR

The preceding chapter describes a peculiar era: the military occupation
of the defeated nations of the Second World War. U.S. soldiers, sailors,
and marines remained in many other lands throughout the world as well,
not as occupying forces, but as combatants whose war had ended. By
1949, the GIs in the liberated countries of Europe and Asia by and large
had returned to their homes. The remaining soldiers assigned to the occupied lands, including South Korea, Austria, Italy, as well as those in Allied
host nations like the Philippines, Guam, and Panama, had been given
peacetime duty overseas. Although the occupation of Germany lasted until
1949 (with an additional six years of supervision under the U.S. High
Commissioner) and that of Japan continued until the formal peace treaty
in 1951, the number of troops overseas declined dramatically. By 1950
only 79,000 GIs remained in Germany, with further cuts expected to
follow.

This withdrawal took place in spite of growing signs of hostility and
conflict between the United States and the Soviet Union. The many events
that destroyed the already shaky wartime alliance are well known—the
dissolution of the Allied Control Commission governing Germany; the
Communist takeover of Eastern Europe; the development of a Soviet
atomic bomb; the victory of Communist forces in China; the Berlin Blockade and consequent Airlift. As early as 1946, Winston Churchill referred

to an "iron curtain" descending over Eastern Europe, and diplomat George Kennan described the Soviet Union as determinedly expansionist in his famous "Long Telegram."

Even so, it was not until 1950 that the United States defined the policy of "containment"—preventing any further expansion of communism—in a document known as NSC 68. In that year, the United States was forced to put the policy into action when communist North Korea invaded South Korea, pushing far into South Korean territory. As U.S. policymakers viewed it, not unreasonably, the invasion signaled the expansionist aims of the communists, and the event, magnified by the fact that U.S. troops came to the aid of South Korea, spurred the United States to develop a strategy of military containment.

The strategy, to summarize it in the simplest terms, involved several elements. The first was the establishment of a ring of airbases around the USSR under the Strategic Air Command (SAC), part of the newly independent U.S. Air Force, from which bombers could attack major Soviet cities and military bases. A second part of the strategy used naval forces in the Pacific Ocean, where aircraft carriers could relocate along any coastline and mobilize fighter aircraft. The third element included ground forces of the U.S. Army, mostly in Europe and South Korea, where they would face any potential ground invasion by the USSR. In addition to these major elements, personnel on thousands of small installations collected electronic intelligence, and a huge chain of support provided the equipment and supplies needed by a global force. The early 1950s strategy of containment envisioned a total of 150 airbases, plus naval bases and army installations, at a cost of more than $3 billion.

BUILDING A COLD WAR BASING SYSTEM

It is often said that the generals of any army plan and prepare to fight the previous war. This bromide holds true for the Cold War era as well— the containment policy attempted to avoid the mistakes of appeasement by denying the communists opportunities to expand through conquest. The physical structure of the worldwide basing system developed in the 1950s also revealed its origins in the previous war. Many of the bases used by Cold War forces originated as World War II installations, both Allied and Axis. The SAC bases in Great Britain, for example, had been used by U.S. and RAF bombers, and many U.S. bases in Germany had been Wehrmacht property until their confiscation in 1945.

Postwar settlements, in fact, shaped the overall strategy of U.S. forces in West Germany. Almost all the U.S. bases in Germany were located in the German states (Länder) which had been part of the U.S. Zone during the occupation, while British forces were stationed in the north, where their zone had been. A purely military strategy, however, would have called for greater numbers of troops in the north, where the Soviets were more likely to approach.[1]

The American base system in Germany, including airbases and army ground troops defending the Fulda Gap, proved remarkably simple to develop. The West German government under Chancellor Konrad Adenauer supported the creation of a strong defense against communism as well as closer ties with the United States. Of course, the bases needed a great deal of construction and renovation, but this created little overt controversy; until 1957 the West German government paid all occupation costs including base construction. Ownership remained in German hands, but the Americans retained the right to use the properties indefinitely.

Another case where the creation of a U.S. basing system ran smoothly occurred in Great Britain. In 1948, American flight personnel returned to Britain for the Berlin Airlift, and mothballed airbases reopened. No formal treaty governed the jurisdiction or uses of these troops; the Americans and British simply resumed the close association they had enjoyed during the war. The SAC strategy, however, required new or expanded bases for its long-range bombers and new facilities for housing the families of U.S. personnel. The two nations split the cost of building or expanding the bases, anything beyond stringent RAF standards coming from the U.S. defense budget. To cite just one example, the Americans demanded better heating systems than those available in Europe, a luxury paid for by the American rather than the British taxpayer.[2]

Germany and Great Britain were the easy cases. In some of the most vital regions to the U.S. forces, such as France and Morocco, a large American military presence had not existed during the war, so a new basing system had to be built more or less from scratch. In a few cases, such as Libya and Iceland, where U.S. troops had established a wartime presence, the populace and the postwar governments resisted participation in postwar containment. Only after the outbreak of the Korean War did these nations allow foreign military bases on their soil.

The U.S. forces needed airbases in France, not only as a part of SAC but as part of the transatlantic supply line from the United States to West Germany. In 1952, a bilateral agreement between France and the United States allowed the Americans to take possession of or build airbases in eastern France and to build a supply depot at Chateauroux in central France as well as an army post near Paris.[3] The construction of these important links in the defense of Europe turned out to be more of an adventure than anywhere else on the continent.

Construction delays in France led to huge cost overruns, work undone, and American personnel living for several years in substandard conditions. One of the problems exacerbating the mess was a cumbersome program whereby a French liaison department hired and paid all French contractors. The liaison was slow and inefficient, and interpreted the 1952 agreement quite differently than the Americans did. It objected to paying for many items that the Americans believed were part of the French responsibility under the agreement, and both sides quibbled endlessly. Some French contractors turned down work with the liaison rather than struggle with the tangled bureaucracy, and a few companies even went bankrupt while waiting to be paid.[4] To add insult to injury (in American eyes), the 1952 agreement stipulated that all construction must be handled by French contractors, precluding the use of the Army Corps of Engineers, who, many Americans believed, would have completed the task in half the time.

For its part, the French liaison office argued that it prevented price gouging and fraud by the contractors, protecting the Americans from abuse and the French economy from inflation. The French also pointed out that many American demands, such as the construction of large, modern medical centers, were not realistic in view of the pressing needs of postwar France.[5] The Americans themselves acknowledged that in such a huge program of construction, it was inevitable that there would be some inefficiencies along the way.[6]

Not all the American facilities in France were of recent construction. As in Germany and Great Britain, the Americans renovated already existing buildings whenever possible. Sometimes, however, this turned out to be not such a savings after all; in one case, a headquarters unit took over a building that had been first used as a hospital—in the year 1203.[7] The biggest problem with the construction project was the large number of personnel forced to live in tents because barracks buildings had not been finished. Eventually, as complaints mounted, the military paid for thousands of prefab housing units at the more than twenty-four camps, bases, and depots at which American military personnel were stationed.[8]

The construction program in Morocco was even more chaotic. French Morocco, a colony since 1912 (another part of Morocco belonged to Spain), had hosted Allied bases during the war. In 1951, the French agreed to allow the Americans to use its colony for SAC.[9] The Moroccan authorities complained that they had not been consulted on the agreement, but the Air Force found the region to be so ideal for the long runways needed by SAC bombers that American negotiators simply tried to paper over the issue. Even as Moroccan nationalists demanded independence from France in exchange for the development of the bases, the Air Force began to send over construction materials for building the landing strips, which, they hoped, would be completed in record time.[10] The Army Corps of Engineers and a coalition of American construction companies built the bases with the help of imported American and French skilled workers and Moroccan labor.

As can be imagined, the sudden influx of thousands of well-paid workers, both local and foreign, dramatically affected the poor and underdeveloped colony, even though, to minimize conflict, the bases were situated in the sparsely inhabited desert. In nearby Casablanca, housing prices equalled those of New York City within about six months. Although military personnel were authorized to bring their families over if they found housing for them first, almost no one was able do so.[11] Moreover, the rush to complete the projects meant lax supervision of accounting and quality control; a report to Congress responding to allegations of waste indicated that as much as $50 million had disappeared through fraud and abuse, and at least $2 million worth of equipment had been stolen from the construction sites.[12] Engineers sent over to supervise the construction projects reported that some of the runways were virtually unusable because of shoddy construction—one airstrip, an engineer said, was so poorly constructed that it "looked like it had popcorn strewn all over [it]." And engineers complained that although workers were paid for 60- to 70-hour weeks, they often brought flasks of iced brandy to work, diminishing their productivity.[13]

In spite of the problems, by July 1952 two bases were ready for use, and another three opened at the end of the year. Before the work had finished, the Department of Defense (DOD), successor to the old War Department, cut costs by replacing more expensive American workers with lower-paid but equally skilled Europeans, as it was doing throughout Europe in an initiative called Project Native Son.[14]

The fiascos in France and Morocco taught the DOD valuable lessons in contracting and supervising the construction of military bases. A few years later a series of installations was built from the ground up in Spain, yet no extensive graft or inefficiency marred the construction of the major SAC runways at Zaragoza, Torrejon, and Moron. Spain also hosted a variety of smaller installations, begun in 1953 and completed in 1959. By 1960 about 7,000 U.S. troops were stationed in Spain, almost all of them part of USAF.[15]

Some construction programs were even more astounding. Perhaps the most Herculean effort occurred in Greenland, where Thule Air Base was built in the summer of 1952. Greenland had proven useful to U.S. forces during the war, but Denmark, Greenland's mother nation, did not initially allow the seventeen wartime bases to remain open. Interestingly, the populations around the bases wanted them to stay, as they provided the only means of contact with the outside world. In 1951, after several years of negotiations, Denmark gave NATO permission to use Greenland as a military base site.[16] Most of the wartime bases eventually closed down or reverted to civilian use with the possibility of reactivation in an emergency. Thule, only 900 miles from the North Pole,[17] became the centerpiece of the U.S. presence in Greenland. Materials and workers came in by ship for the six-week-long summer, the only time that construction could proceed. The last of the workers left in November, just before they were snowed in.[18] The buildings at Thule Air Base connected with a series of tunnels so personnel stationed there during the winter never went outdoors.

Like Greenland, Iceland was a possession of Denmark, at least until 1944 when it declared its independence. Also like Greenland, it occupied a strategically important location, relatively close, via the North Pole, to the Soviet Union. U.S. troops had used Iceland for intelligence gathering since 1941, but when the Americans requested permission to establish a long-term presence on the island at the end of the war, Iceland refused. At American urging, Iceland reluctantly accepted a founding membership in NATO with the condition that no troops be stationed there during peacetime,[19] but after the beginning of the Korean War, Iceland realized its vulnerability to attack from the USSR, and it signed a base treaty with the United States in May 1951.[20] The people of Iceland, however, wished to protect their unique culture and traditions from the Americanization spreading rapidly all over the world, so they insisted on strict limits on the number of troops allowed into the country and a severe policy of separation. American men were not allowed to date or marry Icelandic women, and commanders could issue only 100 weekend passes at any time to American soldiers visiting Reykjavik.[21]

FAMILIES AND LITTLE AMERICAS

By the end of the 1950s, approximately 1 million American troops and family members resided on or near overseas bases in all parts of the world.[22] Some installations were tiny outposts with just a few American personnel, far from population centers, as in the Arctic. Most American servicemembers, however, lived on city-like bases housing thousands of men, women, and children, and these concentrations, while required for strategic reasons, posed special problems for armed forces planners and for the communities adjacent to them.

With the arrival of large numbers of women and children at overseas locations, beginning in Germany and Japan in 1946 and spreading to other areas almost as soon as a base had been established, commanders found it desirable to create replicas of American towns to help personnel and families feel at home. These "Little Americas" as they were sometimes called, mostly by those outside the system, included separate, specially built housing areas divided by rank (but within ranks, completely desegregated—it is often said that military housing is the only truly desegregated American living space), shopping centers with commissaries and PXs (Base Exchanges or BXs in Air Force parlance), schools, hospitals, chapels, gymnasiums, playgrounds, and other recreation areas such as golf courses and swimming pools, even beaches and ski resorts. With the establishment of "Little Americas," military personnel and their families hardly had reason to leave the base. It seemed to many, even at the time, that an opportunity for intercultural contact was being lost, but commanders realized they needed to pay attention to quality of life issues in order to retain expensively trained personnel. Without some semblance of natural community life, officers and enlisted personnel would desert the military for better opportunities in the civilian world.

The presence of family members on bases in forward regions became a potent symbol of American commitment to global defense and a sign to allied nations that the United States would not abandon them to their fate in case of conflict. In actuality, this symbol was a bit less than it appeared, because all installations with family members maintained extensive evacuation plans in case of emergency. Still, commanders knew that the evacuation of a military community would never be undertaken lightly. In the Berlin Crisis of 1948 General Clay decided after some reflection not to evacuate American family members from West Germany as a message to the USSR, the Germans, and the rest of the world that America stood by its friends.

Military planners also aimed at minimizing tensions with host communities, ever-present because of the huge economic disparities between comparatively wealthy American personnel and impoverished civilians. In postwar Germany and Japan, for example, the initial reaction to the creation of "Little Americas" was relief, as separate family housing areas for Americans eased the burden on existing housing stock in the neighborhoods around bases. In both nations, many towns and cities had been destroyed by Allied bombing, and in Germany the influx of millions of ethnic German expellees from Eastern Europe and the Soviet Union added pressure to an already chaotic situation. Before the construction of "Little Americas," military families lived in requisitioned neighborhoods, shopped at requisitioned stores, and sent their children to requisitioned schools. By the early 1950s, many Germans had been out of their homes for seven or eight years and were impatient to return. In most German towns with a significant American population, "Victims of Requisitioning Associations" lobbied local authorities to negotiate on their behalf. In 1949 it appeared that the requisitioning problem might be moving closer toward resolution, but a year later that hope dwindled as large numbers of Americans began arriving. By 1953 the situation seemed dire, but it was at this point that large American housing areas began to appear throughout southern West Germany.

Housing was designed in the German three-story apartment style ("stairwell" housing, in American parlance), but with American electric standards, larger rooms, more space for autos, and more lawn surrounding the buildings than found in typical German developments. Not all Germans approved of the new housing areas, which usually were built on requisitioned farmland. Overall, however, "Little Americas" turned out to be a significant step toward reducing and then eliminating the problem of requisitioned housing in West Germany.

A similar situation developed in France, where American families struggled to feel at home in cramped housing far from the bases. One reason for the housing shortage in France was that the large and central base at Chateauroux was activated long before the last construction workers packed up and went home,[23] and significant numbers of personnel and family members arrived in the country without sufficient housing and facilities available for them. Beginning in September 1952, when construction of the largest French bases was just beginning, an additional 10,000 enlisted men and 1,000 officers were deployed to France to oversee construction.[24] Most families lived miles from base,[25] with nothing to do and little contact with the local populace, and American personnel dreaded duty in France because of the miserable housing situation. Rumors spread that deployment to France was a way to get rid of underperforming personnel and officers from units in Germany, and, although this was probably not true, a tour in France could represent a damning label on a career. American personnel believed, with justification, that they were unwelcome in France, and they did not try to reach out to their hosts.[26]

Other problems developed when families arrived with little understanding of what to expect in their new homes. Most military families were flexible, resourceful, and adventurous, characteristics virtually required for the demanding lifestyle of the global military. Even so, unwary families were taken advantage of by landlords and local businesses because of their unfamiliarity with the host culture, traditions, and even systems of currency. This was a particular problem in Britain, for example, not because the British were more unscrupulous than any other nationality, but because Americans came to Britain expecting to find a slightly different version of America, and what they discovered was a foreign country where English happened to be spoken.

Germany became a popular destination, but even the finest "Little Americas" in Germany had their faults, especially in the early years. Americans from small towns, for instance, found to their dismay that locked doors were necessary to prevent petty thievery by impoverished Germans. In many underdeveloped or war-damaged nations, Americans had to learn to keep house differently, make do with military-issue foodstuffs, and take unfamiliar disease prevention measures such as boiling drinking water.

Some observers have asserted that American families also served as role models for political and social life in the host nations. There is even some evidence that American policymakers viewed the families as "ambassadors" to their hosts, expecting them to demonstrate political values such as democracy and freedom in private life. However, this does not seem to be a primary reason for creating the extensive replicas of middle American suburbs that the United States built throughout the world. If anything, the Americans living on overseas bases reinforced a stratified, rank-based social order among themselves. Within the base community, the hierarchy of rank was maintained among wives and children of military personnel. In this sense, "Little Americas" served as a valuable support for the military system itself, encouraging family members to identify with and socialize within the military community. Military planners created "Little Americas," it appears, to maintain morale by making soldiers and their families as comfortable as possible, minimize problems with the host community by removing the economic and social burdens of American populations in vulnerable communities, and to reinforce identification with and involvement in the American community for military personnel and their family members.

What was life like in these communities? In many ways, "Little Americas" were caricatures of the American suburbs, more perfect than the real thing. But there were differences. Personnel and family members showed their ID cards when entering a base or military store, for example. Another distinction was the ever-present awareness of military rank. A more significant difference was the extreme mobility of military families. Personnel were transferred every year or two, resulting in 100 percent turnover every few years.

But by and large, the typical "Little America" was a reasonable facsimile of home. First of all, military planners took care to provide personnel and family members with the opportunity to purchase American food, clothing, and other goods through the PX/BX, Commissary, and other shops. The PX could be the size of a small shop or a large two-story department store. Commissaries, similar to supermarkets, could be found only on larger installations; unlike the PX, which was run by a private company contracting with the armed forces, the Army Quartermaster managed the Commissary. Most items in the commissaries had been shipped from the United States, although many perishables were purchased on the local economy. In the Azores, for example, a large dairy, one of the biggest businesses on the island, supplied the Air Force installation with milk products. The commissaries usually offered a small assortment of local foods— German sausage or Japanese rice, for example, popular among the more adventurous Americans as well as locally-born spouses. Along with the PX and commissaries, large installations also included other types of shops and services—hairdressers, bookstores, dry cleaning establishments, laundromats, and shops peculiar to the military like Military Clothing Stores and "Class Six Stores" selling rationed spirits.

The military offered numerous recreation options on base, albeit recreation that suited the goals and culture of the military. Bowling alleys could be found at bases from Wheelus Air Base in Libya to the Philippines, Okinawa, and South Korea. Golf courses took up a great deal of valuable land but enjoyed great popularity in Japan, Panama, Germany, Turkey, and England. Almost any base of even modest size boasted gymnasiums and other sporting facilities such as tracks and baseball fields. In addition to sports, most installations maintained at least one recreation center, offering organized activities such as classes, hobby meetings, and dances. Even the smallest installations had a movie theater—Chateauroux in France opened a movie theater before it offered base housing. Most bases had some sort of library, even if the offerings were limited. Separate clubs for officers, NCOs, enlisted personnel, and, in the early years, civilian employees formed another mainstay of base recreation. Over the years, as budgetary concerns became paramount, the club system shrank; most separate NCO and enlisted clubs were consolidated, and civilian clubs closed. During the early Cold War era, however, bases of any size could sustain six or seven different clubs easily. The armed forces also maintained a chapel system run by Catholic, Protestant, and Jewish chaplains.

In the 1950s, the military population experienced the baby boom as much as any other American community, possibly even more so, because virtually everyone in a military community was in their early 20s or 30s, the age of most parents with young children. Military dependents overseas required suitable educational facilities, and placing them in host community schools was not feasible. An overseas military school system was developed and run by a subdepartment of the Defense Department known as DODDS (Department of Defense Dependent Schools); it established schools and hired American teachers to teach overseas. Within 10 years of the beginning of the basing system, thousands of DODDS elementary and high schools all over the world educated military children.

Beginning in 1949, colleges and universities began to contract with the armed forces to offer courses and degrees to servicemembers and their families overseas. The University of Maryland was one such school, with a separate branch of the university system devoted to adult continuing education, most of it overseas. Other universities included Embry–Riddle University, the University of Oklahoma, Boston University, and Troy State University; others came and went. Instructors, recruited from the United States, taught courses in quonset huts, in hangars, on ships—in any available space. Personnel could receive two- and four-year undergraduate degrees as well as MS and MA degrees.

In spite of these numerous options, life on a military base could be boring and dreary, especially for family members. For spouses, work outside the home was almost unheard of; most women had small children, and frequent moves made settling into a job difficult. Moreover, many Status of Forces Agreements (SOFAs) governing the rights and limitations of military personnel prohibited family members from taking jobs designated for host nationals. For women, organizations for officers' wives and enlisted wives provided social support and raised money for charity through social events. However, the hierarchy of military rank was magnified in the isolated world of the overseas military base, and it is no surprise that many found the atmosphere stifling. In the early 1950s, one medical officer at an Air Force medical center reported large numbers of neurotic complaints from women who had nothing to do all day but visit the clubs; in Okinawa, military wives, their household chores done by servants, often spent too much time drinking and losing money in the slot machines that were pervasive in overseas military clubs. Even the information from the outside world was controlled—Armed Forces Network (AFN) television and radio programming provided bland uniformity in news and entertainment, interspersed with public service messages and information about upcoming events on base. The Stars and Stripes newspaper remained nominally independent but in practice rarely printed news that deviated too sharply from the official line.

The "Little Americas," then, provided a safe and sanitized environment for American personnel and their families, where they could move from Panama to Okinawa to Great Britain to Libya and find the same recreation options, the same products in the stores, the same information on television and radio and in newspapers that they had become accustomed to in their previous station. The "Little Americas" made life easier for personnel and their families. On the other hand, they isolated Americans from their host communities, and as a result most members of the military community were exposed to foreign cultures only in small and superficial ways, such as tourism, eating in restaurants, and occasional shopping in local stores.

CONTACT WITH THE HOST COMMUNITY

The development of "Little Americas" did not mean that no Americans pursued contact with the local population, however. In fact, during the 1950s a premium was placed on positive interaction with the host communities, in which the Americans were to act as "goodwill ambassadors," reinforcing the alliance against communism and demonstrating positive American values in their private behavior. In reality, interaction between Americans and host populations often proved somewhat rocky, but in the early 1950s the civil affairs office promulgated a new policy of emphasizing the friendship between the United States and its allies though public relations events.

Perhaps the most intriguing of these are the numerous public relations events held in Germany, a nation which, less than a decade earlier, had been at war with the United States and was guilty of truly atrocious crimes against humanity. On the other hand, Germans shared with white Americans certain aspects of culture as well as a racial similarity, which in the eyes of both groups made friendship much easier. Friendship activities in Asia and Latin America never flourished the way they did in West Germany, and, perhaps not coincidentally, Asian public support for the U.S. presence never reached German levels.

In the late 1940s the Americans considered Germans to be in need of re-education and treated the population as pupils, subordinate to their instructors. In the wake of the Korean War, however, the paternalistic policy was revised as Germany became a valuable ally. In 1952, major installations in Germany began celebrating "German–American Friendship Week," a period in May dedicated to friendship between the two nations. Events such as concerts, lectures, and exhibitions drew host nationals and American personnel, although as the years went by some of the more intellectual events faded away. The high point of German–American Friendship Week came at the end of the week with open-house festivals at the main installations. The most interesting of these were the Air Force bases, where the base displayed aircraft from the United States and other NATO nations. The daylong events attracted hundreds of thousands to U.S. bases, and the open house fit perfectly into the German summer festival tradition. Particularly famous were the "individual" containers of American ice cream, which, the Germans joked, provided enough to feed an entire family. Open-house festivals gave Germans a chance to peer behind the walls that blocked off the installations every other day of the year.

Even before official attempts at fostering German–American friendship began, individuals on many installations established German–American friendship clubs. The first advocate of German–American clubs was Merle Potter, an officer at Bad Kissingen; thanks in large part to his efforts, 17 clubs had been founded by 1948. Most were either mens' or womens' clubs. After 1950, womens' clubs outnumbered mens'. The clubs focused on raising money for local charities—in the early years generally relief efforts, later on scholarship funds and exchange programs—and getting to know more about each other's cultures.

Throughout the 1950s and early 1960s, organized activities such as clubs, dances, and charity events provided a common mode of entertainment and social life in civilian communities in the United States as well as military communities overseas, a trend which dovetailed with the German fondness for organized activities. Many activities revolved around Christian holidays and musical performances, which could be enjoyed in spite of language difficulties. At Christmas, military personnel organized children's parties and public concerts, and at Easter chaplains held interdenominational services. In the summer, military bands performed in public parks.

These officially sponsored activities fit in well with German traditions and made Germans and Americans feel as though they shared a common culture. In areas where host and guest did not share a common culture, such points of connection were more elusive. Still, there were occasional successes. In Libya, an Islamic nation sharing little with the United States, the Air Force held a rodeo in the summer, in which American personnel and Libyans, who had a tradition of horse culture, participated. Airmen from Morocco came to participate in the rodeo, a taste of home for some of them.

Some of this activity merely fostered the image of the United States as a "good neighbor" and carried little overt political meaning. Nevertheless, the military wished to reinforce the notion that host communities and Americans appreciated the importance of fighting communism. Unfortunately, some of their hosts seemed not to fear the communists with fervor sufficient for American standards. While countries like Spain under Francisco Franco officially supported the anti-communist cause, others, such as Greece, saw little threat from the USSR, and support for the Americans remained tentative and ambivalent. Hellenikon, the major air base in Greece, lay very close to Athens and provided an uncomfortably visible U.S. presence, of which the Greeks disapproved.[27] Even in nations where the government supported containment wholeheartedly, the people sometimes showed themselves less than convinced of the danger. The British public, not overwhelmed by the amount of anti-communist propaganda washing over the United States, took the threat of communism relatively lightly. This, according to one journalist, was the "main cause of arguments and fights on Saturday nights in local bars." Another journalist in Britain detailed the strangely paranoid anti-communism of the Americans—a young boy afraid to ride his bicycle outside because he might be kidnapped by communists, personnel who never left their families alone because of an imagined threat of communist break-ins.[28] Such eccentricities entertained the European public but made the Americans appear credulous.

All in all, although the subtext of friendship activities was alliance and mutual commitment to anti-communism, local populations took what they valued from the activities—an opportunity for exotic socializing, a chance to sample American food or drink, a relaxing summer afternoon listening to well-performed music. That the Americans sometimes seemed to be the only ones who truly believed in the imminence of the communist menace did not measurably diminish the success of friendship events.

PROBLEMS BETWEEN HOST AND GUEST

The American presence, in spite of attempts at forging friendship, was not always smooth and uncomplicated. Even where the friendship was most cordial, as in Germany and Italy, problems of local interaction needed to be addressed on a regular basis. In most areas of Europe, councils of base commanders and host community leaders met regularly to discuss problems and concerns. In other regions, such as South Korea, these councils did not exist until much later, indicating, perhaps, the relative lack of importance military officials placed on public relations in less developed regions. Each military community developed a different arrangement for dealing with its host, but the most effective ones maintained a regular, organized, and bilateral system of communication.

Generally speaking, the most annoying problems plaguing a military community were strictly local, and thus amenable to solutions, or at least to discussion and attempts at resolving them. In the early 1950s, one of the first challenges to be dealt with extensively in local councils was the issue of requisitioned buildings and lands. In Germany this problem dragged on for years, and the construction of housing areas was an attempt to solve it. But even the housing areas used requisitioned land, and in other places the problem of using land for new base construction was even more severe. In France, thousands of acres were requisitioned for use in building the chain of supply installations across France, and French farmers protested vehemently against the seizure of valuable farmland for such a purpose.[29] Likewise, military officials in Okinawa requisitioned land from traditional subsistence farmers, who had few other options for earning a livelihood. In the case of Okinawa, the farmers fought for and eventually won the right to receive annual rental payments from the U.S. forces, and most of them became strong supporters of the U.S. presence for economic reasons.

In towns and cities near Air Force bases, noise from flying aircraft became one of the most consistent problems raised by local officials. Noise pollution came in the form of the irritating drone of takeoff and landing practice, or the harsh scream of fighter planes, or even the sonic boom, the deafening thunder of an aircraft flying faster than the speed of sound. As early as the mid-1950s host communities complained of the problem. In Okinawa, mainland Japan, the Philippines, South Korea, and Germany, airbases occupied areas much more heavily populated than was customary in the United States, where such bases could be located in sparsely populated western states. Most of the noise occurred during training flights; the military's rigorous system of flight training produced the best pilots in the world, many of whom went on to fly commercial aircraft after their military retirements. The excellence of USAF training was small comfort, however, to those who suffered its side effects. In some regions, airbases did away with flying late at night and early in the morning, during lunch hours, and during funerals, but in other areas where training required noise practice or where the populace could not exert enough pressure to change the rules, the situation persisted.

Another problem connected with flying was the danger of air crashes. In 1968, a plane crash on the campus of a Japanese university, for example, gave opponents of U.S. bases in Japan an ideal talking point. Other dangers from the American presence included accidents involving tanks and other army vehicles; as recently as 2002 an armored vehicle caused two civilian deaths in South Korea. In poor areas like the Philippines, scavengers braved the artillery ranges searching for scrap metal to sell, occasionally suffering injury or death from exploding shells.

The problem of troop misbehavior continued to exasperate local officials. In the early 1950s, drunkenness and fighting became so out of control that bar owners themselves put their establishments "off-limits" to Americans, in contrast to the late 1940s when "off-limits" designations were considered a grave punishment. Different countries had varying levels of control over the behavior of troops in their country. In the Philippines, for example, the local police had no jurisdiction over American servicemen who committed crimes, a flaw in the treaty much resented by Filipinos, especially when they saw other countries, like former enemy Japan, enjoying more favorable agreements. At the other extreme, Iceland exercised strict control over the U.S. troops stationed in that country so the behavior of American servicemembers had no serious impact on Icelandic society.

. A more difficult problem for the Americans and local authorities to solve was genuine anti-American or anti-military sentiment stemming from ideological differences. As the forward embodiment of American power, military personnel, and their families were never immune to anti-American sentiment or actions. In Italy and France the large communist parties scrawled "Ami Go Home!" on buildings near military installations, and in Libya nationalists maintained a similar "Quit Libya" campaign. Sometimes this opposition stretched to violence; military bases occasionally suffered bombing attempts, but in the 1950s, these usually failed and had little overall effect.

Anti-Americanism was fairly common among the young and educated, who responded to the depiction of U.S. forces as agents of imperialism, especially in nations with a history of colonial oppression. Moroccans, while not anti-American in any specific sense, hated the French presence in their country and associated the Americans with it. Arab League pressure not to allow "outworn imperialism" influenced the Libyan government away from the Americans by the early 1960s, but as early as 1952 Egypt introduced a resolution in the UN General Assembly asking that foreign troops be withdrawn from Libya within 6 months.[30] (The resolution did not pass.) In Japan, young people frequently protested the American presence, demanding that the bases leave.

Another ideological problem for the Americans during the 1950s concerned the presence of nuclear weapons on the soil of other nations. In Britain, the Campaign for Nuclear Disarmament (CND) organized a protest against the deployment of nuclear weapons there. In Germany, a similar movement protested not only nuclear weapons, but German rearmament; the Japanese public also objected to nuclear weapons on its soil. The anti-nuclear protests of the 1950s petered out by the end of the decade, but sentiment against the horrific weapons remained dormant, waiting to explode at another more opportune time.

4

★ ★ ★ ★ ★

Challenges to the Global U.S. Basing System

INTRODUCTION

By the end of the 1950s, the worldwide basing system stood more or less in place. The armed forces could look with pride at a number of impressive achievements: installations constructed or expanded, agreements with host nations concluded, military personnel enlisted into the armed services, new weapons systems developed. This equilibrium, unfortunately, could not last forever, and in the decade and a half from the mid-1960s to the end of the 1970s, the U.S. basing system faced challenges from many directions, both internal and external.

The first storm cloud on the horizon involved the economics of military defense. In the early postwar years, the United States stood in an admirable financial position as the only industrialized nation not severely damaged by the war, and as such was able to exert tremendous political and economic influence over its allies. Funding controlled by the U.S. forces overseas stretched far in impoverished host nations; products and services purchased from the host nations came cheaply. However, most overseas military installations were located in Europe or Northeast Asia—first-world nations devastated by war. As host nation economies began to revive, the military found itself at a disadvantage in its dealings "on the economy" (with businesses in the host community), especially when hiring local employees, who earned better pay and benefits from civilian firms. In addition, the United States found itself with an immense foreign trade deficit, in part due to the expenses of maintaining the global military presence, and the Pentagon pressed overseas military communities to tighten belts and save.

In one sense, the military's budget difficulties could be viewed as a sign of the success of the peacekeeping efforts of the U.S. forces around the world—under the U.S. defense umbrella, the economies of Germany, Japan, South Korea, and other allies developed and flourished in peace. Nationalism, another challenge faced by the U.S. forces in the 1960s, could also be interpreted as the result of the growth of democracy and self-determination in the non-communist world, but this problem could not be solved by cutting expenses or making do with less. In some cases poorly conceived Status of Forces Agreements of the early postwar years, overly generous to the powerful Americans, stimulated resentment. In other cases, new governments demanded more favorable conditions for basing agreements. Nationalist movements in North Africa, France, Japan, Greece, Turkey, and Panama pushed for the expulsion of U.S. forces from their soil, an ominous development for the global basing system. In several nations, nationalists achieved their goals, at considerable trouble and expense to the United States and its allies.

By far the most devastating development of the 1960s for the U.S. forces, however, was the Vietnam War. Not only did more than 55,000 U.S. troops and hundreds of thousands of Vietnamese soldiers and civilians lose their lives, but the entire military institution suffered long-lasting harm as a result of the demoralizing conflict. With the Vietnam War came widespread drug use, anti-military activism, racial tensions and increasing crime, all of which debilitated the training and readiness of the U.S. forces. By the conclusion of the U.S. military involvement in Vietnam in 1973, a growing movement in Congress favored drastic cuts in military forces overseas, and the army itself was compelled to move from a draft-based force to the "All-Volunteer Force" (AVF). In the short term, the AVF worsened the standards and quality of the enlisted forces, as only those with no other choice joined the services. Added to this, financial cutbacks put a crimp in attempts at base maintenance and upkeep, pay standards, and training efforts. The U.S. armed forces of the late 1970s were a sorry lot—underpaid, underqualified, demoralized, and living and working in deplorable conditions.

ECONOMIC PROBLEMS

The financial status of military communities is unusual in that, rather than earning money through some sort of production, such as industry or agriculture, they are almost entirely dependent on the federal government both for funds that support base infrastructure and the pay that personnel spend on and off base. The U.S. Congress decides each year the amount of money allocated to the Department of Defense, which, in turn, distributes funds through the different branches of the services according to strategic policy directives and priorities. Military communities must stand in line along with weapons research and development, military aid to other nations, personnel payrolls, and other defense-related priorities. No other significant source of income in a military community exists, whether on the part of individuals working outside the base, or money-making endeavors on the installation itself. (On overseas bases, slot machines found in clubs have been perhaps the most important form of additional income, funding recreation activities and other extras. The money going into slot machines, however, comes from the military paycheck, in effect simply a redistribution of the limited funds already in circulation.) As a result of this dependence, the standard of living in the community can swing wildly, affected by the generosity of Congress, the priorities of the Department of Defense, and the management ability of the base comman-der's office. The military community is also affected by its specific mission; factors such as which units are assigned to the installation, authorized troop strength, training schedules, drawdowns, and other such issues are beyond the control of the community, but can transform the quality of life on a base. Thus, for the individual soldier, family member, or civilian neighbor, the military community is essentially a town created, improved upon, or dismantled by the Department of Defense.

That is not to say that military communities do not develop their own culture, traditions, and personalities. Military communities throughout the world affect and are affected by their surroundings, both in very obvious and also more subtle and unexpected ways. After the first postwar decade during which the worldwide system of bases was established, aspects of the very diverse societies in which military bases were planted began to creep into the workings of the installations. In the early 1960s, for exam-ple, military communities in Germany and Japan began to face an unex-pected challenge from their host societies: the rapid reconstruction and growth of the economies of the defeated nations brought neighboring communities up to and even beyond the level of affluence enjoyed by the military.

During the Occupation and in the early years of the buildup, life was bountiful for the victorious Americans. Installations in Japan and Germany could count on an ample supply of inexpensive skilled civilian labor for a variety of tasks, freeing military personnel and family members from oner-ous or menial tasks. In Germany, security guards from Poland, many of them former DPs, manned the gates at installations; German women with excellent educations and credentials worked as typists and translators, as well as cleaners and wait staff; and skilled carpenters, electricians, and plumbers maintained and improved the installations at low cost. In Japan, Japanese civilians were needed for virtually all situations where the

Americans had to deal with the civilian community, because almost no Americans spoke fluent Japanese. In both Germany and Japan, most families hired at least a maid, and often a gardener, at very affordable wages. In Okinawa, for example, military families could hire a maid for $15 to $20 a month.[1]

Recruiting and retaining local employees was not a problem during the years when a job with the Americans was one of the few places a worker could get a steady paycheck and free meals. In Germany, another advantage of working on a base was that the Americans placed little emphasis on the elaborate system that certified German craftsmen. For the Americans, if a worker could do the job, he or she was hired. As the war years had interrupted the educations of many young men and women, this flexibility was crucial.

However, as the postwar economic boom intensified, and the reconstruction of damaged and destroyed factories and offices meant more jobs and better pay and benefits for all, a job with the Americans lost some of its sheen. Civilian employment was handled through the Civilian Personnel Office, (CPO), and while the CPO was responsible for hiring and firing, it could not adjust pay scales or benefits on its own initiative. As Germany and Japan moved toward full employment, wages and benefits offered by local firms began to improve, but the U.S. Congress set wages for civilian employees through the annual budgets passed each year, and there was little flexibility in these. Increasingly, civilian workers on the bases began to fall behind their counterparts in local firms.

Another problem was the lack of job security inherent in working on a military base. Throughout the Cold War years, frequent rumors of base closings or consolidations made workers fear for their jobs. Ironically, the need for the forces to cut expenses came in part as a response to the growing strength of the German and Japanese economies, so the dynamic was a vicious circle. The more rumors of layoffs circulated, the more difficult and costly it became to hire workers, and the fewer workers could be recruited. Meanwhile, American politicians called for budget cuts and cost controls.

By the mid-1960s, CPOs at American bases in Europe found it exasperatingly difficult to hire qualified employees. The CPO could not even spare the funds to place regular ads in local newspapers as civilian firms did. CPOs resorted to tactics like recruiting English-speaking office help from small towns in Australia and Great Britain where unemployment remained high, and sponsoring workers from Southern Europe. Still, budget constraints limited even these measures, which cost money to implement.

By the late 1950s, another economic development began to worry accounting departments in Congress and the DOD: the "gold flow," or the problem of too many American dollars being spent overseas and not enough foreign currency flowing the other way. The American forces did not create the gold flow by themselves—a major cause of the gold flow was the consumption in the United States of inexpensive imported products without enough U.S. products exported to other nations. Military communities and personnel, however, did contribute to the problem through construction of base facilities, the payment of millions of dollars annually to landlords and utility companies, and the purchase of consumer goods and services from local economies. Much of this was an unavoidable part of the U.S. defense commitment, and succeeding administrations tried with varying levels of success to mitigate the effects of the gold flow through trade treaties and "offset payment" agreements.

At least a small part of the gold flow, however, could be controlled by the individual decisions of American personnel and family members, and as the problem grew during the early to mid-1960s, American officials attacked the problem at the local level. In 1966 base commanders in West Germany began an extended gold flow public awareness campaign, reminding personnel and family members that shopping at on-base facilities, rather than in German shops, kept dollars in the American economy. Unfortunately, gold flow campaigns based on patriotic exhortations would produce only limited improvements as long as the exchange rate was relatively favorable to Americans and the offerings in PXs did not meet the needs of shoppers.

Base commanders also began to examine their budgets more closely, looking for ways to save. As one analyst put it, "A large establishment in continuous operation for over twenty years inevitably accumulates pockets of obsolescence,"[2] and by the mid-1960s, it was high time for a new look at programs and procedures. On many installations, finance officers appealed to military and civilian personnel directly for suggestions on cutting costs, based on the assumption that employees knew their jobs intimately and often could devise more efficient procedures than those in place. More significantly, in 1968–1969, the Department of Defense initiated a plan called Reduction of Costs, Europe (REDCOSTE), which aimed to eliminate unnecessary or excessive programs. At the end of the program, REDCOSTE saved U.S. taxpayers $38.3 million.[3] Other similar cost-cutting efforts resulted in millions more dollars saved. Military communities, especially in developed areas like Japan and Germany, began to shift from an expansive overseas presence intent on making life as pleasant as possible for personnel and families to leaner organizations with less waste. As a result, living conditions on bases became somewhat less attractive for their populations.

In Germany, Japan, and Korea, the question of offset payments plagued authorities on both sides for years. In offset payment agreements, host nation governments promised to balance the amount of money the United States spent in the host nation, sometimes through direct cash transfers but more often with the purchase of goods, usually military hardware, from

U.S. industry at a certain price. Given the large number of military forces stationed overseas, these amounts could be quite significant. All the governments concerned made a point of insisting that offset payments did not constitute rent or payment for American protection, nor were they considered, by the Americans at least, occupation costs. Opponents of the bases, of course, saw it differently. And in a sense, all sides benefited from the balance of trade, which strengthened the global economic system and minimized the problems associated with overheated economies.

Nevertheless, offset payments gave headaches to those who negotiated them. Much of the annoyance stemmed from the differing perspectives each nation brought to the question. In American eyes, offset payments seemed a matter of simple fairness; in addition to assuming the burden of defense of Japan and West Germany, a cost that would be paid in American lives, if it ever came to that, Americans viewed the economic success of their former adversaries as a direct result of the U.S. security umbrella. For the Germans and Japanese, offset payments served as a reminder of the occupation years, almost a punishment for the hard work they had put into rebuilding their economies.[4]

The offset payments did not spring up out of the blue. In the immediate postwar years, Japan and Germany had provided bases to the Americans free of charge, and in fact the two defeated nations had paid all occupation costs through most of the 1950s, including the construction of new bases and renovation of old ones, as well as the salaries of local national workers, including maids and servants for American military and diplomatic families. Even with this extensive contribution, a mild balance of payments deficit developed, but in the 1950s, the deficit did not cause concern.[5]

By 1960, however, the balance of payments deficit began to balloon, and the Eisenhower administration asked the West German government to pay $650 million annually to support U.S. troops in Germany. The request was rejected but the West Germans agreed to purchase military equipment from the United States.[6] During the early and mid-1960s, America and West Germany negotiated a further series of agreements, with the West Germans purchasing ever greater amounts of military materiel needed by the Bundeswehr, the reconstituted German armed forces. But by 1966, the Bundeswehr had purchased all the equipment it needed and then some, and the German economy was experiencing its first postwar recession. Chancellor Ludwig Erhard, the architect of the currency reform of 1948, visited the United States to negotiate a decrease in the payments, but President Lyndon Baines Johnson rejected his requests. In fact, Erhard's failure contributed to his electoral downfall a few months later. Negotiations over offset payments became more and more tense through the late 1960s and into the early 1970s as the Americans, also cash-strapped, demanded that the Germans contribute more to the defense effort. From the German perspective, the Americans were short-sighted and unable to admit the vital role played by the Germans in western defense; a war with the USSR would most probably be fought on German soil. When the West German offset payments program finally ended in 1976, it eliminated a large thorn in the side of the German–American relationship. Japan and Korea, however, continue to make offset payments,[7] in part because Japan, at least, follows a protectionist policy, reluctant to allow foreign imports into the country to balance the deficit. In 1979, for example, Japan made $1 billion in offset payments–about 30 percent of local costs for the U.S. forces in Japan, and by 1990 this amount had increased to $6 billion, or 70 percent of costs.[8] The offset payments issue did not immediately affect military communities in the sense that their relations with their hosts were harmed by this rather obscure controversy. It did, however, have a major impact on the bases indirectly, in the amount of money available for base maintenance and other costs.

The major catalyst for base funding dilemmas during the 1960s was the expanding war in Vietnam. Throughout the 1950s and early 1960s the United States had become involved in a multitude of regional conflicts throughout the world, in keeping with her new position as "global police officer." But nowhere did this policy bear its bitter fruit more abundantly than in Southeast Asia, where the Americans assumed the task of protecting the quasi-legitimate state of South Vietnam. In 1964 the Gulf of Tonkin crisis prompted Congress to grant the president authority to expand U.S. involvement in Vietnam significantly. The following year, large numbers of American troops began to flow into Vietnam, along with correspondingly large amounts of money. Within months, the costs of the Vietnam War began to affect the financial condition of military bases elsewhere in the world. "With the cost of supporting combat forces skyrocketing . . . many items taken for granted in past years, were suddenly labeled as luxuries and were either completely eliminated or drastically reduced," concluded one 1968 report on the subject. Non-mission related budgets, such as base libraries and recreation centers, scrambled for scarce funding. While the inconveniences and shortages experienced on bases outside the Southeast Asian theater of course did not compare with the hardships suffered by combatants during the war, they affected the smooth functioning of overseas bases, and in time their impact would become more severe.

NATIONALIST PRESSURES

In addition to nagging economic woes, the U.S. global basing system began to face problems as a result of increasing nationalism in many host nations. While there has been no case of the United States actually forcing the development of bases in an area without the permission of some authority, in European colonies like Morocco, not to mention the Philippines, a U.S. colony until 1946, the colonial power granted base access without consideration for the needs and wishes of the host population. In most cases, adverse reaction to U.S. bases did not constitute generalized anti-American sentiment; American products, culture, and visitors continued to be welcome. But the United States became entangled in too many complex relationships, whether with unpopular autocratic rulers, colonial powers, or exploitative corporations, to remain unsullied. Charges of neo-colonialism came from North Africa, Latin America, Asia, even Europe; and the military installations often emerged as the most visible symbol of American power.

Morocco

Since their construction and expansion in the early 1950s, the U.S. bases in Morocco and Libya were among the most important for the USAF in the European theater. Unbroken stretches of sunny, clear weather and vast expanses of flat ground were ideal for the training of SAC bombers, and the geography of North Africa suited the technology of the day—within striking distance of Moscow but closer to the Western Hemisphere than other locations. In addition, the bases aided the underdeveloped economies of their North African hosts, providing jobs for local residents and a source of contracts for local construction companies, agriculture, and other goods and services.

When Morocco gained its independence in 1956, the king was reported to be favorably inclined toward the bases as a source of employment and as a means by which Morocco's importance in world affairs might increase. Even so, the U.S. presence did not remain trouble-free. The same year, Moroccan employees of the U.S. bases went on strike for pay equal to that earned by workers at Air Force bases in other nations. The Air Force resisted, insisting on paying the workers according to local pay standards, a much cheaper alternative. The Moroccan workers, not unnaturally, resented the second-class treatment they received.[9] (It must be noted, however, that using local standards to determine wages was not only less expensive but less destabilizing for the local economy.)

In spite of the king's initial goodwill toward the bases, the Moroccan government pushed for renegotiating the original base agreement concluded with France, including significantly increased amounts of aid in exchange for basing rights. The United States continued to stand by its refusal to pay "rent" for bases; its official stance was that the bases existed to protect the host nation and, as such, the burden for them should be shouldered evenly between the Americans and the host nation.

Within a few months of Moroccan independence, the United States became enmeshed in the nation's struggle to expel the French. Local dockworkers, for example, refused to unload French naval vessels, which brought supplies for the U.S. bases.[10] Having made extensive concessions to France in order to gain French agreement for the re-armament of West Germany, the United States found itself on the side of the French in its colonial quarrels, whether it wished to be so or not.

By the summer of 1958, Morocco joined the nonaligned nations, led by former British colony India, rejecting outright alliance with either the West or the Soviet Bloc. Morocco announced that it wanted all foreign military forces out of the country, including the 20,000 French, 20,000 Spanish, and 12,000 American troops stationed there.[11] At the end of 1959, the two nations came to an agreement on the turnover,[12] and American evacuation of the bases took place the following year. After spending millions in the early 1950s to construct bases, the American forces fell victim to Moroccan nationalism directed not against the United States but against Morocco's former colonial masters.

Libya

In Libya, the situation seemed at first to be more stable. American leaders believed that the United States would remain in Libya for the long-term at Wheelus AFB, a large and central installation. In 1959, however, Libya requested and received a level of economic assistance much higher than the $4 million a year in direct assistance, plus about $18 million in development and technical aid it had won under a 1954 agreement.[13] Like many nations, Libya believed that the United States could and should do more in exchange for the right to maintain a basing system in the country. When the 1967 Mideast war broke out, the bases in the Mediterranean region, especially those in Muslim nations, found themselves in an uncomfortable position: the United States wanted to offer assistance to its ally Israel, including help from the bases in the form of supplies or even direct military support. But Muslim host nations objected to any action that might assist Israel. In the wake of the conflict, 600 wives and children were evacuated from Wheelus Air Base to New York City to protect them from becoming victims of revenge attacks.[14] By this time, nationalism had developed as a powerful force in Libya. On September 1, 1969 King Idris I was overthrown in a military coup, and the Revolutionary Command Council (RCC) headed by Colonel Moammar Qaddafi took power. The RCC's priorities mandated the expulsion of foreign military forces. One of Qaddafi's first acts was to halt training maneuvers. The base treaty negotiated in 1954 was scheduled to expire in 1971, and while the United States received no word on the matter, it seemed clear from the new government's public statements that the bases would be forced to close.[15] Meanwhile, the Libyans demanded more control over the bases, in part prompted by several episodes of smuggling, including the alleged smuggling of a Libyan Jew from Libya to Malta in a crate.[16]

On October 31, 1969 Libya officially requested that the Americans vacate Wheelus,[17] and two months later the Air Force began removing equipment. Pressured by Qaddafi and the RCC, at the beginning of 1970 the Americans closed the base and moved its functions to Europe. On June 11, a last contingent of fifty-two Americans lowered the Stars and Stripes over Wheelus for the final time, and the Libyan flag rose over the base. The Libyan government took over the hundreds of buildings, two golf courses, three schools, shopping centers, beaches, riding stables, bowling alleys, clubs, hospital, 440 trailers, and other facilities the Americans had vacated.[18]

With this final act, the RCC had achieved its main goal—to rid Libya of the foreign bases, which brought "not least, the presence of tens of thousands of foreigners with their wicked habits, including liquor and miniskirts,"[19] according to a spokesman. The Libyans changed the name of the installations to Uqbah Ben Nafe, named for an Arab warrior who led his forces across North Africa to the Atlantic in the eighth century. A few weeks later, Arab rulers including Gamal Nasser and King Hussein of Jordan flew to Tripoli to celebrate the withdrawal of the Americans from Wheelus. Wheelus was like "a poisoned dagger in the back of the Arabs," said the new Libyan commander in a speech.[20] In the case of Libya, the Americans were the direct targets of Arab nationalism, tinged with cultural and religious xenophobia.

France

France was another pivotal spot for the basing system in Europe. It was the easiest and most direct route for supplying Germany, North Africa, and the Mediterranean from the United States. In the 1960s, the chain of military depots across France served to cement the nation's importance in the Atlantic Alliance, which France had insisted on at the end of the war.

However, Charles de Gaulle's election in 1958 brought his overarching mission of "restoring the pride and "grandeur" of France," as one historian put it, to the forefront of French policy.[21] De Gaulle viewed France's dependence on NATO, and particularly on the United States, as a sign of weakness and immediately began to disengage France from NATO. In 1959, he announced that nuclear weapons, the mainstay of the U.S. defense umbrella, could not be stationed in France unless France had partial control over their use. The United States would not accept this limitation, so nine fighter and bomber squadrons left the country. The same year, France withdrew its navy from NATO's naval command structure in the Mediterranean.[22] Finally, at the end of March 1966, de Gaulle announced that all foreign forces would have to leave France by April 1, 1967.[23] The extensive supply system across France that the Americans had built with so much effort in the 1950s was dismantled, and most of its equipment and personnel transferred to Germany. Once again, the United States lost its investment because of nationalism—not directed solely at the Americans, perhaps, but certainly they were the most visible target.

Japan

After the Occupation had ended and the Cold War emerged as a long-term, low-intensity global crisis, the Americans continued to view the Japanese as a somewhat shaky ally. For some, this mistrust stemmed from wartime perceptions of the Japanese as unregenerate militarists, but more realistically, U.S. policymakers feared Japanese pacifism and its tendency toward neutrality, which the Americans viewed as an invitation for Soviet domination. As a result, American policymakers acted carefully to keep Japan firmly in the anti-Communist orbit. One strategy involved minimizing the visibility of American military presence, which was a persistent irritant in Japanese–American relations.

By the 1960s, the large number of bases on mainland Japan had become a sore point for many Japanese; they took up valuable land in an over-crowded nation and they represented a painful reminder of the post–World War II American occupation of Japan. To make matters worse, in 1968, the "year of the barricades" as one author put it, several mishaps inflamed popular opinion. On May 6, 1968, radioactivity was discovered in the water of Sasebo harbor after a U.S. Navy nuclear–powered submarine visited the Naval base there. Japanese scientists assured the public that the radioactivity was harmless and was not definitively connected with the submarine, but activists used the event as evidence that the U.S. military presence was dangerous. When a USAF F-4C Phantom jet fighter crashed on the campus of Kyushu University in southern Japan a month later, this view intensified.[24] Partly in response to public pressure and also as a cost-cutting measure, the navy and Air Force shut down twenty-five bases, bringing the number of installations from 148 to 123.[25]

The protests did not end, however. In June 1970, more than 8,000 students and workers organized a nationwide protest against the presence of the remaining U.S. bases in Japan. There were rallies in about twenty-six cities, and 4,500 people demonstrated against a USAF base at Tachikawa, near Tokyo. A small homemade bomb detonated at the base early in the day.[26]

At the end of the summer, officials announced a series of reforms. Some of the 123 bases in Japan would be consolidated or eliminated altogether, and Japan would start sharing control over about ten of the major bases—units from both nations would be stationed together at the same facility. Bases to be affected under the plan included the major naval bases of Yokosuka and Sasebo and the airfields at Yokota, Misawa, and Itazuke. This reform, in fact, corresponded with the Nixon Doctrine of encouraging

U.S. allies in Asia to take over more of the job of defense, bringing American troops home.[27]

While nationalist sentiment among the Japanese populace ran against the bases, many, including officials in the government, believed that the bases should stay. Communist China had developed nuclear weapons capable of reaching Japan, and the U.S. presence served, in effect, as a nuclear umbrella. When *U.S. News and World Report* published a report in 1970 saying that the United States would pull out of Japan and Okinawa and relocate to Guam or the Marianas Islands, the reaction was strong. The story would "create perturbation among [U.S.] allies," said one Japanese newspaper. A commentator in another national paper said that "it is obvious that an American withdrawal will create a big power vacuum in the defense setup in Southeast Asia and the Far East."[28] Informed opinion wanted the bases to stay, although out of the public eye.

Throughout the early 1970s, discussions and plans for consolidation continued. Both the Japanese and American public favored decreasing the U.S. troop presence in Asia, while leaders wanted to be sure that the defense of Asia remained strong. In 1973 the two nations announced a plan to reduce the bases once again, as well as the number of U.S. personnel in Japan. The plan called for Tachikawa to be returned to Japan within three years, but the total strength of U.S. forces, including the forces on Okinawa, would be cut by only 2,100 to 62,500. About 500 civilians and 7,500 dependents would return to the United States, and 2,600 Japanese employees would lose their jobs. The cost of the change would be split by the Japanese and U.S. governments.[29]

Efforts to get rid of the bases entirely died down over time, and no one on either side seriously contemplated the possibility of Japan becoming a neutral nation. The threat from China and North Korea was still too close to make dramatic changes feasible. Complaints about the behavior of U.S. troops continued to spark anti-base sentiment—in 1983, several robberies and a murder in a short period of time led critics to charge the Americans with having an "occupation mentality," even as the overall rate of American crime dropped.[30] The end result of anti-base activism in Japan did not end or even significantly diminish the number of U.S. troops in Japan, but concentrated them on Okinawa, a Japanese island far to the south of the main islands (see Chapter 8).

Greece and Turkey

Greece and Turkey, both NATO members, struggled with special problems in the 1960s. In 1963 and 1964, the two nations clashed over the disputed island of Cyprus, each accusing the United States of favoring the other, resulting in a considerable amount of popular anti-Americanism from both sides. Critics used language similar to that of the French and

North Africans, citing neo-imperialism and domination. With respect to the Cyprus crisis, both nations also wanted the United States to stay out of their affairs: "Americans should give up their outdated imperialist methods. . . . They should not forget they are guests. They should refrain from clandestine activities which should not even be carried out in enemy lands. At any rate, they should refrain from interfering into our domestic affairs and from interfering into political struggles between parties,"[31] wrote one Turkish commentator. Sensitivity toward any perception of U.S. interference in the Cyprus affair became evident in the media of both sides.

A sociological study of the American military community in Ankara, Turkey, dating from 1964 confirms that the American forces encountered a great deal of anti-Americanism, and that American opinions of the host community were poor. Charlotte Wolf, the author of the study, found that most new arrivals had been given unfavorable reports[32] and that apocryphal stories magnified bad impressions: "The accounts of unpleasant "incidents" with Turks were legion in the American military community: spitting, stone-throwing, children slapped by Turkish workmen or janitors, cars scratched, car lights broken, air let out of tires,"[33] although it was impossible to know how many such events occurred. Even if perceptions had been driven by the international situation, many local irritants exacerbated tension: "Turks resented the increased rents, the increased costs for servants, the increased prices for produce; and they blamed the American community members with their high standard of living and their big salaries for causing the inflation. Americans, on the other hand, felt they were cheated, that two price scales existed—a reasonable one for the Turks and a larcenous one for them."[34]

In Greece, similar difficulties faced the much smaller American military community. In 1966 the King of Greece was dethroned and a nationalist government took power. This government used anti-Americanism as a way to gain popularity, especially in 1974 when the second Cyprus crisis developed. Americans in Greece reported petty harassment from neighbors and official obstruction in shipping household goods, inspections, and other matters under Greek control. Stories of malicious food adulteration and vandalism spread—one tale had it that Greeks put gasoline in milk destined for the Americans. Anti-American demonstrations disrupted the daily routine of military bases with some frequency during this period. However, in neither Turkey nor Greece did anti-American public opinion result in changes in the basing agreements.

THE VIETNAM WAR

U.S. involvement in Vietnam affected the U.S. military during the 1960s and 70s to an extent that can hardly be overemphasized. The war decreased readiness by draining experienced personnel and funding away from

NATO bases; it brought a storm of criticism down on the U.S. military itself; and, not least, it destroyed the mental and physical health of hundreds of thousands of men and women, a carryover effect that would have devastating repercussions on bases outside the theater of war.

As discussed earlier, bases in Europe began to feel the effects of the war effort almost immediately. In 1966 and 1967 base commanders found they had less money for maintenance and repair, construction, and recreation activities. Added to the problems of recruiting local employees and the gold flow, the financial demands of the war diminished the quality of life that American personnel and their families had enjoyed. By the early 1970s, barracks and family housing was decrepit, and enlisted personnel lived in conditions that many commentators did not hesitate to call "slums."[35] On the other hand, Asian bases experienced a boom as they expanded with the war effort. Bases in Okinawa and the Philippines supported the forces in Vietnam, and a number of airbases were constructed in Thailand. Asian cities became "Rest and Relaxation" (R&R) spots for soldiers on three-day leave, bringing economic growth as well as severe social dislocation.

More immediately significant from a mission standpoint, the demands of the war effort drained qualified and experienced personnel from their assignments in Europe to Vietnam. Support units found themselves with just a few inexperienced privates and perhaps a civilian employee to manage what had been the tasks of officers and NCOs. Many traditional programs, such as community relations efforts, fell to the wayside as fewer personnel could be spared to carry them out.

As the financial pressures of the Vietnam War placed a heavier burden on the armed forces, public opposition to the war made the effort a thankless task. As early as 1965, protests against the U.S. involvement in Vietnam began to attract support in Europe and Asia. 1968 and 1969 saw the opposition movement peak, as hundreds of thousands of people from all walks of life took to the streets throughout the world, demanding an immediate end to U.S. intervention in Southeast Asia. Military bases became the focus of some protests, and violent demonstrators targeted military headquarters and high-ranking officers for arson attempts and bombings. By and large, however, low-ranking personnel themselves were not viewed as oppressors; if anything, activists viewed them as victims of an unjust policy.

Perhaps one reason GIs did not experience anti-Americanism directed at them personally was that many soldiers, sailors, and airmen supported or even joined the antiwar movement. Antiwar activism attracted many draftees in the army, but studies show that it was even more common among "draft-motivated" enlistees in the army, Air Force and navy[36]— recruits who enlisted rather than be drafted into the army. Between 1968 and 1973 the "GI movement," a loosely organized and often ephemeral anti-military and antiwar movement, flourished on bases in Europe, Asia, and the United States. A plethora of underground newspapers and magazines publicized anti-military sentiment, with titles such as FTA (Fuck the Army), RITA (Resisters Inside the Army) and PEACE (People Emerging Against Corrupt Establishments). Bases from Germany to Japan, from Iceland to Australia, as well as stateside installations, saw their share of GI protest. On major installations in Germany, such as Heidelberg, Frankfurt, and Berlin, a number of different groups spread their views. Most GI protest groups lasted only a short while before their members were discovered and reassigned to faraway bases, an easy method of destroying resistance. Some groups, however, such as PEACE, founded by Vanessa Redgrave and other activists in Britain, which boasted branches on all eight Air Force bases in England,[37] survived for several years. Other efforts to improve the lives of low-ranking military personnel included attempts to organize servicemen's unions and the recruitment of lawyers for soldiers facing courts-martial, organized in groups like the Heidelberg Lawyers Military Defense Committee.[38]

In many cases, personnel acted on their disapproval of the military by simply leaving their units, "going AWOL" (absent without leave) or deserting. Cultural isolation, language difficulties, and racial differences made escape very difficult in Asia, but in Europe, a network of sympathizers helped young men flee and go to France or Sweden. As David Cortright, author of a history of the GI movement, wrote: "Throughout 1967 and 1968, thousands of GIs deserted their units, often causing severe personnel shortages; some units, such as the 509th Airborne Battalion, in Mainz, experienced a 10–20 percent AWOL rate."[39] These figures may be exaggerated, but AWOL and desertion did become a serious problem in the early 1970s.

In large part the GI movement addressed issues unique to the armed forces, such as treatment of enlisted men by officers and NCOs and reform of military justice. In addition to these concerns, however, unrest and social change roiling civilian society in the United States and elsewhere began to take their toll on the U.S. forces. Racial tension, crime, and drug use diminished the effectiveness of all the services, especially the army, and made life on or near military bases unpleasant and even dangerous.

Racial conflict in the military, a serious crisis during the early 1970s, could be dealt with, in the short term at least, using methods unavailable to the civilian community. Military authorities could reassign troublemakers or arrest and incarcerate them on charges relating to military discipline. They could compel personnel to attend racial awareness training programs, and they instituted, from the top down, changes such as offering culturally diverse products in the PXs, extending coverage of race issues in base newspapers, and expanding entertainment options geared toward African Americans in clubs and on radio and television. Still, even with all these measures available, the military struggled with racial unrest all over the world. Some outbreaks of racial violence became extremely dangerous; in Germany, for example, one base was closed for three days because of a race riot, and white personnel were instructed to go off-base and stay in hotels.

The use of drugs grew into another serious problem during the Vietnam era. Much of the drug use in the military had originated in Vietnam, where marijuana and opiates were easily available and commonly used. It spread to Europe as soldiers with time left to serve after their one-year tours in Vietnam were transferred to European bases. These soldiers, some with serious addiction problems, others with the habit of social drug use, became the source of innumerable discipline problems. Drug trafficking reached crisis proportions in Germany; some who resisted involvement were forced into cooperation by criminal gangs. Drug arrests of GIs appeared almost daily in most host community papers, and GIs were popularly believed to have introduced the use of drugs to Germany.

Along with drug abuse came crime, which escalated in the early 1970s. Muggings, rapes, robberies, and vandalism committed by GIs plagued host communities, and American soldiers began to be perceived as dangerous criminals. The social effects of the Vietnam war and other social changes on the U.S. forces could be seen all over the world, but the large concentrations of troops in places like the Philippines, Okinawa, and Germany magnified the problems in those areas. Towns adjacent to large military installations, especially army and Marine Corps installations in less-developed regions, became vice-ridden pits of crime, drug abuse, prostitution, and violence.

Not only was the military dissolving from the bottom up, but support from the top also began to waver. Beginning in 1966 and continuing through the 1970s, Mike Mansfield, a Democratic senator from Montana, argued that the military commitment overseas had become unnecessarily large, and he advocated the withdrawal of thousands of troops from overseas bases. While the Mansfield Amendments never quite gained enough support to pass in the Senate, they did earn attention from Congress and the public. Whatever their intent, the Mansfield Amendments sent a strong message to the armed forces that military service was not a valued occupation. In 1973, the unpopularity of the military led the DOD to abolish the draft and institute an all-volunteer army, with predictable results. With military service at an all-time low in the eyes of the public, it became difficult, if not impossible, to recruit enough qualified volunteers to fill troop authorizations; as a result, less qualified applicants entered the armed services and, especially in the army, the overall quality of military recruits went down.

One final action by the government hurt military personnel overseas perhaps more than anything else, although it was certainly not designed to do so. In 1971 the Nixon administration took the nation off the gold standard, which freed exchange rates to float to their "natural" levels. Almost immediately the dollar lost up to half its value against many other currencies, especially in Europe, which meant that goods and services "on the economy" cost more for U.S. personnel and family members. Off-base rents and utilities payments rose precipitously, leaving personnel with little money left for savings, or recreation, travel, and enjoying their stays overseas.

Taken as a whole, developments in the 1960s affected the U.S. forces overseas in many ways, almost all negative. The economic strength of host nations forced commanders to cut back on base activities and programs, and nationalist movements challenged the wisdom of the U.S. presence altogether. Vietnam had especially devastating effects. By the mid-1970s Americans overseas were plagued with poor morale and discipline, marked by mistrust between the races, petty crime, drug abuse, and the demoralizing effects of a lost war. They lived in shabby, outdated installations where fantastic problems were commonplace—vermin infestations, no heat, dripping water, mold and crumbling plaster. Their money was not worth what it once had been, confining them to the meager options on base. The effects of this decline could be seen in military–civilian relations around the world; to increasing numbers of people, the U.S. troops seemed to be a scourge on the local population.

5

★ ★ ★ ★ ★

Rebuilding the U.S. Forces: Germany in the 1980s

INTRODUCTION

In the aftermath of the Vietnam War, the U.S. forces overseas, as well as on bases in the United States, suffered from demoralization, poor military readiness, and a low standard of living. Among the troops in West Germany, the largest American military population in the world outside the United States, the problem became especially severe; West Germany had developed into a strong, affluent society in the postwar decades, and by the 1970s the U.S. forces appeared impoverished compared with the Germans. The military forces in Germany, moreover, consisted of a large proportion of U.S. Army troops rather than Air Force or Navy personnel, and the army suffered from post-Vietnam disintegration more than any other branch of service. While recognizing the importance of national defense, many Germans viewed the army as an unwelcome scourge and demanded that American military commanders assert firmer control over their unruly troops. Other Germans, however, remembered the benefits the U.S. forces had brought in the lean postwar years and reached out to the soldiers now isolated on their posts, ignorant of German customs and language and too poor to venture far from home.

A rash of political crises in the late 1970s refocused attention on the necessity of maintaining a strong defense. First, the Soviet Union placed SS-20 missiles in Eastern Europe as part of a nuclear modernization program. Then in 1979 came the Soviet invasion of Afghanistan, while around the same time Islamic revolutionaries occupied the U.S. Embassy in Iran and held fifty-two Americans hostage for more than a year. It seemed to many that the West had let its guard down, with disastrous results.

One response to these crises was a crash program of NATO modernization, improving and expanding the military power of the NATO allies. As the largest component of NATO, the U.S. forces benefited correspondingly from the modernization plan, including new weapons systems, both conventional and nuclear, and upgraded equipment and facilities. Personnel in the army and other branches of service enjoyed substantial pay hikes and better living conditions, and the quality of recruits improved dramatically.

Unfortunately for the U.S. armed services, modernization efforts sparked heated opposition. In West Germany, a huge protest movement against the deployment of U.S. Pershing II and cruise nuclear missiles engaged the German public for several years. The protest movement remained overwhelmingly peaceful, but a few individuals on the fringe engaged in terrorist violence, and the 1980s saw several spectacular terrorist attacks on U.S. installations, personnel, and civilian businesses catering to Americans; dozens or hundreds more were detected before damage occurred. Some terrorist attacks were carried out not by German left-wing terrorists, but by Libyan or other Middle Eastern groups, adding to the sense of vulnerability and danger.

Although terrorist violence certainly forced Americans to be careful and aware while traveling in Europe—Sylvester Stallone ("Rambo") famously cancelled a planned trip to Italy because of the threat of terrorism—American military personnel, civilian employees, and family members by and large remembered the 1980s as a golden time in Europe. Pay increases had brought living standards up to comparable civilian rates, and the strong dollar of the early 1980s made enjoying Europe easier than ever. The high quality of recruits and the corresponding drop in drug use and crime improved life for everyone. In spite of continued and occasionally violent opposition to modernization and expansion measures, military–civilian relations grew closer and stronger.

MORALE AND READINESS IN THE 1970s

By the middle of the 1970s, the U.S. armed forces and the army in particular had suffered from a collapse in readiness, morale, discipline, and overall quality, comparable only to that of the late 1940s when occupation soldiers in Germany and Japan spent their days drinking and chasing women. According to late 1970s research by sociologist and career officer Larry Ingraham, young enlisted men used drugs as a social bond, rarely ventured off base to participate in civilian activities, and suffered loneliness and alienation as they waited to be discharged.[1] Ingraham's study focused mostly on enlisted men in the United States, but his conclusions applied to bases overseas as well. A German journalist, Signe Seiler, studied GIs at an army post in Mainz, Germany, and came to the same conclusions as Ingraham. She found enlisted men largely ignorant of German customs, unable to speak the language, and in any case with so little money in their pockets that they had no choice but to spend their evenings at the base clubs drinking cheap American beer.[2] While anti-war activism had dried up by 1975, crime and drug use persisted as stubborn problems. All in all, the armed forces of the 1970s, especially the army, did not offer many signs of hope.[3]

Among the many reasons for the disturbing trend, several stand out as especially influential. Above all loomed the transition from a draft army to the AVF in 1973. Nixon's decision to abolish the draft came reluctantly and for political rather than strictly military reasons, and many critics predicted that an AVF would never provide the necessary levels of acceptable manpower needed by the army. In the short term, the critics proved to be correct, as qualified young men in the United States avoided military service *en masse.* The recession of 1975 eased by 1979, and those who could find work in the better-paying civilian sector did so, leaving other less able young people to join the services. The two most commonly used predictors of successful performance in the military—scores on the standardized Armed Services Vocational Aptitude Battery (ASVAB) and rates of high school graduation—declined precipitously among army recruits during the 1970s.

A second reason for the deterioration of morale and readiness was the relative poverty in which members of the armed forces, especially enlisted personnel, found themselves. Military pay had fallen far behind civilian pay both for enlisted personnel and officers as a result of pay caps instituted during the inflation years of the 1970s.[4] In Germany, a weak dollar exacerbated the money problems of American servicemembers, particularly those in ranks E-4 and below. Stories of soldiers and even non-commissioned officers qualifying for food stamps and other government aid spread to the civilian public and discouraged qualified young men and women from considering the military as a career. The military's method of categorizing pay was partly to blame for this—military housing benefits did not count as take-home pay—but even so, American personnel were indeed forced to watch their pennies carefully.

A third reason for the military's predicament was the decline in confidence and morale resulting from American involvement in Vietnam, admitted by many to have been a debacle. Public criticism of U.S. policy and the military became a constant, depressing factor of life for those in the armed services. Stories of Vietnam veterans being spit upon as they walked through airports may have been urban legend, as some suggest, but the idea that it was shameful to have served in Vietnam lingered for years after the United States withdrew from Southeast Asia. In fact, Vietnam vets experienced such alienation from the American Legion and the Veterans of Foreign Wars that they formed their own organization, the Vietnam Veterans of America. Vietnam vets' rejection from civilian institutions such as higher education was even more severe. In short, Americans serving in the military no longer projected the optimistic self-assurance of earlier decades and were less inclined to see themselves as "ambassadors" to the world or to behave as such.

Judging from the experience of the 1970s, then, the AVF appeared to be a failure. One factor that buoyed the depressing performance was the armed forces' expanded recruitment of women, whose numbers increased from 20,550 in 1973 to almost 53,000 in 1978. According to defense analyst Martin Binkin, it would not be an exaggeration to say that women saved the AVF by propping up test score averages and other statistics. In the first ten years of the AVF, for example, 92 percent of enlisted women in the army had completed high school, but fewer than 62 percent of the men had done so.[5] Similar comparisons between women and men could be seen in ASVAB scores,[6] and Binkin suggests that without the contributions of women, the AVF would have been abolished as an unsuccessful experiment by the 1980s. Interestingly, German defense experts noticed the increasing number of women in the U.S. forces with alarm and worried that the quality of America's defense commitment to Europe would be weakened with large numbers of women in the ranks.[7]

By and large, the 1970s saw the Americans in Germany, both officers and enlisted personnel, withdraw behind their walls and recede from sight. The extended German–American Friendship Weeks and huge open houses of earlier decades had long since disappeared. German–American clubs still had their stalwart memberships, but new energy ceased to flow in, especially on the American side. In many German garrison towns, the Christmas sing-alongs, Fasching balls, summer band concerts, charity drives, wine tastings, torchlight parades, and other evidences of German–American contact on an official, friendship-sustaining level began to fade away. Germans and Americans did not entirely lose contact, but as the postwar generation who remembered and appreciated the American contribution to German security aged and a new generation saw only Vietnam, drug use, and poverty, connections between Germans and Americans grew more tenuous than they had ever been. German–American councils during the 1970s wrestled with the growing problem of discrimination against U.S. personnel, most commonly in clubs and bars that designated themselves "off limits" to Americans, especially black Americans. German authorities battled this problem with varying levels of success throughout the decade.

To be sure, the army recognized the problem. During the 1970s, many installations in Germany founded "Kontakt Clubs," where Germans and Americans could meet each other and learn more about each culture. Unlike the German–American clubs founded in the late 1940s, however, which acted as an outreach to the Germans, the Kontakt Clubs of the 1970s aimed to bring young enlisted personnel out of their barracks and clubs and expose them to German culture, acting, in effect, as outreach organizations to soldiers. Germans living near U.S. installations also tried to reach out through efforts to invite troops into their homes for Christmas. A sign of the increasing distance between young American enlistees and the often older, more affluent Germans who supported the American presence could be seen at some of these attempts. GIs often did not understand the more formal rules of dress and behavior expected by their German hosts, and friendship efforts sometimes ended in disaster.

These efforts were fundamentally different from earlier German–American relations activities. In previous decades, clubs and special events brought together Germans and Americans of similar social classes and educational levels who were genuinely interested in socializing with each other and fairly knowledgeable about each other's culture and expectations. Germans and Americans viewed each other as equals—if either side took the role of social superior during the early years, it would have been the more affluent Americans. Efforts during the 1970s to reach out to GIs, by contrast, served an educational and relief function. The GIs were assumed, correctly in most cases, to be largely ignorant of German customs, history, and language, and German participants understood their involvement as a charitable activity rather than an opportunity to become acquainted with people like themselves. In this sense, the transformation of German–American activities in the late 1970s highlighted the change in the status of American personnel after Vietnam.

POLITICAL CRISES

Even if the state of the AVF in Germany seemed to be at a low point, the tense struggle of geopolitics moved along, demonstrating the need for a strong and well-prepared military force. In the early 1970s, Nixon pursued the policy of détente, during which tensions between the USSR and the United States noticeably eased. The West German policy of Ostpolitik improved relations between the FRG and the nations of the East Bloc. For a few years, it appeared that perhaps peaceful coexistence might be a possibility. Arms limitation agreements—the ABM treaty of 1972 and SALT—evoked the hope that endless defense spending and the threat of nuclear war might ebb. For an America exhausted and demoralized by the Vietnam War, a shift away from military matters seemed a welcome change.

In 1975, however, the USSR deployed the new intermediate-range nuclear SS-20, a weapon unlimited by arms talks, pointed toward targets in Europe. West European leaders feared that the United States would pursue an arms control strategy that protected the Western Hemisphere while leaving Europe on its own without a substantial nuclear defense, and that the American commitment to defend Europe would weaken.[8] President Jimmy Carter made a painful political error with his advocacy of the neutron bomb, a nuclear weapon that allegedly would kill people but leave buildings and structures intact. West German Chancellor Helmut Schmidt supported the creation of the controversial weapon at great political cost, but in the face of American public outrage Carter canned the idea, leaving Schmidt, whose SPD constituency tended toward anti-militarism, angry and embarrassed. The Cold War in all its complexity had not yet ended.

In 1979 the USSR invaded Afghanistan, bolstering the arguments of hawkish critics that a state of "normalcy" was a costly illusion. To make matters worse, in 1980 Reza Pahlavi, the Shah of Iran, was overthrown by radical Islamist students who occupied the U.S. Embassy in Teheran. The students held fifty-two Americans hostage for 444 days, a decisive humiliation for the Carter administration. In the 1980 election, candidate Ronald Reagan positioned himself as a tough, no-nonsense leader who would shape things up at home and abroad. He won a landslide victory.

The early 1980s saw the Solidarity movement in Poland crushed by the communist government as well as increased communist activity in Central America. SALT II ended in failure. In 1982 Reagan famously called the Soviet Union the "evil empire," and it seemed that the United States had chosen a path of forceful anti-communism. But it was difficult to take a strong military position with the disorganized forces available.

NATO MODERNIZATION

In later years, the Reagan administration took credit for a variety of sensational events of the 1980s, from freeing the hostages in Iran to engineering the collapse of the USSR. Not least, Reagan claimed to preside over the rejuvenation of the U.S. armed forces from their deplorable state in the late 1970s to an enthusiastic and highly trained professional force of the 1980s. It can be fairly argued that Reagan did deserve credit for many of these developments, but the foundations for the improvement of the armed forces, particularly in Germany, had been laid during the Carter administration.

As early as 1976, Helmut Schmidt, realizing the possibility that the United States might drift from its strategic commitments in Europe, pressed Carter for a NATO modernization plan that improved the U.S. forces in Germany and bolstered the German–American alliance.[9] The NATO modernization plan called for larger numbers of forces in Western

Europe, mostly in Germany, and improvement of living conditions, pay scales, housing, and thus the quality of the troops. It also incorporated vast updates of conventional weapons—helicopters, fixed-wing aircraft, tanks, armored vehicles, air-defense weaponry.

The most famous, or notorious, aspect of the plan, however, was the December 12, 1979 "dual-track" announcement. The first track mandated disarmament talks between the United States and the USSR, and the second was a 572 weapon Intermediate-range Nuclear Force (INF) to be deployed in western Europe in 1983 should the talks fail to reach a conclusion. The weapons, produced in the United States, consisted of 108 Pershing II land-based missiles and 464 ground-launched Tomahawk cruise missiles; ninety-six of the cruises and all of the Pershings would be located in West Germany. The Netherlands, Britain, Belgium, and Italy would also receive cruise missiles.

PROTESTS AGAINST THE PERSHINGS

Almost as soon as the NATO plan was announced, German anti-missile protesters coalesced around the issue. Largely made up of the left wing of the SPD and the recently formed environmentalist Green Party,[10] opponents accused the Americans of involving Germany in its militaristic plans and using the continent as, in the words of the movement, "Schlachtfeld Europa"—slaughterhouse Europe—expecting to fight the worst of a world war in Europe rather than allowing it to touch American soil. Even Willy Brandt, the respected chairman of the SPD and former chancellor of West Germany, allegedly claimed that the United States treated Germany "like a colony."[11]

The anti-missile movement must be viewed as part of the complex and diverse West German protest scene, active since the first anti-re-armament movement of the 1950s. A decade after that first burst of activity, protesters opposed what they saw as the authoritarianism of German society, as well as the Vietnam War and other apparent examples of western imperialism. In the 1970s, some branches of the movement turned toward cultural change with a vibrant alternative scene creating an economy and society outside mainstream norms. Other protest forms addressed specific local ecological or social issues in the citizens' initiative movement. Very few activists turned to violence. In the late 1970s and 1980s protests encompassed environmental crises, nuclear energy, and the women's movement, among other themes, mostly focusing on political and economic issues in German society itself. In most cases protests had little to do with the U.S. armed forces stationed in the country. However, "America" became a powerful symbol to this sprawling movement, a symbol of ecological devastation, exploitative capitalism, and, most of all, unrestrained military might.

Thus, the anti-missile protest movement attracted many groups and individuals with a wide range of experience in activism and a variety of differing perspectives. Some activists simply opposed the specific Pershing and cruise missile deployments; others identified with extreme pacifism and advocated a new social, economic, and ecological order. The organizational structure of the movement, often called the peace movement, remained loose and flexible, and many of the groups joining it had been founded for purposes predating the missile protests.[12] However, as many as 4,000 local initiatives sprang up to oppose the missiles.[13] The "minimal consensus" of the movement settled on opposition to the deployment of cruise and Pershing II missiles in Europe.

Because the SPD officially supported deployment of the missiles, opponents could not use that political party as a vehicle for protest, and the Green Party's "fundamentalist" positions did not appeal to everyone. As a result, activists were forced to turn to unconventional means. In any case, many of the protesters leaned in the direction of alternative protest because of their past experiences in activism. According to Alice Cooper, an analyst of West German peace activity, the movement, while extremely diverse in approach throughout the entire period, moved through several phases in its preferred tactics. In 1980 and 1981, opponents disseminated information about the missiles and collected signatures for petitions.[14] The second phase involved mass demonstrations. In October 1981 the first massive demonstration was held in Bonn, in which about 300,000 people participated. Another occurred in June 1982, at the same time that Ronald Reagan visited Germany and made his famous stop at the Bitburg cemetery. Some demonstrators went further; in December 1982 protests at fifty bases blocked gates and temporarily prevented employees or servicemembers from entering or leaving the installations. At this point, however, most opponents tried to use tactics that would attract the largest amount of support and alienate the smallest number of people. In the early 1980s, the Easter march, a mass peace demonstration tradition beginning in 1959, grew in popularity, and Easter marches all over Europe drew tens of thousands of participants.

The third phase, at the movement's peak, took place during the "heisse Herbst" (hot autumn) of 1983, in the months and weeks before the final Bundestag vote on whether to accept the plan. Demonstrators launched Heisse Herbst in September 1983 with blockades of U.S. Army bases at Mutlangen and Bitburg, likely sites of the missiles. The protests, which involved non-violent civil disobedience, began in the early morning at the exact hour when Hitler's armies invaded Poland. About 1,000 people at Mutlangen were joined by the novelists Gunter Grass and Heinrich Böll, Green Party leader Petra Kelly, SPD maverick Oskar Lafontaine, and American peace activists Daniel Ellsberg and Philip Berrigan.[15]

When the Bundestag voted in favor of the missile deployment at the end of 1983, opponents turned to nonviolent resistance, including blockading missile sites and forming human chains around military bases. By and large, however, the affirmative vote for the missiles took the steam out of the movement. Many supporters of the opposition considered it a lost battle and dropped out. Those who remained bickered about the direction the movement should take—the Green Party advocated criticism of the East Bloc for its transgressions as well as opposing the American missiles, while the small German Communist Party resisted any such critique. The Communists comprised a tiny element of the peace movement, but as a highly organized group with substantial funds (from the Soviet Union and East Germany) and time to contribute, they played an outsized role. Others expanded their opposition to U.S. military policy in Europe from condemning the specific Pershing and Cruise missile deployments to a more general critique of Airland Battle 2000, a new strategy entailing a massive counterattack of the Warsaw Pact if NATO nations were attacked. The broader critique, however, failed to galvanize opposition as the missiles had. Furthermore, popular opposition to the missiles had burgeoned as a result of the apocalyptic imagery used by the movement; descriptions of the atomic destruction at Hiroshima and Nagasaki, visions of nuclear winter, and similar scenarios spurred the public to oppose the missiles. When the missiles were deployed and the dreadful predictions did not come to pass, little remained with which to work.

In other parts of Europe, opposition movements developed as well. Britain's movement was especially strong, with a "women's peace camp" outside the gates of Greenham Common Air Force Base blockading the gates and obstructing maneuvers and training. Still, after the cruise missiles arrived in the UK as planned, the movement lost its momentum, and fewer and fewer showed up for demonstrations and rallies. Only in the Netherlands did the opposition movement maintain its strength into 1984 because the government postponed a vote on the missiles until the summer of that year.[16]

By the middle of the decade, the only visible signs of the peace movement in Germany were the Easter marches, which continued to be the largest, most organized, and most accessible options for public protest.[17] During the 1986 Easter marches, which combined anti-military activism with concerns about nuclear waste and other environmental issues, police arrested a total of 280 people at a "peace village" in Bavaria, claiming they had amassed chemicals and other materials for use in making explosives; the protesters countered that the materials were normal items used in camping.[18] The debacle suggested an increased willingness on the part of the police to crack down on demonstrators, perhaps because the Easter marches during the second half of the decade turned out to be a shadow of their former selves.[19] By 1987, Easter marchers praised the efforts of

Mikhail Gorbachev to move forward with arms talks and focused on far-flung issues like U.S. treatment of the Sandinistas in Nicaragua. The INF treaty of that year mandated that the missiles be removed, ending the need for an anti-missile protest movement.[20]

VIOLENCE AND TERRORISM

Organized opposition to the missiles maintained an overwhelmingly peaceful character from its inception in 1980 to the conclusion of the INF treaty in 1987. To be sure, disruption of military training maneuvers and temporary delay of daily activities on military bases proved inconvenient, but it harmed no one.

A small minority of activists went further with their protests, however, incorporating vandalism, arson, and even bombings in their methods. These protests, very much outside the mainstream of opposition, seemed to target the U.S. forces in general and included as their goals not only the end of the missile deployment but also the end of NATO and the German–American military alliance. Needless to say, the threat of terrorism lent a certain atmosphere of tension to the experience of the U.S. forces in West Germany during the 1980s.

On August 31, 1981, protesters burned vehicles owned by U.S. personnel in Wiesbaden, bombed the USAFE headquarters in Ramstein, injuring twenty, and torched the offices of the SPD in Frankfurt. The arsonists involved in the Frankfurt attack painted anti-American slogans on the partially gutted office building.[21] A short time later, members of the Red Army Faction (RAF), a leftist terrorist group, attacked General Frederick J. Kroesen, commander of the U.S. Army, Europe (USAREUR) near USAREUR headquarters in Heidelberg.

On June 1, 1982, an organization called the Revolutionary Cells Terrorist Group organized a coordinated bomb attack on four bases in Bamberg, Frankfurt, Gelnhausen, and Hanau. No one was hurt by the blasts, which occurred at 1:30 A.M., but the army estimated the costs of the damage at about $120,000. The bombings came a week before Ronald Reagan came to visit Germany, and the Revolutionary Cells intended to disrupt the trip. "As the start of what we hope will be a noisy, eventful and unforgettable reception, we today attacked some nests of the U.S. military," they reported in a letter.[22] All in all, authorities counted fifty-three bomb attacks against U.S. installations during 1982.[23]

Even after the Bundestag laid the missile controversy to rest by endorsing the plan, the threat of violence continued. On July 2, 1984, the German police raided an RAF hideout in Frankfurt and found lists of offices, clubs, and living quarters used by the U.S. military that had been designated as possible targets for attacks,[24] and in December of that year the RAF tried without success to blow up the NATO Shape School in Oberammergau.

In 1985, six bomb incidents occurred on U.S. bases, but all were discovered by the police, and no damage was done.[25]

The most daring attack of the decade against the U.S. forces in Germany came on August 8, 1985, when RAF terrorists detonated a car bomb on Rhine–Main Air Base. Two Americans were killed and eleven wounded. Investigators soon connected the case with the mysterious murder of Private Edward Pimental, a soldier stationed at a nearby army post, whose body was found in the Taunus mountains in the morning of August 9. He was last seen with a woman he had met in a Wiesbaden bar frequented by Americans. The woman, it turned out, belonged to the RAF. The terrorists had lured Pimental to the isolated spot in the Taunus, killed him, and took his military identification card and license plates. They used these to gain access to the heavily guarded Rhine–Main Air Base. In a later communique, the RAF explained the act as a strike against the American war machine and dubbed it "Kommando George Jackson," after a member of the Black Panthers killed in a prison riot in 1971.[26]

AMERICAN LIFE IN EUROPE

How did American personnel in Europe manage to negotiate the complicated mixture of heated protest and warmhearted outreach that characterized German attitudes toward them? Certainly the anti-missile demonstrations and rallies, not to mention discrimination and violence, had serious and detrimental effects on many Americans. By 1982, the third year of mass protests, military officials reported that the peace movement had led soldiers to conclude that Germans did not appreciate their efforts in defending the West and that they were not welcome in Europe. In spite of improvements in conditions on most bases and the superior quality of most recruits, officials decried the isolation of American soldiers stationed in West Germany and condemned the all too common discrimination in bars and restaurants. Many Americans experienced minor harassment such as individual Germans accosting them in the streets.

In general, the 1980s saw an upsurge of criticism, sometimes heated, of Americans and American policy. This came from many directions, including developing nations that decrying what they interpreted as the neo-imperialism of the United States, as well as leftist groups in Europe and in America itself. Sometimes this critique seemed to unite enemies of the United States with critics from friendly nations. During a 1982 meeting with European leftist groups including the West German Green Party, for example, Colonel Moammar Qaddafi encouraged the anti-missile movement to try to close European bases during the protests, urging them to cut off water and supplies to the installations to force them out.[27] It will come as no surprise, then, that many Americans in Germany believed that young Germans, close in age to most military personnel, harbored feelings of anger and resentment toward the United States and against them personally. In response, American personnel in Germany, energized by the new spirit of somewhat jingoistic patriotism of the Reagan era, tended to view younger Germans as "soft on communism," idealistic, and naïve. In contrast to the Vietnam era where anti-military sentiment was shared by Germans and younger American enlisted personnel, and hostility divided the older and the younger generations, in the 1980s young American personnel stood firmly on the side of their nation against their German peers.

At the same time, most Americans with any experience in Germany knew that the majority of the population, and without question the mostly older Germans and other Europeans employed at the bases, fundamentally supported the American presence. In some cases, non-American employees felt more strongly about the value of the U.S. military presence than most Americans did. Employees of Polish extraction, for example, who had begun their careers with the Americans as liberated DPs, noted that they owed their lives to the Americans and sometimes claimed that they would leave Germany should the Americans withdraw.

Whatever the frequency of pro- or anti-Americanism during these years, and every American experienced instances of both, life in Germany and all over Europe took a marked turn for the better as the dollar increased in strength. Between 1980 and 1984 the Deutschmark traded at over 3.25 marks to the dollar, and the British pound lost 40 percent of its value against the dollar. Suddenly travel, entertainment, and large purchases fell within the reach of even lower enlisted personnel.[28] Americans bought furniture, appliances and even BMW and Mercedes automobiles, traveled across Europe, and ate in fancy restaurants. Along with the Reagan administration's famous military pay hikes, which went far in bringing military pay rates up to the level of comparable civilian employment, the strong dollar made military service an economically attractive option.

In addition to increased affluence among individual personnel, military communities themselves received more dollars through generous Reagan Administration budgets. Base commanders renovated barracks, expanded office buildings, and constructed new bowling alleys, movie theaters, and sports fields. Restaurants and clubs improved. Installations and housing areas became more comfortable and attractive, much less like the notorious "slums" of the previous decade. As a result, even though personnel and their families could spend money in off-base establishments without hardship, military recreation provided enticing alternatives.

Another change in military life, less quantifiable but nevertheless evident to those who had spent the 1970s in the army, was a dramatic upswing in morale and pride. No longer did the army seem like a dumping ground for the rejects of society; rather, the personnel of the 1980s were more likely than ever to view their service with pride and to see themselves as turning back the tide of degeneracy of the 1970s. Along with this change came a marked turn to the right in political attitudes, unsurprising in the self-selected AVF. Ronald Reagan became a hero to many, both for his practical efforts to improve military life and for his strong anti-communist stand, which gave the military something around which to rally.

The cultural change in the military could be seen in many small ways: in the base bookstores and video rental shops which did brisk business in books and movies with military themes; in the scornful attitudes of many military personnel toward the German anti-missile movement, and in voting behavior. More substantively, military measures of qualifications, intelligence, and readiness also improved from the 1970s. By the mid-1980s, a high-school diploma was virtually required for enlistment, and college students found themselves turned away from ROTC scholarships. The numbers of enlisted personnel scoring on the upper ranges of the ASVABs rose, resulting in a more qualified, better motivated military than ever before.

6

★ ★ ★ ★ ★

The Demands of Sovereignty: Panama

INTRODUCTION

In many regions, the U.S. armed forces have been an essential element of a broader Americanization effect encompassing diplomatic, business, cultural, and other influences. Nowhere, however, has the military played so integral a role in advancing U.S. interests as in Panama. The creation of Panama was itself accomplished through military intervention when, in 1903, U.S. Marines aided Panamanians in achieving independence from Colombia. That same year, the U.S. Army created the Panama Canal Company, a government-owned corporation that built and ran the Panama Canal and acted as its largest "stockholder." The 10-mile-wide swath running from the Atlantic to Pacific on either side of the Canal, known as the Canal Zone (CZ), was technically a U.S. military reservation for most of the twentieth century (although thousands of civilians lived on it). In 1977, President Carter's controversial treaty returning the Canal to the Panamanians sparked a wave of patriotic indignation in American conservative circles; the main argument for retaining the Canal lay not in its economic value, however, or even its symbolism for the grandeur of the nation, but in its strategic and military utility.

During the long decades of discontent leading up to the 1977–1978 treaty, civilian Americans living and working in the Zone, known as Zonians, suffered the brunt of Panamanian and U.S. censure for what many alleged to be a colonial lifestyle, privileges and attitude. Indeed, the notorious "silver"

(Panamanian) and "gold" (American) pay scales sharply illustrated the inequities of the traditional order. At the same time, however, the communities of the U.S. Army, Air Force, and Navy, with much less public criticism, enjoyed a similar if not identical lifestyle and busied themselves with training and supporting military rulers throughout Central and South America. On the eve of the 1977–1978 treaty setting a timetable for turning over the Canal to Panama, the U.S. forces used the CZ, in contradiction of the original 1903 agreement, as an central hub of the global military system.[1]

Whether because of its wide–ranging military mission or its economic dominance, the Panama Canal appeared to the people of Panama and their sympathizers in other nations as a symbol of American colonialism more powerful than almost any other American endeavor. The Canal, an American creation, was administered by Americans in an American–run zone, with most of the revenues going to Americans. On the other hand, proponents of the Canal defended the U.S. military and civilian presence there as a matter of right. As a candidate in the Republican primary in 1976, Ronald Reagan summed up the sentiments of conservatives throughout the country: "When it comes to the canal, we bought it, we paid for it, it's ours, and we should tell [Panamanian leader Omar] Torrijos and company that we are going to keep it."[2]

A BRIEF HISTORY OF THE CANAL

Almost from the nation's birth, American leaders viewed Latin America as a legitimate part of its sphere of influence and defended America's exclusive rights in the region. In the Monroe Doctrine, American leaders articulated the policy that no European or Asian power had the right to interfere with relations between the United States and Latin American nations. These relations spanned the vast area from the Gulf of Mexico to the tip of South America: in the nineteenth century, the U.S. armed forces, usually the Marines or the Navy, intervened more than forty times in conflicts or unrest in the Caribbean and Central or South America.

Panama was one of the many areas receiving American attention. Originally the narrow isthmus attaching Central America to the large land mass to the south had belonged to Colombia. However, considerable sentiment in favor of independence roiled the area during the closing years of the century, and the Panamanians embraced a nationalist identity even before American intervention,[3] attempting dozens of unsuccessful rebellions before the Marines stepped in.

The idea of building a canal connecting the Atlantic and Pacific oceans was not a new idea, nor was it exclusively American. As early as the seventeenth century, Hernando Cortez, the Spanish conqueror of the Aztecs, had suggested the notion. Two hundred years later the Americans considered it, and after the Mexican War of 1848, when the borders of the United States spread from the Atlantic to the Pacific, the project gained some urgency. Initial attention focussed on Nicaragua to the north, but a French company led by engineer Ferdinand de Lesseps chose the narrow section of what would become Panama as a more suitable site and began digging. The company went bankrupt in 1889; in 1902 the United States bought the rights and property of the New Panama Canal Company, the successor to the French company, for $40 million, and work began anew.[4]

The United States approached Colombia with an offer to buy the land that the French had begun excavating, but the offer was turned down. In response to this rejection, the United States encouraged independence activists in Panama to lead a revolt against Colombia with the military support of the U.S. Navy and Marines. The revolt succeeded, aided by American gunboat diplomacy, and a few days after the new nation was established, the Americans approached the new Panamanian government for permission to build a canal.

The American offer for the use of the land presented a rude shock to the Panamanians—it was much less generous than earlier proposals made to the Colombians. (In 1923 the United States compensated Colombia for the loss of Panama—$25 million in a settlement that indirectly acknowledged the American role in the affair.[5]) Although they were disappointed, the leaders of the tiny new nation had little choice but to accept the proposal of their patron, who threatened to abandon them to the Colombians if they resisted. In 1903 the United States and Panama signed the Panama Canal Treaty, which gave the U.S. rights "in perpetuity" to a 10-mile-wide zone, "as if they were sovereign" in the zone. In later decades this somewhat obscure wording would come back to haunt both sides.

Whatever chicanery and bullying may have characterized the negotiations for the use of the land through which the Canal was cut, there is no denying that the Panama Canal was an engineering marvel for its time. A series of locks raised ships 85 feet above sea level, and a huge man-made lake spread through the center. The Canal took several years to build, involved 45,000 workers, mostly from the Caribbean, and cost millions of dollars. Hundreds of workers died from malaria and yellow fever during the construction, but it was finally completed in 1914.

After it opened for shipping in August 1914, the Canal enabled the United States to develop a two-ocean navy, brought a great deal of revenue to the Panama Canal Company, and provided income to about 4,000 employees of the company.

THE CANAL ZONE

According to the 1903 treaty the status of the Canal Zone resembled that of an American state, its only reason for existence being the Canal. In 1904 the Americans set up a Zone government, separate from the parallel

Panamanian government, with headquarters only blocks away in the old section of Panama City, the nation's capital.[6] Administration of the Zone was conducted with an eye toward maintaining the privileged position of American residents and employees. Housing areas, schools, shops, and recreation separated the Americans from their Panamanian neighbors and from the lower-status workers from the West Indies and Southern Europe.

Employment practices in the Zone rapidly became a controversial matter and remained so for the better part of a century. Two pay structures existed side by side—the "silver" and "gold" rolls. The silver roll consisted of manual laborers and craftsmen, while gold workers included engineers, pilots who navigated the large ships through the Canal, managers, and other white collar workers. Gold workers were white in more than their collars, however, as the two rolls divided employees by race. In 1906, chief engineer John Stevens reported that "the 'gold' men there are the white men. . . . The 'silver' men are the black men."[7] Most of the silver workers came from Barbados, Martinique, Guadeloupe, or Spain, Italy, and Greece; very few were Panamanian, at least in the early years, and almost no silver workers were American.[8] Silver workers earned less than their gold counterparts, even for similar work,[9] and they did not enjoy the benefits gold workers did. In 1903 a commissary was built to provide for the needs of gold workers, for example, but silver workers were not allowed to shop there. When Panamanian shopkeepers inevitably began to overcharge the silver employees—which became a problem as early as 1905, well before the Canal was finished—the Company built separate commissaries for the silver workers.[10]

The U.S. Army protected the American presence from the beginning. Under the 1903 agreement, the U.S. armed forces could intervene when the safety of the Canal or the safety of U.S. citizens was endangered, although this role risked involvement in Panamanian politics. The Marines, after supporting the independence movement, policed the CZ for a short while but withdrew in 1904 and thereafter played almost no role in the Zone.[11] The 10th Infantry Regiment, the first army detachment sent to the CZ, arrived in October 1911. Numbering only 985 personnel, the 10th Infantry was small and lightly armed—hardly capable of defending the Canal against a serious attack from another power. Rather, the army protected Americans in Panama, and, against its will, it sometimes monitored Panamanian elections and performed functions that the Panamanian security forces, known as the National Guard, could not or would not do. In the 1920s, for example, the army began a campaign against the vice flourishing in and around the Zone.[12] The army fit into neither the gold nor the silver rolls exactly, receiving its own funding from the War Department; before World War II, this funding was not generous. In the 1920s and

1930s soldiers lived in wooden shacks, and the garrison never had the full contingent of authorized personnel.[13]

During World War II the War Department viewed the Canal as a potential target for enemy attack and devoted considerable numbers of personnel to its defense. A system of eighteen military bases eventually spread through the CZ. In 1945, the United States wished to retain the bases, but the idea proved unpopular among Panamanian students and the general public on nationalist grounds. In 1947 the Panamanian assembly unanimously rejected the U.S. request to keep all the bases, resulting in a marked decrease in American spending in the Zone although smaller numbers of American forces did remain in Panama. The postwar demobilization caused a recession in the Panamanian economy, but the nationalist sentiment behind the demand for withdrawal did not ebb.

By the postwar period the Zone, the wealth, and the inequities it had created had left a deep mark on Panamanian society and economic life. With the passage of time, workers from the Caribbean had become Panamanian citizens, intermarrying with the local populace. However, they maintained a unique identity, neither culturally Panamanian nor accepted as Americans by the whites. Their descendants worked for the Canal as silver roll workers, an institution that survived the war, although in the late 1940s the names were changed to "U.S. rate" and "local rate."[14] Local rate workers lived in segregated housing areas in the Zone, and their children attended Zone schools taught in English rather than Spanish.

Spanish–speaking Panamanians lived near the Zone as well. By 1950 about 300,000 Panamanians—out of a total of 800,000—lived in the CZ cities of Panama City, Colon, and David. Most endured horrible poverty as well as the degradation and vice seen in camp towns throughout the world. The inhabitants of the Zone cities subsisted in whatever ways they could, mostly from the Americans. The few black American employees usually took unskilled, local rate jobs and lived in the segregated Zone housing areas with other local rate workers. Local rate workers, while better off than their Panamanian neighbors, clearly suffered from discriminatory treatment. In 1947, for example, the minimum wage for gold workers was $1.07 per hour, while silver workers received a minimum of 44 cents. In fact, the parallel systems created a number of duplicate jobs. Two separate school systems for the children of American and local workers necessitated two sets of teachers— the U.S. teachers earning three times that of their local rate counterparts.[15]

White American workers of the Panama Canal Company enjoyed a privileged existence, receiving the rankings and pay scales of the U.S. Civil Service. In addition, about 1,800 American civilians worked for the U.S. military in the Zone, also as civilian employees. At the end of the war, approximately 12,000 military personnel, mostly army, were stationed at the fourteen bases remaining in the Zone (the number of bases dipped further in the 1950s). No longer did soldiers live in flimsy wooden huts; their standard of living improved dramatically, and after the war the military shared the benefits of the white employees in the Zone. Many of the employees and military personnel had families living with them, bringing the total number of white Americans in the Zone to about 22,000.[16] They lived in company housing—Americans were not allowed to own property in the Zone or in Panama—and, like military families everywhere, they attended American schools and churches, shopped at American–style company stores, relaxed at company movie theaters, golf courses, and bowling alleys, and were looked after by American police and firefighters. U.S. employees enjoyed benefits superior even to those of most of their compatriots back home, such as free health care.[17] The United States, not Panama, had legal jurisdiction over the Zone, including the right to investigate crimes, so in essence the CZ existed as a separate nation in the center of Panama. In general, white Americans, known as Zonians, lived comfortable, if not luxurious, American lives isolated from the Panamanian population. Like the local workers, the Zonians developed their own multi-generational subculture, determinedly American, yet with a peculiar flavor of European colonialism.

The military personnel, of course, were only one part of this unusual society, but the military had its own uses for the CZ. As a tropical area under U.S. jurisdiction, the Zone proved ideal for staging jungle exercises and maneuvers, and Panama's location gave the military a foothold in a region where it did not enjoy any other significant base access. As Cuba fell to Communism and Communist movements spread elsewhere in Latin America, the Zone became more important to the U.S. forces, and military strategists increasingly factored the base system in Panama into the overall strategy of containment. The military took advantage of U.S. sovereignty in the Zone to develop military installations whose rationales went far beyond the defense of the Canal.[18] The Canal, in other words, gave the military an excuse to remain in Panama, but the Canal was not the most important reason so many military units were deployed there.

The U.S. Armed Forces Southern Command (SOUTHCOM), the headquarters for the combined military forces in Panama and Latin America, sat overlooking the bay at Quarry Heights in Panama City. SOUTHCOM had wide-ranging if vague responsibilities; in addition to commanding an army combat brigade of 2,000 men, it oversaw guerilla-warfare training by U.S. Army Special Forces units, jungle-rescue exercises with the Air Force Tropical Survival School, the Army Jungle Warfare Training Center, a marine squadron that stopped in for port calls at Balboa; it also gave military assistance and advice to U.S. allies in Latin America.[19]

Perhaps the most notorious project undertaken by the armed forces in the Zone was the U.S. Army School of the Americas, founded in 1946. The school, housed at Fort Gulick, trained officers from various Latin American countries allied with the United States. While the purpose of the school had been to train officers to lead effective, professional, and presumably law–abiding armed services in their own countries, more than one graduate of the school strayed from the straight and narrow path in later life. One of its most infamous graduates, Panamanian general Manuel Noriega, later became a thorn in the side of the Reagan Administration and was removed by U.S. troops in a controversial military action. A number of other Latin American military dictators graduated from the school as well. Altogether, the role of the U.S. military in Panama, which had little to do with the defense of the Canal, still less with the defense of the country itself, became an exacerbating factor in the ongoing controversy over the CZ and the U.S. presence there.

By the mid 1950s, Panamanians had had enough of the Americans, military or civilian, in the Zone. They objected to double standards and segregation in employment and the affluent standard of living of white employees in contrast to Panama's grating poverty. The Company kept the bulk of the profits from the Canal, leaving the Panamanians with what they rightly considered a measly percentage. In the early 1950s, for example, the Canal brought in $5 to $7 million, of which Panama received about $430,000 as annual reimbursement.[20] To add insult to injury, the impoverished Panamanian government desperately needed even this small amount of revenue; the Panamanians depended on the Americans for a large part of their total economy, and this dependence rankled. More important, perhaps, than economic injustice was the insult to national sovereignty the Zone represented. Panamanians wanted the right to shape their own desting all the more fiercely because the nation had been in large part a creation of the U.S. Marine Corps.

The Panamanians were not alone in criticizing the more offensive aspects of the Zone. In the era of postwar decolonization and independence movements, the Zone stood out as an anomaly, especially since the system contradicted everything the United States professed to stand for in foreign relations. By the early 1950s, a number of articles and magazine exposés reported on the allegedly sumptuous lifestyles of the Zonians, an embarrassment that compelled the American government to implement austerity measures in the Zone. Cutbacks in spending pinched the Zonians, but the real sufferers were the Panamanians, whose fragile economy depended on the Canal.[21] Throughout the Cold War decades, the Panamanians agitated for a more equal distribution of wealth and opportunity as well as increased sovereignty, while on the other hand the Zonians demanded protection of their privileges and lifestyle.

Balancing the two opposing pressures was not easy. Another challenge came from competition for funding from myriad American financial commitments throughout the world—foreign aid, development assistance, military spending. In the mid-1950s, as the expanded U.S. basing system began to soak up money and the gold flow problem emerged, administrators in the Canal Zone tightened belts further and looked for ways to save money. One austerity measure decreased the workforce by at least 2,000, almost entirely at the expense of silver roll workers.[22] In 1954, the Zone administration announced that it would try to shift almost 1,500 local workers and their families from their housing areas in the Zone to privately owned homes "on the economy" in Panama; in addition, teachers would begin using Spanish as the language of instruction in the eight Zone schools for local rate workers, presaging an eventual shift from Zone schools to Panamanian schools. This was not a popular move: the workers, while Panamanian citizens, had spent their lives in the Zone as English-speaking Americans. The Zone administration's solution to financial challenges and to silver roll complaints about segregation and discrimination was to move the silver roll population out of the zone and out of its jurisdiction.[23]

Dissatisfaction among local workers over discrimination and poor working conditions and among the Panamanian populace in general over their lack of control over the Canal was rising to dangerous levels. The United States at last agreed to discuss reforms in the 1903 treaty, and in 1954 a treaty of "mutual understanding and cooperation" and a "memorandum of understanding" were signed by U.S. President Eisenhower and Panamanian President Jose Antonio Remon. The treaty dealt with many specific issues of contention, but the United States refused outright to discuss the fundamental reason for the existence of the Canal Zone, that is, the granting of sovereignty in perpetuity to the Americans. Negotiators did agree to increase the annual payment to Panama from $430,000 to $1.93 million. In addition, the treaty abolished the separate U.S. and local wage systems and created one system for all. This concession, however, was less than it appeared. The U.S. workers received a 25 percent increase in their pay, regardless of the job they performed—because, it was argued, Americans would need an incentive to leave home and come to Panama. In addition, the salaries of positions that Americans were likely to take were set to standards prevailing in the United States, so that an American employee coming to work in the Zone would not suffer a substantial pay cut. The pay for local jobs, on the other hand, was set to local rates, substantially lower. Thus, although there was now legal equality—no longer were jobs restricted to Americans or local workers—the dual system remained alive in spirit.[24] Under the treaty, moreover, local workers were pushed several steps farther away from the American culture of the Zone and toward Panamanian society. Workers not living in Zone housing areas lost commissary privileges and, in a victory for the Panamanian government, were required to pay Panamanian income tax.[25] In spite of opposition from Zone residents of all types, the treaty was ratified by the U.S. Senate and passed into law in 1955.

The revised treaty did not satisfy Panamanian nationalists any more than Zone residents, however, because it did not address the basic issue of national sovereignty. While nationalists could not hope in the short term to dislodge the Americans from the Zone entirely, they did expect that progress could be made on symbolic issues, such as the flying of the Panamanian flag in the Zone. Since the Zone had been created, the only flag to fly there was the Stars and Stripes, marking the CZ as U.S. territory. Nationalist activists fought to fly the Panamanian flag instead of or alongside the American flag. The issue grew into a rallying cry for nationalists, students, and others near the Zone, and hoisting the Panamanian flag, even for a few minutes before it was hauled down by police, became a popular act of defiance.

FLAG RIOTS

In 1958, flag flying as a method of protest began in earnest. That year, students from Panama University initiated an effort called "Operation Sovereignty," in which they defiantly planted flags at various points in the Zone. In the first of many episodes, fifty flags were removed immediately by Zone police,[26] and the National Guard attacked the students. One student was killed in the fighting,[27] and riots ensued. Unrest spread through Panama as enraged opposition groups tried to overthrow the government.

On November 3, 1959, the anniversary of Panama's declaration of independence, student protesters made another attempt to plant flags in the Zone, just over the border of Panama City on the Pacific side of the Canal. This time, former Foreign Minister Aquilino Boyd spearheaded the protest, which involved large numbers of participants, as many as 2,000 by some estimates. This protest, too, led to violent clashes with law enforcement. After the first attempt to plant the flag, U.S. police in riot gear pushed the demonstrators back to Panamanian soil. The students marched along a street on the border singing the Panamanian anthem, while Panamanian National Guardsmen and U.S. Canal police stood by. About an hour later, a young student stepped too close to the border and was pushed back by the Canal police. At that point, fighting broke out, and the youth was arrested and put in a Canal Zone vehicle. Students began to throw rocks, and the Canal police responded with tear gas and water hoses.

As the rioting continued, protesters burned American cars in a parking lot and threw stones at American businesses and government agencies, including the U.S. Embassy. Army units were called out after Zone officials determined that Panamanian National Guard troops had not taken sufficient action to protect U.S. property. About thirty-six protesters and police were injured in the rioting, and several students were arrested.[28]

Several weeks later, more rioting occurred after crowds tried to enter the Zone, but U.S. infantry troops and the National Guard pushed them back. When the crowd of 1,000 was repulsed, they looted and vandalized U.S. businesses in Panama City once again. The riots claimed thirty more casualties.

U.S. observers blamed the rioting on Cuban revolutionaries egging on the leaderless crowd and noted that many demonstrators carried banners with revolutionary slogans and pictures of Fidel Castro.[29] The U.S. military, which against its will had been an integral factor in the unrest, concluded that the latest waves of riots were "better organized, involved larger crowds, and were more violent in their expression of anti–U.S. sentiments" than earlier ones.[30] However, the rioters dispersed within four hours of the outbreak of violence, and the following day saw no repetition of the unrest.

The agitation settled down by January 1960, but it alerted the U.S. to serious problems in and around the Zone. In September, Eisenhower ordered Panamanian flags to be flown along with the American flag at Shuler Triangle in the Zone.

Eisenhower's order to fly the flags of the two nations did not go to the root of Panamanian dissatisfaction, however, and President John F. Kennedy's 1962 order extending the policy to all public buildings in the Zone did not help. The very presence of a large American community, affluent, uninvolved in Panamanian life, and (in many cases) aggressively nationalist, served as a constant reminder of the limits on Panamanian sovereignty. Moreover, the American community in Panama did not shrink as a result of the changes and unrest; rather, it grew larger than ever. According to statistics from the Department of Defense, in 1964 more than 36,000 Americans (excluding local employees) lived in the Zone, including 9,750 active duty military personnel and 11,800 military family members, 3,905 civilian employees of the armed forces and their families, and 10,700 company and CZ government employees and their families.[31] In addition, the company employed 5,000 Panamanians and the military employed 10,000.[32]

Members of the American community itself caused the worst outbreak of violence in the century of American involvement in Panama. On the afternoon of January 7, 1964, U.S. high school students raised an American flag outside the Balboa High School in the Zone and vowed to continue flying the American flag unaccompanied by the Panamanian flag as a protest against the Kennedy order. The governor of the Zone, General Robert Fleming, ordered that no flags be flown at the school, but the students disobeyed the order.[33] Two days later Panamanian high school students marched into the Zone and tried to put up their flag, which, they correctly pointed out, should have been flying with the Stars and Stripes. The U.S. students jeered at the Panamanian students as they hoisted their flag, and to avert a scene the Zone police began to move the Panamanian students back across the Zone border. According to most witnesses, some pushing and shoving occurred on both sides, and the Panamanian flag was torn.[34] The DOD report on the incident also said that the Panamanian students committed minor acts of vandalism, such as overturning garbage cans and breaking lights, as they left the Zone.[35]

The border between the Canal Zone and Panama was open, or at least fluid—anyone could cross into the Zone or leave the Zone without passing through gates or checkpoints. The boundary in Panama City was a major thoroughfare known after 1964 as the Avenue of the Martyrs. The street itself was part of the Zone, but the sidewalk lay in Panama City proper. As news of the student confrontation spread, an angry crowd of Panamanians gathered along the sidewalk and attempted to cross the street into the Zone. About thirty Zone police were on hand to keep order, which became impossible as the mob threw stones and advanced on the officers. What happened next is difficult to determine, but according to later reports by Maj. Gen. Andrew O'Meara, the commander of SOUTHCOM, the police were pushed back 400 yards into the Zone by the crowd and had used up their 100 tear gas canisters to no avail.[36] The Zone police shot into the air and on the ground, hoping to disperse the mob, but instead, many demonstrators were injured and some killed by flying bullets. At 8 p.m., the situation had deteriorated so severely that SOUTHCOM was called to take over. O'Meara ordered troops from the 193rd Infantry to secure the Zone and break up demonstrations. All unauthorized persons were ordered to leave the Zone or face arrest, Americans were to stay in their homes, and schools were closed for several days.[37] O'Meara announced that the rioters had been dispersed by 9 p.m., but he spoke too soon. Riots erupted all over Panama after reports that six people had been killed, and snipers took aim at U.S. soldiers guarding the Zone border, killing three. Soldiers were ordered not to shoot—one witness reported seeing an officer striking a soldier to stop him from shooting[38]—but considerable fire was exchanged.

When the dust cleared on January 12, twenty people were dead, including three American soldiers and a civilian, and hundreds had been injured. The president of Panama, Roberto Chiari, severed relations with the United States in protest against what the Panamanians believed was inexcusable aggression. During the several days of riots, life in Panama came to a halt as citizens focused their attention on the crisis. Panamanian radio stations broadcast denunciations of the Americans,[39] and anger ran so hot that more than 2,000 Americans living in Panama moved into the Zone as refugees.[40] Additional refugees, mostly employees of the United Fruit Company, fled to Costa Rica, which announced that it would accept them without the usual documentation necessary to cross borders.[41]

Although the presence and privileges of the Zone in general were the underlying cause of the riots, the U.S. armed forces came under especially sharp scrutiny for their role in the violence. O'Meara denied that the soldiers had panicked, blaming the deaths on inexperienced Canal Police and on the actions of the rioters themselves. Four rioters, he said, had been killed in a fire at an office building set by Panamanians.[42] The ease, however, with which the U.S. military stepped in and put down civil unrest among

Panamanians indicated to critics of the Zone—virtually all Panamanians—
that the U.S. forces exercised an unacceptable level of power, leaving
Panama weak and dependent.

The Zonians, too, received unwelcome publicity in the wake of the riots.
European observers, mostly on the left, decried U.S. imperialism in Latin
America. More substantively, the U.S. Congress laid the blame for the
explosive situation on two groups, first the oligarchic government of
Panama, which deflected criticism from its own failings onto the American
presence in the Zone and led Panamanians to believe that all would be well
were the Americans to vacate the property, and second, the Zonians, who
resisted any attempt to reform their privileged position.[43] A *Time* magazine
article published in the wake of the riots described the life of the Zonians in
terms virtually guaranteed to win them no friends: "Few Americans abroad
lead a more comfortable life or are more self-consciously American . . .
[Zonians live] in model company towns with look–alike houses, bargain–
priced groceries, liquor and clothing from Government commissaries, bowling and Hollywood movies at the service centers. They have their own schools
(including a junior college), country clubs and well-kept golf courses; 1,600
boats are registered at the yacht basin."

Zonians resented the accusations of Panamanians and outside critics
that they lived a life of colonial ease, noting that although conditions in
the Zone were better than in surrounding Panama, they were hardly sumptuous, and in any case, Zone employees did not own any property.[44]
"Whatever you write, don't say we have manicured lawns," a public relations official begged a reporter in 1973, explaining that the image of
ordered luxury gave an inaccurate impression of life in the Zone. The
homes and buildings in the Zone were carefully maintained, Zone residents said, because otherwise they would quickly deteriorate in the tropical jungle climate. The "manicured lawns" of many a magazine article
were simply malaria prevention measures. In fact, most of the buildings in
the Zone, like so many buildings on military installations throughout the
world, were rather old and built along the same patterns as barracks—
hardly luxurious.[45] Many Zonians, moreover, protested that they had deep
roots in the area. In the early 1970s, about a quarter of the Americans in the
Zone were second or third generation Zone employees, and about 13 percent
were married to Panamanians.[46]

ATTEMPTS AT REFORM

However, in the aftermath of the riots, the U.S. community quietly
began to make changes, especially by bringing increasing numbers of
Panamanians into the system. The Canal Zone Personnel Policy Coordinating
Board, which had overseen hiring of local and American workers since
1955, actively recruited and trained Panamanians for the more skilled

Canal positions in technology and administration. By the late 1960s, about 11,000 Panamanians worked in the Zone.[47] The traditional separate housing areas for the descendants of "silver roll" workers survived, as well as the "Latin" or Spanish–language school system, but the new policy was one of attrition. Children of workers were not allowed to take over their parents' homes as the older generation retired, and in the decade after the 1964 riots, the number of children in the "Latin" schools dropped from 3,500 to 1,300.[48]

Economic changes were welcome, but still did not address the question of sovereignty. Panamanians marked the "Day of the Martyrs," as January 9 was known, with protests and demonstrations, although police attempted to keep memorial services dignified and peaceful. More significantly, Brig. Gen. Omar Torrijos Herrera, one of a group of officers who seized power in 1968 and later became a military dictator, set himself the goal of renegotiating the treaty, demanding to know "What people can bear the humiliation of seeing a foreign flag planted in the very heart of its nation?"[49]

With the action of the Panamanian demonstrators, however, came an equally determined reaction from many Americans, and talks dragged on for years. Military leaders tended to view the 1964 riots as a Communist–inspired plot, embracing the idea that the Panamanian students had been guided by Communist agitators,[50] and they rejected any suggestion that the military presence in Panama be decreased. Civilian Zonians also received support from conservative groups in the United States who feared that a change in the Panama treaty would be another step in the degeneration of American power, so clearly revealed, in conservative eyes, by the Vietnam debacle, the antiwar movement, and the 1960s culture wars. During the Senate debates over the Canal in 1978, Senator Bob Dole called it the "latest in a series of foreign policy retreats by our government."[51] Maintenance of American power and strategic influence was the key to conservative reaction. The Canal was no longer the goldmine it once had been— it had operated at a deficit for years, subsidized by the U.S. government. Still, many Americans disliked the image of their nation being "pushed out" against its will and pointed to the strategic value of the region.

If the military value of the Zone was one reason many opposed reform, the U.S. forces in Panama struggled with their own problems. In the 1970s, the U.S. Army in Panama suffered the same morale and discipline problems faced by the military everywhere—in 1974 a large clash between black and white soldiers, for example, injured several; investigators believed the violence was drug related.[52] Panama enjoyed a reputation among military officers as a restful, easy assignment in a tropical paradise, a "rehabilitation center" for officers returning from hardship tours,[53] and, according to a *Wall Street Journal* report, the military hierarchy in Panama was bloated to the point of absurdity; with a population of about 10,000 active duty personnel, SOUTHCOM enjoyed the services of ten generals and two admirals—whose fleet consisted of two 45-foot fishing boats.[54] Even these beneficiaries had to admit that life in Panama could not remain as it had been.

In 1974–1975, more serious negotiations on the Canal finally began between Secretary of State Henry Kissinger and Panamanian Foreign Minister Juan A. Tack. One important achievement was the draft of a SOFA for the military bases in Panama, a measure the Panamanians had been requesting for years and the Pentagon agreed must be completed before serious negotiations over the future of the Canal could take place. A SOFA, both sides concurred, would place the military bases on the same status as those in Europe and Asia, a position they deserved in view of the wide-ranging missions they performed. In February 1975 the negotiating teams signed an agreement, which clarified the status of U.S. troops and consolidated fourteen military bases to four.[55]

The slow pace of negotiations throughout the late 1960s and early 1970s had been criticized by other Latin American nations as well as the UN, and in September 1975 students attacked the U.S. Embassy in Panama City, demonstrating their frustration and anger. This time, the Panamanian government did not suspend relations as it had in 1964, but apologized to the Americans, revealing the importance the government placed on the negotiations. By 1975 the two sides had agreed in principle that there should be a fixed date whereby the United States would end its dominant role in the Canal Zone. The steps made thus far would not go unchallenged, however. In the presidential election of 1976, candidate Reagan brought the issue to the public, standing against revision of the treaty and charging that the United States "owned" the Zone, an incorrect statement but one which made intuitive sense to many Americans. Although Reagan did not win the primary, he forced Republican Gerald Ford to move to the right on the issue, and little progress was made until Carter took office in early 1977.

THE PANAMA CANAL TREATIES

One of Carter's stated goals was to solve the festering Panama problem, not only for the sake of Panamanian–American relations but also to improve America's image throughout the Western Hemisphere.

The Carter negotiating team addressed two major sets of issues, first the ownership of the Canal, financial arrangements for its transfer, and the fate of the Zonian community, and second the defense of the Canal and the military bases in Panama. On the first issue, the proposals detailed the gradual transfer of responsibility for running the Canal from the United States to Panama, a process that would end at noon on December 31, 1999 with Panama's final assumption of sovereignty. Although they would retain most existing privileges, U.S. employees would be replaced with Panamanians as they retired or transferred out of the country. Panama would benefit much more substantially from the Canal, and the Americans would assist Panamanians in acquiring the skills and experience to operate it. In terms of defense, the two nations would work together to defend the Canal, with the United States assuming primary responsibility until the end of the treaty; at the end of the century the Panamanians would defend the waterway.

On September 7, 1977, after months of intense negotiations, President Carter and General Torrijos signed two separate documents: the Neutrality Treaty, pledging the neutrality of the Canal and joint defense responsibility of the United States and Panama, and the Panama Canal Treaty, the agreement in which the United States would relinquish the Canal in 1999. Senate ratification was a tough and bruising fight and was almost derailed at the end of the debates when Democratic Senator Dennis DeConcini added an amendment granting the United States the right to protect the Canal after 2000. The Senate ratified the treaty with this change, a change the Panamanians did not accept. Carter and Torrijos, however, added a clarification that noted that the amendment did not allow the United States to intervene in Panamanian internal affairs, and there the matter stood. The treaties passed the Senate in March and April of 1978, and their provisions became law on October 1, 1979.

During the debates and immediately after, a spate of books and articles appeared condemning the Canal treaties for giving American property away, harming the defense capabilities of the United States, allowing Communism to spread, going against the Constitution, betraying the trust of Americans, and other complaints. Most Americans, it appeared, opposed the treaties, and the Zonians repatriated to the United States in large numbers. Soon the majority of Americans in the CZ were connected with the military.

However, during the next decade, the Canal and its operations were gradually turned over to Panama without incident. Apprenticeship programs and training helped Panamanians to take over the jobs of Zonians who left, and a unified pay system adopted in the early 1980s gave the same wage scales to all employees regardless of nationality. The DOD used the same system for the employees on military bases, which made the transfer easier and less disruptive. In 1984, Canal company employees lost PX, Commissary, and APO mailing privileges, but this blow was eased by the fact that many of them continued receiving these privileges through spouses working for the DOD.[56]

OPERATION JUST CAUSE

It appeared that the long American presence in Panama was coming to an end. But a final chapter to the strange story remained, a chapter that encompassed all the conflicting motivations and entanglements of the

United States in Panama. This last act was known to the military as Operation Just Cause, a name chosen to illustrate what the army hoped would be the philanthropic nature of the action—removing a dictator who had seized power illegally and terrorized the Panamanian people.

Manuel Noriega had enjoyed long and close ties with the United States, first as a graduate of the School of the Americas and later as a CIA informant. As a member of the National Guard, he had become involved in drug smuggling in the late 1960s and early 1970s. He served under Torrijos in the 1970s and rose through the ranks, becoming the head of the Panama Defense Forces (PDF), which replaced the National Guard in 1983.[57] He was, by all accounts, corrupt through and through—involved in drug- and gun-running, extortion, and political murder. However, he maintained his American support because he participated in efforts to arm the Contras, the guerilla opponents of the Communist Sandinista regime.[58] As head of the PDF, Noriega also received generous funding from the Pentagon, which hoped that the PDF would become a stable military force that could replace the U.S. forces guarding the Canal. Panama's gradual move toward military dictatorship was indirectly assisted by the United States, which pursued its own goals in the country, seemingly unaware of the monster it had created.

In 1985, Noriega seized power and ran Panama as a military dictator. In 1986–1987, Panamanians and U.S. observers began a campaign of opposition to Noriega, publicizing his crimes and criticizing those who supported him. By 1988 even the CIA realized that Noriega was a liability, and the Department of Justice indicted him for drug smuggling in the Florida courts. Washington imposed sanctions on Panama, and the Panamanian people began a huge campaign of demonstrations and protests against the dictator. For two years the Panamanian people tried to pressure Noriega to resign, but he resisted. By the summer of 1989 relations between the Americans and Noriega deteriorated to the point where the 10,000 U.S. servicemen in Panama and the 10,000 U.S. civilians in the business community, all potential hostages in a showdown, began to come under threat. The U.S. bases experienced vandalism, infiltration, even sniper attacks on soldiers. In September 1989, the United States broke off diplomatic relations with Panama, and in October rebels within the PDF captured Noriega.

The wily general escaped with the help of loyal followers in the PDF, however, and was soon back in control. In December, several U.S. soldiers were fired on as they drove by the PDF headquarters, and one was killed. Shooting continued over the next few days. The Pentagon sent reinforcements to Panama, and on December 20, U.S. forces began taking over PDF facilities. Within a short time the American forces had gained control of much of the PDF establishment, and Noriega escaped into hiding. He spent a week at the Vatican Embassy, where the papal nuncio tried to convince him to surrender. He finally did so in early January 1990.

The crisis appeared to end quickly and quietly, but the questions and problems it had raised remained, especially the legality of the U.S. action in removing Noriega; the United States had specifically promised in the 1977–1978 treaty that it would not interfere in Panamanian affairs. Although by most accounts the intervention was popular among Panamanians, who supported it and were happy to have Noriega gone, a prolonged U.S. presence would not have been welcome. The United States in any case was committed to leaving Panama, and Panama needed to build a civil society on its own. There was no place in this situation for any kind of World War II–style military occupation or reconstruction period. The age of military-sponsored nation building, it seemed, had passed.

7

★ ★ ★ ★ ★

Freedom from the Colonial Legacy: The Philippines

INTRODUCTION

The history of the U.S. military presence in the Philippines and the controversy it engendered in the 1980s illustrates a number of the contentious issues that bedevil many installations in the global basing system. Host communities in the Philippines displayed the most extreme effects of the U.S. military presence overseas, which were particularly severe in developing regions.

The U.S. bases in the Philippines, above all, stood as a painful reminder of a colonial history from which most Filipinos wished to dissociate themselves. Americans ruled the Philippines as a colony from 1898 to 1946, but even after the Philippines received its independence on July 4, 1946, the United States demanded a base agreement very favorable to U.S. interests and dismissive of Philippine sensitivities. The colonial legacy, then, did not disappear with independence but remained real and present in the form of the sprawling Subic Bay Naval Base, Clark Air Base, and a number of other installations. Moreover, the Americans supported the corrupt but pro–American Ferdinand Marcos, connecting the United States in the eyes of many Filipinos with a criminal, dictatorial regime. America's determination to retain the bases appeared to drive policy to a disturbing extent, and Filipinos began to view American decisions through the lens of the bases, "assuming that the bases are the motivation behind every American act," as one newspaper described it.[1]

Economically the bases proved, in the short term at least, a godsend for the desperately poor nation, pouring millions of dollars into the Philippine economy through the paychecks of thousands of local employees of the Americans as well as through the notorious bar culture patronized by soldiers and airmen. On the other hand, the social degradation of the camptowns humiliated and shocked the socially conservative Philippine population.

Irritations stemming from the bases bothered even those otherwise favorably disposed to the U.S. presence. Criminal jurisdiction over American servicemembers remained in U.S. hands, which allowed Americans committing crimes on or off base to be investigated, charged, and tried under the military court system, rather than that of the Philippines. In the 1950s, Filipinos objected to the U.S. flag flying over military areas and demanded that the flag of the Philippines fly next to, or instead of the Stars and Stripes. Some critics charged that the bases displaced other industries that might have developed had the installations not been there, although certainly the economy of the Philippines had much room for improvement, bases or no.

Paradoxically, while dissatisfaction with the U.S. bases grew steadily during the Cold War, Filipinos maintained a long and close relationship with the United States. A four-decade wait for immigration visas to enter the United States was but one sign of the widespread Filipino acceptance of things American. Many Filipinos enthusiastically followed American current events, sports, and culture.[2]

During the 1980s, however, a growing anti–base movement pressed for changes in the Philippine relationship with the United States. When President Marcos lost power in 1986, the push to remove the bases intensified, and a left–wing guerilla group added violence against U.S. personnel to the generally peaceful movement. President Corazon Aquino tried to maintain a balance between the bases and their supporters and the anti-base movement. In the end, though, the U.S. bases in the Philippines were swept away by the forces of nature in the form of the volcano Mount Pinatubo. Clark Air Base disappeared under layers of ash and rock, and while Subic Bay did not suffer directly from the volcanic eruption, the Americans seemed to lose the energy to fight for the base, and it closed in 1992.

A BRIEF HISTORY OF THE UNITED STATES IN THE PHILIPPINES

In 1898, the United States took control of the Philippines from the Spanish as a result of victory in the Spanish–American War. On May 1, 1898, Commodore George Dewey sailed into Manila Bay, destroyed the Spanish fleet, and began a century of American influence in the archipelago.

The Americans, however, did not have an easy time subduing the Filipinos, who fought fiercely for their independence for three years and continued to press for freedom even after the violence ended.

In 1935, the United States granted the Philippines commonwealth status and scheduled independence for 1946. As part of this gradual transfer of authority, the U.S. forces transferred defense responsibility to the Philippine government, although in reality the Filipinos had few resources to spare on such an effort.[3] Nevertheless, in 1935, a year in which the Japanese threat loomed, the Philippine National Assembly proposed the creation of a large reserve force to supplement the small Philippine Regular army, and two years later, on his retirement, General Douglas MacArthur arrived to supervise the establishment of this reserve force. In addition to Philippine reserves and regular forces, a U.S. Army garrison had been stationed in the Philippines since the turn of the century. By the mid-1930s, however, this force had shrunk and could not hope to hold out against an attack by the Japanese, an event which appeared increasingly likely. War with Japan probably meant war with Germany as well; the Americans settled on a "Germany first" policy and faced the prospect of abandoning the Philippines to the Japanese. The plan created by the army and navy to address such an eventuality called for the U.S. Army forces in the Philippines to withdraw to the Bataan peninsula on the main island of Luzon and then to the tiny island of Corregidor. In July 1941, FDR authorized the development of a combined Philippine and American force, known as U.S. Armed Forces, Far East (USAFFE), to organize a defense of the island. MacArthur returned to active duty to lead this force and prepare a stronger defensive posture.

At the beginning of December 1941, the one development that gave real hope for an extended defense of the Philippines centered on the large number of U.S. aircraft, including 35 B-17 Flying Fortress bombers and 107 P-40 fighters, that made up the new Far East Air Force. They were grouped together on Luzon at Clark Field, an airstrip on the grounds of the former Fort Stotsenburg, the old horse cavalry post used in the Philippine war of 1898–1902.

It was probably unwise to concentrate the aircraft at one airfield in the first place; to make matters worse, in the hours after the attack on Pearl Harbor on December 7, no emergency order came to move them. Nine hours later, the Japanese 11th Air Fleet attacked and destroyed almost all the aircraft parked at Clark Field, demolishing in a single raid any realistic possibility of defending the Philippines.[4] The Japanese invaded Luzon on December 22. The Philippine Army forces deployed to resist the Japanese were easily overcome by the invaders, and four days later, December 26, MacArthur ordered a withdrawal to Bataan and Corregidor. About 65,000 troops and 25,000 civilians retreated to the Bataan peninsula, where the Japanese held them under siege. Unfortunately, because of the tardiness in planning for defense, USAFFE had not made preparations for a long stay in Bataan and had inadequately stockpiled food and supplies. For months, the men and women, Philippine and American, on Bataan subsisted on half rations, succumbing to malaria and other diseases that could not be treated, but they held firm against Japanese attacks. By order of the president, on March 12 MacArthur evacuated to Australia to avoid capture, but the other American and Philippine personnel stayed on. They held out until early April in increasingly grim conditions. When they finally surrendered on April 8, the Japanese marched them 65 miles to an evacuation point, an event later known as the Bataan Death March. Between 6,000 and 10,000 people died, all but about 600 of them Filipino.[5] The Japanese occupation of the Philippines was a dark time for the islands, not only because of harsh treatment from the Japanese, but because Filipinos disagreed on whether to resist or collaborate. Many resisted, refusing to work for the Japanese or even joining guerilla groups such as the Hukbalahap (Huk). Others, won over by Japanese anti-western propaganda, or simply seeing no alternative, worked with the Japanese.

On October 20, 1944, MacArthur waded ashore on the island of Leyte, fulfilling his famous promise to return to the Philippines, made in 1942 as he and his staff evacuated Corregidor. The battle for Leyte, a smaller island to the south of Luzon, proved to be even more dramatic than MacArthur's staged landing; it was a fight to the death between the Japanese and American naval forces. Kamikaze attacks inflicted horrible damage on U.S. ships, but in the end the Americans eliminated the Japanese navy as a factor in the war. Japanese ground forces resisted the American advance, but by the beginning of January 1945, U.S. army combat units landed on Luzon, approaching Manila a month later. The final two weeks of fighting for Manila proved to be the fiercest struggle for the Philippines, the brunt of the battle borne by Filipino civilians. In the final days Manila was virtually destroyed by American artillery, and as many as 100,000 Philippine civilians died.[6]

Even before the war drew to a close, the Americans eyed the Philippines as a prime location in a postwar basing system. In May 1945 the president of the Philippines, Sergio Osmeña, agreed to American demands for basing rights, in return for desperately needed reconstruction aid.[7] In addition, the United States successfully pressed for an exclusivity agreement; no other nation would receive basing rights in the Philippines.[8]

THE DEVELOPMENT OF A COLD WAR BASING SYSTEM IN THE PHILIPPINES

Soon after the war ended, the presence of U.S. forces in the Philippines began to chafe American and Filipino alike. As in virtually every other overseas military garrison during the first months of peace, soldiers remaining in the Philippines smoldered with discontent at the slow pace of demobilization. In an effort to improve morale, commanders allowed soldiers to use jeeps and trucks to travel the countryside in their leisure time. Unfortunately, their poor driving skills and lack of consideration entangled them in numerous traffic accidents with Filipinos, which brought up the issue of jurisdiction.[9] Other serious incidents arose between U.S. sentries (who were Filipino) and Filipinos trying to gain access to U.S. installations; the Americans called them thieves, but the local media claimed they were merely poor scavengers. In any case, guards who were ordered to deal sternly with pilferage and scavenging threatened intruders with arrest or worse. On several occasions, conflicts escalated to violence, and civilians were wounded or killed. Such episodes could not be investigated by Philippine police, nor could the sentries be charged with any crime under Philippine law because they occurred on base and so fell under U.S. jurisdiction. The question of who exercised authority in these matters quickly led to claims of neo-imperialism.[10] On the eve of independence, the United States insisted on its right to handle American suspects in its own way, much to the chagrin of the Philippine government. The thorny issue of criminal jurisdiction became the first, but not the last, of many disagreements between the U.S. military and the Filipinos.

In addition to the jurisdiction issue, other drawbacks made the idea of an enduring U.S. military presence less than attractive to the Philippines and to the United States, among them numerous incidents between soldiers and Filipinos that earned the U.S. Army a poor reputation among the populace, the existence of other more advantageous sites for base development such as Okinawa and Guam, and nationalist sentiment that rejected a huge and enduring U.S. military presence. Many Filipinos objected above all to the U.S. garrison in Manila, the capital of the nation, an insult that even the most pro-American Filipinos could not tolerate. Yet Filipino leaders, like their American counterparts, saw the need for a continuing military presence, albeit a less visible one. To a greater or lesser extent they believed that the United States would serve as a defense umbrella, but much more importantly the military presence would help maintain American interest in the nation, essential if the Philippines were to benefit from U.S. economic aid.

The Military Bases Agreement (MBA), concluded in March 1947, reflected the ambivalence of U.S. policymakers toward the use of the Philippines as a forward basing location and the desire of Filipino leaders that the Americans remain in their country, giving the U.S. forces extremely favorable terms at a small and easily bearable cost. For a period of ninety-nine years, the U.S. Air Force received the use of Clark Field, soon to be redesignated as Clark Air Base, and the U.S. Navy took possession of Subic Bay near the city of Olongapo. The U.S. Army left the country, but the Air Force and navy received more than nineteen other installations.

Several points in the 1947 treaty disproportionately benefited the Americans. The Americans placed quotas on Filipino products entering the United States while U.S. corporations could invest freely in Filipino natural resources. Criminal jurisdiction over American personnel by and large remained with the Americans: crimes committed on base (even those involving a Filipino national), *inter se* crimes (American perpetrator and victim) off-base, and off-base crime that "threatened the security of U.S. installations" all fell under American jurisdiction.[11] Under the terms of the treaty, Filipinos accused of crimes that the Americans determined to be threats to base security—for example, guerilla activities—would find themselves in the hands of U.S. authorities for trial and sentencing. For its part, the Americans agreed to minimize the number of troops deployed to the Philippines,[12] and promised a package of economic aid to the islands.

The 1947 MBA suited both sides for a few years, until the Korean War focused U.S. policy on the strict containment of Communism. When the United States began to put the containment policy into practice in the early 1950s by creating a worldwide basing system, many nations with little or no historic connection to the United States, such as Turkey, Greece and Spain, drove hard bargains in their negotiations over basing rights. Even former enemies received favorable treatment; the Japanese treaty allowed the Japanese more jurisdiction in criminal incidents than the Philippine MBA did. When Filipinos learned what other nations received for base rights, in many instances bases much less important than those in the Philippines, they demanded that the United States compensate the Philippines appropriately.

As outraged Filipinos questioned the fairness and good faith of their former colonial overlords, the Americans were discovering the Philippines to be a vital strategic location, one that neither the Air Force or the navy could do without. At the same time, a guerilla rebellion by the Huk, who continued their struggle for independence after the Japanese left, sent the cold warriors of the Truman administration into a panic. In 1949 the CIA sent the famous counterinsurgent Edward Lansdale to the Philippines to assist the government in suppressing the rebellion, a mission that Lansdale and the Philippine forces achieved within a few years. But the Americans evaded any discussion of reforming the MBA. While the government of the Philippines under Ramon Magsaysay aligned itself with the United States to the point of obsequiousness, Philippine nationalists like Senator Claro Recto criticized Magsaysay's apparent unwillingness to stand up for Philippine rights.

By 1956, the "year of nationalism" according to one Filipino magazine,[13] public dissatisfaction bubbled over into demands that the government address the glaring inequities of the U.S. presence. Issues ranged from U.S. Navy administration over Olongapo, which had continued after independence, and charges of American abuse of Filipinos, to concerns that the bases made the Philippines magnets for nuclear attack.

Magsaysay died in a plane crash in 1957, and the new president, Carlos Garcia, followed his pro–American policies. He could not, however, ignore public discontent over the American presence in his nation. In discussions with the United States throughout the late 1950s, the Philippine government attempted to raise questions of compensation, jurisdiction, sovereignty, and consultation in the use of the bases—simply speaking, it sought to renegotiate the 1947 MBA. For his part, Eisenhower advised compromise on symbolic issues, such as flying the Philippine flag next to the American flag, which began in 1957, and the reversion of Olongapo to Philippine rule occurring in 1959, but insisted on maintaining the military integrity of the bases. All in all, U.S. policymakers refused to take Philippine demands particularly seriously, dismissing complaints as communist–inspired, as they tended to do elsewhere.

In 1964 several tragic incidents spurred Filipinos to renew demands for a revision of the MBA. First, an Air Force sentry shot and killed a Filipino civilian collecting shell casings for scrap metal on a U.S. target range. A few weeks later Marines killed another Filipino who approached them in a boat. Demonstrations and protest marches ensued. Activists claimed that thirty-one Filipinos had been killed by the Americans since 1952; American authorities acknowledged thirty deaths, twenty-one of which had been committed by Filipino guards employed on the base. The Americans implicated in civilian deaths, however, had all been cleared of wrongdoing and sent back to the United States. The appearance of leniency for Americans accused of crimes against Filipinos put the Americans on the defensive. In 1965, the Philippine government won jurisdiction over off-base crimes, as well as on-base crimes in which the suspect was Filipino, and the ninety-nine year lease became a twenty-five year commitment ending in 1991. The conflict did not vanish entirely. In 1968, a U.S. guard was court-martialed for a shooting similar to the 1964 incidents, but like the others, he was acquitted and returned to the United States.[14] More protests and demonstrations erupted, but with time anger died down, at least temporarily.

THE MARCOS REGIME

In 1965 Ferdinand Marcos successfully ran for president of the Philippines. His election would have grave consequences for the U.S. bases in the Philippines, but for the moment, the Johnson administration welcomed his pro-American, anti-communist stance and rewarded him with $80 million in aid.[15] In return, Marcos promised to send a few units of Philippine soldiers to fight in Vietnam. Marcos' dishonesty soon disappointed the President, but the Philippine bases played an important part in the Vietnam effort, and Johnson did not press him to improve. Given a free hand,

Marcos made no effort to rein in widespread graft or to reform the oligarchic traditions of Philippine politics and economic life. In fact, he revealed himself to be as adept in corruption as any other Philippine politician, although the truly spectacular levels of theft occurred only later.

Opposition to Marcos, from street demonstrations to the armed guerilla activity of the communist New People's Army (NPA), flourished, and inevitably some of the muck spattered on the Americans. In 1970, as antiwar protests engulfed Manila, demonstrators called Marcos a puppet of the Americans in Vietnam and linked American support of Marcos to his regressive policies and corruption.

Affairs in the Philippines went from bad to worse when Marcos declared martial law in 1972. The Americans grumbled but did not cut off aid; the communist insurgency led by the NPA continued to gain Marcos time and support. Meanwhile, problems with the bases aggravated Filipino sensitivities. One commentator called the bases "sociological mistakes" for placing large numbers of middle-class, white Americans with the masses of desperately poor Filipinos who lived in the surrounding towns.[16] Lingering jurisdiction issues and camptown social problems topped the list of complaints. Marcos did not address the issue of the camptowns directly but pressed for a renegotiation of the base treaty with an emphasis on increasing the amount of money the United States paid for the privilege. When President Ford rejected Marcos' overtures, the Philippine president decided to wait for a better opportunity.

The "better opportunity" came with the election of Jimmy Carter, possibly the only president to care sincerely about human rights violations in the Philippines. Carter pressured Marcos to improve his dismal record and in return negotiated a new deal on the bases. The agreement, signed in January 1979, compromised on the demands of both sides. Clark and Subic Bay were to be reduced in size and some smaller installations would be relinquished entirely; in all, the United States gave up the use of 100,000 acres. Philippine sovereignty over the bases was acknowledged and joint flags flown. The bases were to be administered jointly by Filipinos and Americans. Filipinos were to provide security for the bases, reducing the problems occurring when American guards confronted Filipino trespassers or scavengers. Every five years the treaty would be reviewed until 1991, when the earlier twenty-five year treaty was set to expire. Perhaps most importantly, Carter promised to make his "best effort" to provide a generous aid package for the Philippines, including $50 million in Military Assistance, $250 million in Foreign Military Sales credits, and $200 million in Security Supporting Assistance—a total of a half a billion dollars, if it all came through.[17] Carter did make his best effort to get the money Marcos wanted, but Marcos did not markedly improve his human rights record, except in the optimistic and perhaps self-deluding rhetoric of Carter administration officials who wished to justify the additional funds.

THE BASES DURING THE MARCOS ERA

By the 1980s, Subic Bay and Clark Air Field were the largest U.S. installations in Asia and among the largest in the world. About 6,000 Naval personnel, families, and civilian employees lived at Subic Bay, and the base hosted nine major commands, including the naval command of the Pacific. Clark housed about 10,000 personnel and served as the headquarters for the 13th Air Force, a major unit in charge of the Pacific and Indian Oceans. The two installations brought about 40,000 Americans to the Philippines.

American advocates of the bases could point to many advantages of the installations. At the top of the list came the Philippines' strategic location, which had assumed great importance during the Vietnam era and continued its relevance when the Soviets invaded Afghanistan in 1979. Second, Marcos, in spite of his criminality and his occasional advances toward America's adversaries, had proved himself a reliable, if not especially attractive, ally. Third, over the years, polls showed that the population of the Philippines, by and large, supported the presence of the bases, mostly for economic reasons, but also because they felt a genuine tie to the United States. Fourth, Subic Bay was one of the only deep-water ports in the region large enough to accept the huge aircraft carriers which were the mainstay of the U.S. Navy. Finally, a large pool of skilled, English-speaking craftsmen repaired and maintained naval vessels at about one-seventh the cost of U.S. workers.[18] A combination of strategic, political, and economic factors, then, made the bases appear indispensable.

The bases also provided benefits to the Philippines, most noticeably economic benefits. Between 50,000 and 60,000 Filipinos earned their paychecks directly at Clark and Subic Bay, and several thousand more worked at the four smaller installations. In fact, after the Philippine government, the U.S. military was the largest employer in the nation, and poured about $507 million a year into the Philippine economy.[19] The bases were said to account for at least 3.5 percent of the Philippines' private income from GNP.[20]

Although the bases brought in a great deal of money, it could not be said that they were universally loved. Some Filipinos, especially intellectuals and leftists, feared that with such a large concentration of American forces, the Philippines might serve as a target for conventional or nuclear attack by the Soviet Union, a danger they would not be likely to face without the bases. Nationalist groups also objected to the lack of sovereignty and independence the bases implied—the United States continued to act as a colonial power, these critics charged, and the Philippines remained a colony. The general public did not seem to agree with these views entirely, or, more likely, economic need tempered anti-base resentment for most people. In any case, Filipino newspapers tended to criticize the bases harshly and advocate their removal, a view more extreme than that held by most Filipinos.

By the 1980s it was evident, however, that the most symbolically vivid objection to the U.S. military presence hinged on their extremely pernicious social and cultural impact on the areas around Subic Bay and Clark. The base towns of Olongapo and Angeles City had long since degenerated into seedy districts of bars and brothels. Filipinos were appalled by the extent of the sex trade, of which child prostitution made up a much larger element than was generally admitted by Americans. While "sex tourists" from Japan, Europe, Australia, and the United States visited the islands on package tours, servicemen made up the majority of sex trade consumers.[21] By some estimates, about 20,000 child prostitutes worked in the Philippines, many of them near the bases.[22] The sex trade proved impossible to eradicate because poverty in the island nation was so widespread. "Hostesses" and "entertainers," common euphemisms for prostitutes, could make almost $800 a month, while government employees made $100.[23] Most prostitutes supported large extended families, often rural dwellers on other islands who chose to believe their daughters and sisters worked as waitresses or maids. In the late 1980s, 25,000 to 30,000 young women and girls earned their livings as "entertainers" around the bases.

Philippine health services regularly checked sex workers for venereal disease, but when AIDS began its inexorable spread in the 1980s, neither the Philippine government nor the military monitored the disease among Filipina prostitutes. Servicemen received AIDS tests, but sex workers did not, and education about the disease in the Philippine community did not exist.[24] Only beginning in 1989–1990 were women tested regularly for AIDS.[25]

Not surprisingly, the rate of unintended pregnancy was extremely high among sex workers. Most women who became pregnant through a U.S. airman or sailor did not want or could not afford abortion, so they carried their children to term and then gave them up for adoption. Interestingly, however (and fortunately for the children), Amerasian parentage held virtually no stigma in the Philippines, in contrast to the situation in other Asian nations such as Korea, Japan, and Vietnam, where the problem assumed horrific proportions. Amerasian children were eagerly adopted by Filipino or American couples, and according to one nun working with abandoned infants, her orphanage maintained "a long waiting list" for Amerasian babies. Amerasians blended easily into Filipino society, achieving success as entertainers, athletes, and politicians. The longtime mayor of Olongapo, Richard Gordon, was a third-generation Amerasian. "It's a hangover from the colonial experience," Gordon speculated on the popularity of Amerasians in the Philippines. Anything associated with the United States was valued, including an American bloodline—especially if it brought with it the possibility of obtaining American citizenship.[26]

Amerasians in the Philippines may not have experienced the discrimination and rejection suffered by such children elsewhere in Asia, but their ubiquitous presence signaled a serious maladjustment in Philippine society. Left wing critics like the *Guardian* of London warned that the "moral collapse" brought by the presence of U.S. troops in the Philippines created an explosive situation in which a revolutionary movement could gain a great deal of support.[27] While the complex and contradictory views of Filipinos toward Americans and American culture made these sorts of statements too simplistic, it was nevertheless true that the peculiar and unsettling social conditions brought by the U.S. bases were a potentially powerful source of discontent.

THE OPPOSITION MOVEMENT

Unlike Jimmy Carter, who twisted and turned to square his criticism of Ferdinand Marcos' human rights violations with American quid pro quos for the bases, Ronald Reagan had no difficulty explaining his support of the Philippine dictator. Reagan believed that as a true anti-communist, Marcos stood on the side of the angels. Besides, Marcos lifted martial law in 1981, eliminating the most egregious human rights offense, and voices of protest could speak with slightly more freedom. Reagan's uncompromising anti-communist, pro-military political philosophy had a number of short- and long-term repercussions in domestic politics as well as international relations, and an upswing in anti-base protest all over the world emerged as one of the most immediate and visible effects of his presidency. Nowhere was this more true than in the Philippines.

In the early 1980s, as discontent with the U.S.–Marcos connection began to spread, pacifists and opponents of nuclear weapons began to organize protests against the bases. In February 1983 Lorenzo Tanada, a longtime foe of the American bases in the Philippines, formed the Anti-Bases Coalition (ABC), a group that for eight years would stand in the forefront of the popular movement against the bases. Meanwhile Marcos made a serious blunder in August, when someone, almost certainly an agent of Marcos or one of his cronies, assassinated opposition leader Benigno Aquino as he stepped off a plane returning home from the United States. The Aquino assassination revealed to the world and to Philippine opposition groups how corrupt and desperate Marcos had become, and illustrated to U.S. policymakers the type of leader they supported. In the wake of the assassination, police halted public rallies for a while, but new opposition parties sprouted almost overnight, providing a more fertile ground for criticism of the bases. Lorenzo Tanada led the Nationalist Alliance for Justice, Freedom and Democracy and spoke out against the "U.S.–Marcos dictatorship," clearly linking the dictator to the Americans. One of Tanada's chief goals was the expulsion of U.S. forces in the Philippines. In October, he led the first rally allowed by the police since Aquino's assassination, an anti-base demonstration at the U.S. Embassy.[28]

Critics in the United States added their voices to the growing chorus of demands to re-examine Cold War priorities and decisions. Many noted the destructive effects of the links between U.S. bases and dictatorial regimes, pointing out that the Americans tolerated unjust, potentially explosive situations in order to keep the base structure intact. In 1984, the *Christian Science Monitor* suggested that this dynamic was dangerous and unnecessary—comparing the Philippines to Ethiopia, Iran, and Libya, where the United States had once maintained important installations but where the price to keep them was U.S. support of undemocratic, unpopular regimes. Eventually the regimes could no longer hold on, even with American help, and the United States was left with nothing but a residue of resentment.[29]

In an atmosphere of growing crisis, the government called elections for February 7, 1986, in which Marcos ran against Corazon Aquino, the widow of the assassinated Benigno. The U.S. bases quickly emerged as a major election issue, with Marcos supporting the presence of the bases and warning that Aquino would remove them should she be elected. Aquino herself took a more equivocal stance, saying that she would respect the base agreement that expired in 1991, after which she would negotiate a new agreement. Her moderate position was probably a wise one, because although the nationalist left demanded an immediate expulsion of the U.S. presence, most Filipinos realized their importance for the nation's economy.

When Aquino was elected, Marcos at first attempted to cling to power by falsifying the election results claiming victory. The military joined with the civilian population to overthrow the dictator, and he and his cronies were forced to flee to Hawaii—on a U.S. aircraft from Clark Air Base—where they caused additional scandal by spending over $10,000 of U.S. government money in a Hawaiian PX.

THE BASES AFTER MARCOS

With the overthrow of Ferdinand Marcos, the anti-base movement gained a new lease on life. A Constitutional Commission charged with forming a new basic law for the Philippines considered clauses declaring the Philippines a neutral state and banning foreign military bases and nuclear weapons.[30] The proposed clauses were defeated, largely because the nationalist members who had pressed for a total ban on foreign bases abstained from voting. However, the commission did adopt a law requiring any future base agreement to be ratified by the legislature.[31]

During the campaign and after, Aquino pledged to respect the base agreement for the time being and renegotiate the compensation package when it came time for review in 1987. This did not satisfy the most militant base opponents, including Tanada, who advocated immediate removal of the bases. Opposition to the bases grew louder in the absence of Marcos' strong-arm tactics, and the United States could not afford to assume that the base treaty, due to expire in 1991, would be renewed automatically. U.S. officials scouted for alternatives to Subic Bay and Clark, but the other non-communist nations in Southeast Asia, while privately supporting the continuation of the U.S. presence in the region, proved reluctant to share the defense burden with the Philippines and allow bases on their own soil. Indonesia insisted that it could take care of itself, while New Zealand passed a law prohibiting vessels with nuclear weapons to dock on its ports, thereby excluding the U.S. Navy. Thailand had hosted a large number of U.S. bases during the Vietnam War, but the last of them had closed in 1976, and the Thais, perhaps remembering the social turmoil they had caused, had no desire to reopen them. Only tiny Singapore volunteered to allow U.S. ships to dock at its facilities.[32] Several factors, including the apparent warming of the Cold War, numerous trade disputes, and U.S. "meddling" in domestic politics—a buzzword for calling attention to human rights abuses—made many Southeast Asian nations less than willing to accommodate U.S. military demands or sympathize with American interests.[33]

Meanwhile, in the Philippines, voices raised in protest against the bases grew ever louder and more persistent. On July 4, 1986, a holiday celebrating Philippine as well as U.S. independence, 5,000 protesters battled with police in front of the U.S. Embassy. In a reprise of Marcos-era tactics the police dispersed them with tear gas and water hoses.[34]

In addition to the nationalists and peace groups who wanted the bases out, the NPA began stepping up its activity. The rebels demanded, among other things, the immediate closing of U.S. military bases; the group's political arm, known as the National Democratic Front, fought for land reform and demilitarization of the Filipino political system.[35] The NPA developed a harsh approach to the social problems of prostitution and exploitation exacerbated by the bases. In one resort town, for example, where the sexual exploitation of young boys by foreign tourists flourished, the NPA seized the town, arrested the municipal leaders believed to tolerate the situation, and publicly executed them.[36] Most Philippine citizens disapproved of such tactics, but they also hated the rampant exploitation and degradation of Filipino men, women, and children in the sex trade.

The NPA suspected that the United States, through the bases, interfered with Filipino political life, especially through support of right wing activities and coups (they were probably correct in this belief). NPA spokespeople warned that if the United States were to continue its involvement in such activities, the NPA would begin attacks on Americans.[37] They made good on the promise when they killed three American Air Force personnel in separate but coordinated ambushes on the evening of October 28, 1987. The NPA took responsibility for the killings and promised more.[38] The deaths ushered in a new level of lethality in the anti-base opposition, a level that pacifists like the anti-war Tanada never condoned.

When the five-year review of the base treaty approached in 1987, both American and Philippine negotiators knew the discussions were particularly significant. Not only was the review the first under the democratically elected Aquino, but its outcome would indicate whether the Philippine government planned to renew the treaty in 1991.[39] For a while it looked as though the review accord would fall under the weight of Philippine opposition, but finally negotiators hammered out an agreement in which the United States agreed to provide the Philippines with $962 million of assistance in the two years before the treaty lapsed. The money represented a huge increase, nearly tripling the amount the Philippines had received before the renegotiations. It included $481 million in hard cash, $176 million in military assistance, primarily to support the government against the communist guerillas, $160 million in economic support, and $121 million in food aid and housing loan guarantees. The deal was subject to approval in Congress, which left it somewhat less than 100 percent certain to achieve ratification, and many Philippine legislators were disappointed that Raul Manglapus, the Philippine representative at the negotiations, did not get the $1.2 billion in compensation he had publicly announced as a goal.[40]

In spite of the last-minute successful renegotiation of the economic portion of the base treaty's last two years, it appeared increasingly unlikely that the overall agreement would be renewed in 1991. While Corazon Aquino seemed to favor a plan to phase out the bases over a period of 5 to 10 years, more than half of the Philippine Senate stood firmly opposed to extending the base treaty even for a short while, and a relatively small but vocal and influential minority of citizens continued to demonstrate against the bases.

Unrest continued in early 1989 as base opponents staged several large public protests. Philippine police and troops attempted, with some success, to hinder the progress of the rallies by "dirty tricks," such as insisting on numerous and time-consuming checkpoints that delayed the proceedings until after the rally permits had expired. Naturally, this angered protesters who justifiably felt that their rights had been violated.[41]

Not surprisingly, most Filipinos living in the base cities of Olongapo and Angeles City did not support anti-base activism aimed at closing the bases. When 2,000 base opponents gathered for one rally in January 1989, for example, 10,000 supporters of the bases held a pro-base demonstration, which included a band playing "God Bless America." Bar girls frequently participated in protests in favor of the bases, because they depended on the bases to support their families. People who lived near the bases perhaps developed extra sensitivity to well-meaning anti-base activists from outside the Philippines, who appeared to be interfering in matters not affecting them. Pro-base demonstrators attacked an Irish priest, Father Shay Cullen, with rocks, for example, after he testified in favor of removing the bases.[42] It is unclear, of course, how much of this protest may have been sponsored or incited by right-wing Philippine groups or even U.S. covert organizations like the CIA; on the other side, questions were raised about communist support of the anti-base demonstrations.

The rebel movement began a new offensive in the spring of 1989. In April, the Communist guerillas killed another American military adviser outside of Manila. The NPA targeted Col. James "Nick" Rowe for his role as part of an advising team helping the Philippine Army in counterinsurgency activities.[43] In early September, the guerillas blew up a communications facility near Baguio, and on September 27, two American civilians working for an Air Force communications facility were killed, bringing the total of American dead to six. The deaths were all the more ominous because they came on the eve of a visit by Vice President Dan Quayle, and police expected more violence, possibly against the vice president himself. "The ground rules have changed," said one American official. "There's a willingness to hit us" that hadn't existed before. In fact, American murders formed but a small part of NPA guerilla violence—Philippine authorities blamed the rebels for more than 3,600 deaths in the previous year,[44] but violence from the guerillas and other groups of protesters, including shootings, grenade attacks, and detonation of homemade bombs, rose alarmingly in the days leading up to Quayle's visit.[45]

The increased level of violence had its effect on the 80,000 Americans in the Philippines, including many Americans whose activities did not relate to the military. The Peace Corps sent its workers home after the NPA announced it would target any Americans in the country,[46] and embassy personnel received extra protection because of similar concerns. Americans with any connections to the military, including family members and civilians, were ordered to avoid travel outside the bases, and several thousand former military personnel who had retired in the Philippines left for other regions in Asia or returned to the United States.

The basing controversy grew more complicated at the end of 1989, when U.S. forces intervened to protect the Aquino government from an attempted coup. U.S. F-4s based on Clark patrolled Philippine airspace with orders to shoot down any rebel aircraft after rebel planes shot at the presidential palace and other strategic locations. This was an unusual event—while U.S. forces occasionally intervened in such affairs in other nations, generally the troops and equipment came from offshore vessels or from bases in the United States. By using U.S. forces based on Philippine soil to protect the Philippine government, the action gave rise to charges that Aquino would be pressured to extend the base treaty past 1991.

Aquino herself recognized the danger. In February 1990 she refused to meet with Secretary of Defense Dick Cheney, saying that she was "tired of seeing herself portrayed as an American lackey."[47] While the American action to protect her government was perhaps well-meant, the Americans negated any possible benefit by reneging on $96 million of the $481 million of increased funding they had promised during the 1987 review of the base treaty. The agreement had been subject to Congressional approval, and President George H. W. Bush, attempting to trim the budget, did not push hard to convince Congress that the full amount of funding should be authorized. Cheney insisted that the Americans would pull out if they were not wanted, but officials continued to try to find a way to keep the bases on the cheap.

In the spring of 1990, as preliminary negotiations over the future of the expiring base treaty approached, demonstrations against the bases intensified. To participate in a protest meant risking life and limb, as activists endured beatings and abuse from the police, but most were undeterred.[48] On May 13, one day before negotiations were to open, another pair of American personnel died at the hands of guerillas. The NPA warned: "We will not stop until abuses by American officers and soldiers have ceased. We will not stop until U.S. imperialism has been finally driven out of our shores."[49] Protesters rallied in neighborhoods throughout Manila, where violence continued to rise; forty-two people were injured in demonstrations.[50] The NPA sent another warning through a statement sent to Filipino news agencies, telling the American forces to "go home or suffer the agony of attrition."[51]

On the day negotiations began, hundreds of demonstrators clashed with police and eighty-one people were arrested. The talks opened on an acrimonious note, as Raul Manglapus accused the United States of failing to pay $222 million of the $481 million it owed, and proposed delaying the talks until the money was paid. The United States acknowledged a shortfall of $96 million and said that President Bush would make "best efforts" to get the money from Congress. The chief of the U.S. negotiating team, Richard L. Armitage, added curtly that he did not "stand next to a cash register when conducting foreign affairs,"[52] and if separation was what the Filipino people really wanted, then the United States would accept that. His comment about cash register diplomacy incensed the Philippine negotiating team, who considered it insulting.[53]

On the second day of the talks the Filipino negotiators said that they wanted U.S. forces to be withdrawn *by* 1991 if an agreement was not signed before then. In other words, the Americans could not stay on in the absence of a treaty while negotiators tried to work something out. This put them in a difficult situation, because a withdrawal would take at least a year to complete; U.S. officials would have to judge whether the talks had irretrievably broken down, and begin a withdrawal immediately, or gamble that they would succeed, and stay put. Outside the meeting rooms where the talks took place, more groups from diverse strata of Philippine society joined the anti-base movement, including the Young Officers Union (YOU), a radical segment of the armed forces which promised violence against the bases if they were not withdrawn; and the Reform the Armed Forces Movement–Soldiers of the Filipino People (RAM-SFP), a coalition of mid-level army officers and former Marcos supporters in the military, which had attempted the coup against Aquino in December. The YOU demanded that the United States withdraw and let the Philippines "run their own government and their own lives."[54]

The Americans, in turn, protested that security outside the bases, a responsibility of the Filipino police and military as defined in the 1979 treaty, did not adequately protect the American population. Indeed, life for Americans in the Philippines changed dramatically in the late 1980s, as attacks necessitated stricter security measures. Americans were ordered not to wear uniforms in public, even traveling from home to the base.[55] During base treaty talks, Americans were restricted to the bases or their off-base homes from 7 P.M. to 7 A.M. As a result, the thousands of bars, discos, and massage parlors catering to Americans waited in vain for customers. Some closed their doors permanently, and most had to lay off workers. Bar girls began to drift back to their homes in the provinces. For the sex workers who lost income, this was at least a short term disaster. But for others who cringed at the sleazy honky-tonk strips around the bases, it was a positive first step. Father Cullen, the controversial Irish priest, called Olongapo "the most vicious form of human exploitation that can be imagined," and noted that while the U.S. armed forces were in the Philippines to defend the American way, that way included, judging from the behavior of the troops, child sexual abuse. "If American parents knew what their boys were up to, they'd be outraged," he said.[56] Most exposés of the culture of sexual exploitation in Asia, however, focussed on sex tourism from Japan, Europe, and Australia, and sidestepped American military involvement.

Even opponents of the bases realized that an abrupt withdrawal would spell economic disaster for thousands, by some estimates as many as 80,000 directly employed by the Americans. The question of the bases took yet another turn in the summer of 1990, when the Philippines suffered an earthquake and the American forces rushed to provide aid and rescue. The efficient help was welcome, but suggested to Philippine nationalists that their nation could not stand on its own two feet without the help of the Americans. The earthquake aid reminded many Filipinos that the Americans represented good as well as bad, but the anti-base movement rolled on.

As negotiations continued, it became increasingly clear that the United States would be forced to mothball at least one of the bases, but an extended period of transition likely would be incorporated into the agreement so that the regional economy would not collapse. Only left- and right-wing extremists continued to object to this compromise, standing by their demands for an immediate withdrawal. Most members of the Philippine Senate leaned strongly against the U.S. presence, as did the media and intellectual elite, students, and some labor unions. On the other hand, pro-base opinion ran very high in many areas, and *The Washington Post* reported that "a huge majority of Filipinos still support a continued presence." A poll taken by the U.S. Embassy showed that two of three people in Manila wanted to keep the bases.[57] Protests, many of them violent, continued outside the U.S. Embassy and in the vicinity of the bases, but they were countered by police officers and also supporters of the bases, especially local women who depended on the bases for income.[58]

The anti-base activists, if not in the majority in the Philippines, at least had history on their side: as the Cold War wound down, public opinion in the United States expected a "peace dividend" and government officials acknowledged less need for extensive and costly facilities throughout the world. "Those bases are not as valuable as they used to be," said one official commenting on Subic Bay and Clark. In September 1990, the Bush administration announced that it would not seek a renewal of the 1991 treaty but was ready to begin phasing out the bases. The drawdown would be accomplished over a period of years to minimize the economic consequences for the surrounding areas. Filipino leaders, however, hoped that the bases would close by the symbolic date of June 12, 1998, the centenary of the Philippines' declaration of independence from Spain.[59]

The Bush administration's announcement that the Americans would work out a gradual withdrawal of the bases handed a major victory to moderate base opponents. Rafael Alunan III, the spokesman for the Philippine negotiating team, said that the goal of the talks was "to regain our dignity, to demonstrate sovereignty and establish self-esteem," and that with the U.S. announcement, this goal had been achieved.[60] As the talks on specific points continued, officials restricted the American military community to a 9 P.M. to 5:30 A.M. curfew and limits on off-base travel during the day.[61] The talks were not smooth or easy; the Philippine team demanded $825 million a year for continued use of the bases, including about half that ($400 million) in cash and the rest in debt relief and assistance. In return, the Philippines would guarantee a 7-year extension in leases of the bases. For its part the Americans offered $360 million, and wanted at least a 10-year lease on the bases.[62] The Americans proposed various other aid, but the Filipino negotiators refused to count much of it toward the "price" of the bases. At this stage, the debate centered only on Clark and Subic Bay; the Americans had already agreed to release the remaining four smaller bases. Negotiators resolved many minor issues, such as the possibility of a new name for Clark Air Base and decisions on who would run the taxi service and deliver mail. Another sticking point was whether the agreement would be presented in a formal treaty, as required by the Philippine constitution, or a more informal agreement, as the Americans desired. The U.S. team objected to a formal treaty because a treaty would have to go to the Senate for ratification, taking time and introducing the possibility of failure. The negotiations became increasingly frustating as the two sides bickered.[63] By the spring of 1991, the Philippine Senate appeared ready to veto any agreement made, as more than half of the senators were opposed to the bases in any configuration.

MOUNT PINATUBO AND THE END OF U.S. BASES IN THE PHILIPPINES

On June 9, 1991, Mount Pinatubo, a long-dormant volcano about 10 miles west of Clark, began to shoot hot gas, ash, and rock fragments into the air from two vents in the face of the mountain. The area around the volcano quickly disappeared under a thick layer of ash, and the smoke was so heavy that day seemed like night. Helicopters flying over the volcano reported an eruption of magma, or melted rock, from an opening near the summit. While the magma did not threaten to cover Clark itself, the ash and smoke made the base inoperable.

Thousands of Filipinos were evacuated from their homes and farms, including aboriginal people who lived on the mountain. The population of Angeles City, next to Clark, fled in busloads in the early morning. In the early hours of June 9, 15,000 American personnel, families and civilians left Clark for Subic Bay, leaving only 1,000 personnel to guard the base.[64] A few days later, on June 14, a series of eruptions shot a column of ash 98,000 feet into the air, and base opponents worried that the explosions would trigger nuclear weapons that were rumored to be stored at Clark.[65] The following day the volcano appeared ready to blow its top, and scientists established a danger zone of 18 to 25 miles around the mountain, encompassing Subic Bay and Olongapo. While neither city received orders to evacuate as yet, the remaining 1,000 Americans abandoned Clark Air Base, and authorities made hasty arrangements to fly Air Force families back to the United States. To make matters worse, torrential rains from Typhoon Yunya drenched the area and turned the ash into heavy mud, which collapsed flimsy buildings where refugees had gathered. The growing violence of the volcano created panic among the residents of the base cities, resulting in disorganized flight by any means possible.[66]

By the middle of July, U.S. officials announced that the Americans would permanently give up Clark rather than attempt to rebuild. The volcano had partly buried Angeles City, and even after the worst of the eruptions ended, rainstorms created severe mudflow hazards. The negotiating teams continued to discuss the future of Subic Bay, which the Americans suggested might still be of some use. Negotiators slashed the original offer of $360 million to $203 million for the use of Subic Bay alone, which the

Philippine Senate called offensive. In the end, the Philippine Senate rejected the base agreement on Subic Bay by a vote of 12–11.[67] The Americans, while expressing disappointment, did not seem particularly devastated—they made no attempts to renegotiate or sweeten the deal. Corazon Aquino, who in the end wanted the bases to remain because of the dire economic plight of the islands, organized a pro-base rally, expected to draw 1 million supporters. Only 100,000 to 200,000 showed up, however, and Aquino's second suggestion—a nationwide referendum—was rejected by the Senate.[68] While many in the Philippines and the United States saw the Senate's vote against the Subic Bay deal as impractical, even those who supported the bases said that a withdrawal of the Americans would force the Philippines to stand on its own feet, solving its problems for itself. Some noted that the closure of Subic Bay might not be the calamity that many expected—that the nation's economy, while not as strong as that of a developed nation, might be resilient enough to absorb the blow.[69] Others wondered how the Philippine economy could be any worse without the bases than with them; at least a base-free nation created a new opportunity.[70] On December 31, 1991, the Philippines formally requested that the Americans withdraw all its forces from the island by December 31, 1992.

On November 24, 1992, a Marine Corps honor guard lowered the U.S. flag flying over Subic Bay, and Philippine President Fidel V. Ramos hoisted a giant Philippine flag. The new flagpole was exactly 94 feet high, representing the 94 years of the American presence in the Philippines. Hostesses hugged Marines and waved farewell to the last contingent of Americans left at Subic Bay as they boarded a ship headed for Okinawa. "The Party's Over" served as an ambiguous slogan as the Americans said goodbye.[71]

When the Americans abandoned Clark Air Base to the ash and dust, the extensive facilities were looted by residents of Angeles City, making any serious salvage attempt pointless and destroying the possibility of reconstructing Clark for Filipino use. Olongapo Mayor Richard Gordon prevented a similar waste at Subic Bay by stationing thousands of unpaid volunteer sentries to guard and maintain the base. Gordon's prudence paid off, as the city found itself in a better position to actively recruit international businesses to the new Subic Bay Freeport. The former naval base had much to offer: a large airport, a huge deep-water port with ship-repair facilities, more than 1,000 industrial buildings and offices, an oil depot, 1,876 residential homes, all air-conditioned, with the recreational facilities typical of a large U.S. base—movie theaters, tennis courts and gymnasiums, an eighteen-hole golf course—and highly trained, inexpensive labor with a knowledge of English.[72] Moreover, the designation of the area as a free port meant that many economic advantages ensued: duty-free imports, exemptions from many taxes, and elimination of government red tape.[73]

The story did not have a truly happy ending, however. The U.S. Navy and U.S. Air Force left behind catastrophic messes of pesticides, arsenic, asbestos, heavy metals, petrochemicals, mercury, and other toxic substances in the land under Subic Bay and Clark. Contamination ran deep due to the long and intensive U.S. presence at the bases; the Philippine government during the Cold War had set no standards for proper waste disposal.

Shortly after Clark closed in 1991, around 20,000 evacuee families were moved by the government onto the base as a temporary measure before they found permanent substitutes for the housing destroyed by the volcano. In the end, some families remained at Clark for years, during which time they drilled wells and planted food crops near abandoned runways. A few months after the first families took up residence at Clark, they began showing signs of illness, including stomach pain and skin problems. Women suffered miscarriages and stillbirths at unusually high levels. Over the five years that evacuee families lived on Clark, a large cluster of children were born with neurological problems, brain damage, and birth defects, the result of mercury poisoning. By 2000, Philippine authorities counted 100 deaths due to poisoning by toxic waste at Clark.[74]

When the Philippine government demanded that the U.S. forces pay for cleanup, however, the Pentagon first denied the problem, then simply refused to pay, insisting that it had no legal obligation to do so, having merely followed Philippine law. In any case, Congress was not eager to fund cleanup efforts; in 1999 the U.S. spent only $17 million to clean up overseas bases, or .001 percent of its spending on domestic base cleanup.[75] Even taking into account the higher expenses of cleanup in the United States, the amount of money spent on overseas bases was miniscule.

Since September 11, small numbers of U.S. forces have returned to the Philippines to assist the Philippine army in tracking down Islamic terror groups using the southern island of Mindanao as a base. Not surprisingly, the American troops in the Philippines have caused great controversy, and many critics of the government vow to prevent any expansion of the U.S. presence.

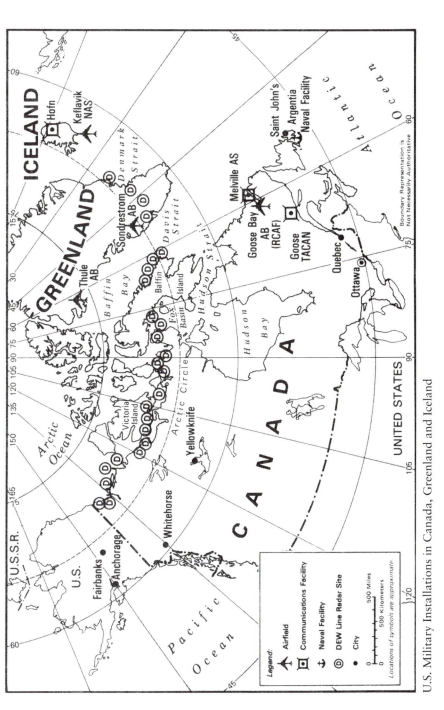

U.S. Military Installations in Canada, Greenland and Iceland

Major U.S. Military Installations in West Germany

Major U.S. Military Installations in Japan and Korea

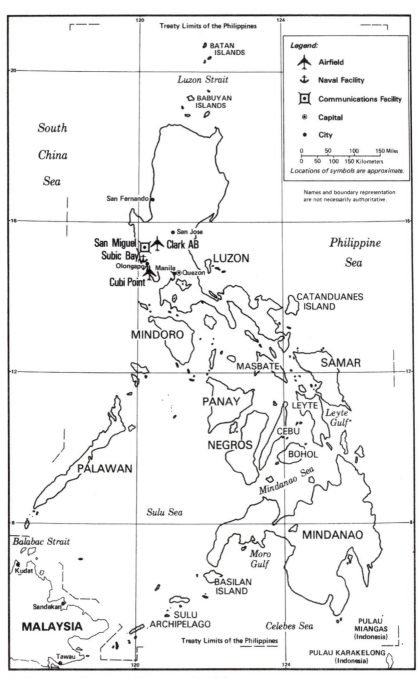

Major U.S. Military Installations in the Philippines

Major U.S. Military Installations in the United Kingdom

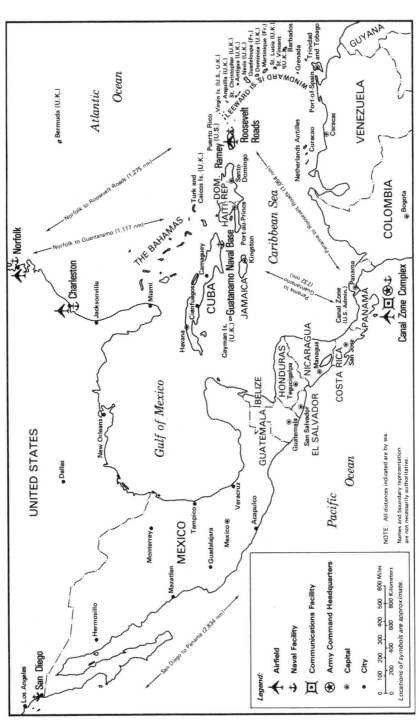

Central American Region

American soldiers prepare to go back to the United States with their German wives after the occupation of the Rhineland. Courtesy of the National Archives Still Picture Collection.

American soldiers overseas in Egypt during WWII. Courtesy of the National Archives Still Picture Collection.

GIs and their Austrian girlfriends after the war. Courtesy of the National Archives Still Picture Collection.

The sight of military vehicles and Allied soldiers was common in postwar Germany. Courtesy of the National Archives Still Picture Collection.

Building an airstrip on a Pacific atoll. Courtesy of the National Archives Still Picture Collection.

Anti-American rioting in Panama, 1959. Courtesy of the National Archives Still Picture Collection.

Japanese wives of American soldiers register for a class on American customs. Courtesy of the National Archives Still Picture Collection.

American Cub Scouts entertain a group of elderly Germans. Courtesy of the National Archives Still Picture Collection.

The ice chapel at Thule Air Base, Greenland. Courtesy of the National Archives Still Picture Collection.

A 1980 REFORGER (Return of Forces to Germany) exercise in Germany. Courtesy of the National Archives Still Picture Collection.

Construction of missile launchers in Okinawa. Courtesy of the National Archives Still Picture Collection.

American military communities used already existing buildings whenever possible. Courtesy of the National Archives Still Picture Collection.

Antiwar hitosubo (landowners) in Nara, Okinawa. Head bands read, "Life is a treasure." Courtesy of Joseph Gerson.

Banner announcing anti-base conference, Korea. Courtesy of Joseph Gerson.

Demonstrators protest against an artillery range on Mount Fuji used by the U.S. Marines. Courtesy of Joseph Gerson.

Anti-base activists plan campaign against the expansion of Yokota Air Base near Tokyo. Courtesy of Joseph Gerson.

Homeless Filipino family sleeping outside Clark Air Base gate. Courtesy of Joseph Gerson.

8

★ ★ ★ ★ ★

Bearing the Burden of Defense: Okinawa

INTRODUCTION

During the Cold War and after, Okinawa was one of the most strategically significant locations for the U.S. forces. U.S. Army maps showed Okinawa, the largest island in the Ryukyu chain, south of mainland Japan, 620 miles from Korea, 970 miles from Tokyo, 920 miles from Manila, almost next door to Taiwan—and 6,000 miles from the continental United States. From Okinawa the U.S. forces could reach almost any city in Asia within a short time. Not surprisingly, the U.S. military considered Okinawa a geographic treasure, and the U.S. Army governed the island for 27 years after World War II ended. The island reverted to Japanese administration in 1972, but the American military remained. At the time of reversion, the U.S. forces held approximately thirty installations, from training areas and firing ranges to beaches and memorial sites. The Americans also shut down bases and airfields on mainland Japan in response to public protest, and moved units to Okinawa. Thus, by the 1970s, the island hosted about 75 percent of all U.S. military installations in Japan.

The preponderance of military bases in Okinawa did not sit well with the population of the island. To most Okinawans, it appeared that the Japanese government in effect sacrificed Okinawa to the Americans, concentrating the U.S. forces in one economically marginal island separated by geography and culture from the majority of Japanese. From the Okinawan point of view, the Japanese desired the protection that U.S. forces offered but refused to shoulder the burdens—inconveniences, social problems, and physical dangers—of hosting the troops, forcing the problem on the Okinawans far away to the south.

Beginning in the 1960s, sporadic anti-base movements emerged but generally waned with time, especially in light of the island's economic dependence on the Americans. In the 1990s, however, the brutal rape of a 12-year-old girl by three servicemen outraged Okinawans and spurred a huge protest movement against the U.S. presence. The movement initially focused its attention on the Americans but also appealed to the Japanese government for support. When this support was not as forthcoming as expected, the Okinawans viewed the maneuvering of the Japanese government as further evidence of a mainland betrayal of Okinawan interests.

The difficulty of the Okinawan conundrum has stemmed from the belief of most Japanese citizens, including Okinawans, that aggressive neighbors truly did put the island nation at risk, even after the Cold War ended. Until recently, few Japanese outside leftist student groups have argued for a total removal of the American military presence. However, political developments in Asia have brought even this consensus under question, and increasing numbers of Japanese argue that the bases do not provide a real deterrent and are unnecessary. As long as Japan's economy continues to stumble, the American forces will be tolerated, but once their economic value recedes, a renewed call for the removal of U.S. bases is likely to emerge once again.

A BRIEF HISTORY OF OKINAWA

For thousands of years the Ryukyus had been an independent kingdom, with their own ruler and a separate language and customs. The kingdom of the Ryukyus gravitated toward the great civilization of China more than toward Japan, and Ryukyu culture showed strong influence from that empire. In 1609, however, a Japanese warlord invaded the island, and the Ryukyus began to move closer to the Japanese. Until 1879, the Ryukyu kings remained independent, paying tribute to the Japanese shogunate, but after Japan modernized its political system the Ryukyu kingdom became a prefecture renamed Okinawa. From that point the people of the islands maintained an uneasy colonial relationship with the Japanese. Although Okinawa was politically a part of Japan, the Japanese government did not treat Okinawa as truly Japanese, and the people did not view themselves as such.

During World War II, the Japanese used Okinawa as a shield against a possible invasion by the Americans, stationing thousands of Japanese troops on the island. The battle of Okinawa, in 1945, was one of the fiercest and bloodiest of the war, above all for the Okinawans. Up to a quarter of the population—about 237,000 men, women, and children—were killed by the American forces or forced to commit suicide by the Japanese.[1] Apparently, many suicides feared the American troops, a result of years of government propaganda as well as real-life experience of the depredations of Japanese soldiers. Thousands of Okinawans jumped off the cliffs on the southern tip of the island, so many that, according to local legend, the water turned red.[2]

After the war, the Americans occupied Okinawa as they did the rest of Japan and ruled through military government. In 1952, Japan gained its independence, but the U.S. Army continued to administer Okinawa through a high commissioner. Many Okinawans suspected betrayal: they believed that Japan encouraged the Americans to maintain their occupation of Okinawa while terminating the occupation of Japan. The Americans, it was assumed, would end military government in Japan only if they felt sure that, first, containment of communism could be carried out in Asia and, second, that a resurgence of Japanese militarism would not occur. An American occupation of Okinawa served both these goals. The arrangement would benefit Japan as well; Japan would receive American military protection while placing the burden of hosting the forces mainly on Okinawa, a poor and remote prefecture.

Okinawans resisted the appropriation of their land by the U.S. military even though they understood and appreciated the economic gains they received from the forces. The island was desperately poor before and during the war, relying on subsistence agriculture and sugar cane. The Americans brought money, but they also exacted a high price in land requisitioned from Okinawan farmers. The farmers received a lump-sum payment for their property, which, the farmers argued, did not represent the value of the land. In the late 1950s, Okinawans objected to the expansion of bases, runways, and practice areas used by the U.S. forces. They formed the shima-gurumi (whole island) campaign to fight the development,[3] which, however, did not result in removal of the bases. However, opposition did finally force the armed forces to make some concessions; in 1958, the United States agreed to end lump-sum payments for the use of requisitioned land, and began making annual rental payments.[4] Paradoxically, the switch to annual payments probably bound the Okinawans closer to the army and Air Force because many older islanders depended on the annual rents for income and could not countenance a U.S. withdrawal.

REVERSION TO JAPAN

Nevertheless, agitation continued, especially over the occupation issue. During the late 1960s bases in Japan and Okinawa formed one of the loci of student and left-wing protest along with the Vietnam War and other issues. Opponents of the base system demanded the removal of all U.S.

installations from mainland Japan in 1970, when the base treaty signed in 1951 and revised in 1960 was to come up for renewal. Okinawa drew more attention, not only from students but from Okinawans who wanted the American military presence decreased and an end to military rule on the islands. The Japanese government also wished the mainland bases to close and pushed for a return of Okinawa to Japan while tacitly tolerating the huge military presence on Okinawa. As the wrangling wore on, diplomats from both nations pointed to the controversy over Okinawa's status as the biggest stumbling block in U.S.–Japan relations.[5]

The U.S. installations on Okinawa proved essential in the air war against Vietnam and vital as well to containment of North Korea.[6] In February 1968, the Americans stationed B-52s on the huge Kadena Air Base in Okinawa "temporarily" in response to the Pueblo incident with North Korea in which a U.S. intelligence ship was seized and its crew captured. The B-52s were also used to bomb Viet Minh positions in South Vietnam. In November, one of the B-52s bound for Vietnam crashed on takeoff from Okinawa, and the bombs loaded on board exploded, shooting flames 450 feet into the sky; 139 houses were damaged. The accident seemed to illustrate yet again that the Okinawans exercised little control over their destiny.[7] However, they had recently elected a socialist mayor, Chobyo Yara, who pledged to oppose the bases. In the wake of the B-52 explosion, Yara asked the U.S. High Commissioner of Okinawa to remove the B-52s from the islands. Lt Gen. James B. Lampert replied that the decision was made in Washington, and he had no power to make such a move. However, the Department of Defense did plan to remove the B-52s as soon as was feasible, concerned that protests might spin out of control and push the United States and Japan toward a change in the status quo.[8] The reversion debate continued, and in June 1969 the Foreign Minister of Japan, Kiichi Aichi, traveled to the United States for opening negotiations on the return of the Ryukyus.[9]

AMERICAN INFLUENCE IN OKINAWA

Okinawa was, along with the Philippines, among the most Americanized of all regions in Asia. In the early years, U.S. influence extended to formal legal issues; until the islands were returned to Japan, Okinawans drove on the same side of the road as Americans, used dollars as currency, and needed passports to go to Japan.[10] But American influence could be seen in all areas of life, formal and informal. Ryukyu glassware, a popular art form, was made by local craftsmen from Coca-Cola bottles discarded by American servicemen. American foods, such as ice cream, instant coffee, and Spam were common in Okinawa—60 percent of American products imported to Japan went to the island.[11] Americanisms in Okinawan speech made the Okinawan language, already district from Japanese, even more different.[12] Even the American pastime of relaxing at the beach spread to Okinawa where such leisure habits had been unknown.

Many Okinawans depended on the bases, directly or indirectly, for their livelihoods. In 1970, as anti-base protests in mainland Japan raged, 7,000 Okinawan workers went on strike to protest U.S. plans to cut almost 2,000 jobs, a result of budget cuts from Washington.[13] The All-Okinawa Military Workers Union represented 21,000 employees of the armed forces and fought for increases in severance allowance and longer notice for dismissed workers. Job security was a serious issue among the Okinawan workers, as it was for all employees of military installations, whose jobs depended in essence, on the state of worldwide tension which necessitated a global base system. Proposals to reduce the number of U.S. military installations in Okinawa always included discussions and disagreements over the effect of base closings on the workers and on the Okinawan economy in general. Because the bases prevented prefecture leaders from developing the area economically, an extraordinary number of Okinawans continued to depend on the bases for their livelihoods even as the rest of Japan competed with the United States for economic dominance. In the late 1990s, almost 8,000 Okinawans worked directly on the American installation, and many more depended on American patronage of their businesses and services.[14]

A more negative influence on the island was the large number of illegitimate babies left by U.S. personnel. Each year an estimated 200 Okinawan babies were abandoned by U.S. servicemen. Mothers had no way to win child support or assistance from the fathers, who simply transferred back to the United States after their tours were over. Some activist groups and individuals worked to improve the lives of women who were abandoned by the fathers of their children, but the situation remains dire to the present day. It has been very common in Japanese schools for biracial children to be bullied and ostracized. In 1998, a group of mothers joined together to form the AmerAsian School in Okinawa, specifically for biracial children, a move that gave a new lease on life to many children with virtually no future in the highly structured society of Japan.

Okinawan culture seeped its way into the subculture of the American military as well. In San Diego, host to a number of large naval and marine bases, an association of Okinawan Americans was founded in 1979, comprised mostly of women who married American soldiers. Similar organizations were established in other cities and towns with large military populations.[15] Okinawa, along with South Korea and the Philippines, has been one of the regions of Asia most familiar to non-Asian Americans because of military service there.

POST–COLD WAR REVISIONS

When the Berlin Wall fell in late 1989 and the Soviet system collapsed, the global security picture began to change. While the effects of the "New World Order" became apparent most quickly and clearly in Western Europe where forces had been deployed to guard against the USSR, questions about the number of troops needed to defend Japan also arose even though communist China remained a threat. Of course, the fate of the Japanese defense posture affected Okinawa above all. The situation in Okinawa had improved somewhat since 1972—Japanese investment aid had helped to create modern water, sewage, and medical systems, and while unemployment was twice as high in Okinawa as in the rest of Japan, this too represented an improvement.[16] Still, the U.S. bases overshadowed all attempts to bring Okinawa to the levels of the rest of the country. Tourism and industry, potential avenues of economic development, could not flourish in the shadow of the huge military presence. The island makes up only .06 percent of Japan's land mass, but 75 percent of the Japanese territory used by U.S. installations was on Okinawa—about 20 percent of the land mass of the main island. Moreover, a substantial amount—estimates ranged from 33 percent to 75 percent[17]—of the land the bases occupied was owned by private citizens, not the government. About half of the U.S. personnel in Japan were stationed on Okinawa. The U.S. Marine Corps presence had decreased by several thousand in the early 1990s, but not significantly enough to make a difference. In the mid-1990s, about 28,600 of the 47,000 Americans stationed in Japan lived and worked on forty-four American facilities in Okinawa.

THE 1995 RAPE

On the evening of September 4, 1995, a 12-year-old schoolgirl in Kin, a town in northern Okinawa, went shopping for a notebook. She went alone, as was common; the violent crime rate in Japan was infinitesimal compared to that of the United States, and she had no reason to be afraid. She wore her school uniform and carried a bag of books from school. Having made her purchase, she began the walk home.

Meanwhile, three young American servicemen maneuvered their white rental vehicle along the streets of Kin, looking for something to do. They had been driving around all afternoon, debating their options. The three—22-year-old Navy seaman Marcus Gill, a Texas native, and Marine Pfcs. Rodrico Harp and Kendrick Ledet, ages 21 and 20, respectively, both from Georgia—had thought about cruising one of the sleazy bar strips and finding a brothel, but Gill complained that he had no money and that paid sex was "no fun." He suggested a different plan. Evidently he had been contemplating an alternative earlier in the day, because he had purchased a roll of adhesive tape and packets of condoms from the PX. Ledet and Harp did not take him seriously at first. But a fourth man who had been with them did and left the three because he did not want to take part in the plans.[18]

The men came across the 12-year-old walking home. Ledet grabbed her and forced her in the car while Harp bound her eyes and mouth with the tape and drove to a nearby beach. There, Gill, a 260-pound former football player, climbed in the back seat and raped the girl. Then Harp and Ledet took their turns. When they were finished, they dumped her out of the car and drove back to the base. The girl, crying and bleeding, made her way to a nearby home where she called her parents.

News of the atrocity roiled Okinawa and all of Japan. "All Okinawans are shaking with anger," said one long-time opponent of the bases, 81-year-old Fumiko Nakamura. In Japanese polls before the rape, 75 percent of those interviewed supported the bases; polls in the weeks after showed that up to 70 percent wanted changes in the security arrangement.[19] For over a week thousands of Okinawans marched outside Camp Foster, the central Marine Corps installation, demonstrating their anger and demanding an immediate removal of the bases.

The Americans quickly made public apologies. Lt. General Richard B. Myers, commander of the U.S. forces in Japan, said that the crime "makes all of us wearing the U.S. military uniform deeply ashamed." Okinawans noted that the Americans had even more to be ashamed of—in the past year three rapes had been reported, although the number of actual rapes was much higher, according to women's groups and police. In the years since 1972, American forces had been convicted of twelve murders and 4,500 other crimes.[20]

Within a month, Japan's prime minister, Tomiichi Murayama, announced that he would demand a reduction of the U.S. presence on Okinawa, although he and other national political leaders had always strongly defended the American presence. The reaction to the rape was so intense that politicians everywhere were compelled to respond, even if they fundamentally supported the bases. Some pro-base politicians, in fact, criticized Murayama for not articulating the need for the bases with sufficient clarity.

A few days after Murayama's announcement, a huge anti-base rally was held in Okinawa. Estimates of the crowd ranged from 58,000 to 85,000, far exceeding organizers' expectations. More than 300 groups participated in the rally, from political parties—all the political parties in the Okinawa Assembly signed on as sponsors of the rally—to business and social organizations. The protesters called for compensation for the girl who was raped, closure of some bases, revisions in the SOFA, and improved discipline of the troops.[21]

One of the many legal provisions grating on Okinawans was that under the SOFA, U.S. authorities did not turn over American suspects to Japanese

law enforcement officials until they were formally indicted; criminal investigations, in other words, remained to a large extent in the hands of the
American military police. This was viewed as a slap in the face of the
Japanese justice system and led to suspicions that the Americans received
special treatment. Many Okinawans believed, incorrectly in most cases,
that Americans accused of crimes were free to go about the base until their
indictments.[22] In October 1995, the Americans promised to expedite the
transfer to Japanese police of all U.S. suspects accused of murder or rape.
To many American officials, however, Japanese methods of interrogation,
such as roughing up suspects, depriving them of sleep, or interrogating
them for hours on end, did not entirely coincide with U.S. legal protections
of the accused.

Okinawan insistence that the suspects be turned over to Japanese
authorities was not, however, attributable to a desire for the harshest punishment possible; U.S. military courts generally handed out stiffer sentences to criminals than did Japanese courts. Rather, certain aspects of the
military justice system, such as the influence of the commander in deciding
whether to press charges, and the closed court, were viewed as soft on sexual crime. Many Japanese and Okinawans believed that the military tolerated their soldiers' abuse of women while harshly punishing crimes that
directly affected military discipline—AWOL or desertion, for example, or
disrespect to an officer. More importantly, perhaps, the Okinawans
resented the lack of sovereignty and independence that the military court
system represented. A crime might occur off-duty in an off-base location
against a civilian, but the suspects were still arrested by military police and
held by military authorities until they were indicted.

Because of the especially shocking nature of the 1995 rape, however,
and the outraged response of the public, American authorities did not
quibble about handing the three men over to Japanese police; they were
formally charged on September 29 and turned over a few days later.
Before their formal indictment, they had been held in a U.S. prison for
more than 20 days and interrogated by Japanese police for up to 10 hours
a day.[23] A court date was set for November 7.

THE RISE OF THE ANTI-BASE MOVEMENT

As the trial date approached, Okinawans began to speak more sharply
about the burden placed on them by the heavy American military presence.
The outrage of the rape in September and other crimes committed by servicemen was one aspect of this burden. American forces committed about
1,000 crimes a decade, counting the crimes that were reported. The crime
rate was decreasing, and in any case the rate was lower than comparable
communities in the United States but very much higher than that in Japan.
The fact that the military police were involved in investigating and arresting

American suspects, even when the suspects had committed crimes against civilians, simply added insult to injury.

Another burden borne by Okinawans was the constant noise of American jets, which, according to neighbors, began at 4 A.M. and ran long into the night. In addition to being deafeningly loud, the jets posed the danger of accidents; since 1972 there had been thirty-six crashes on or near the island.[24] In addition, the activities of the bases took up air and sea lanes, thereby making off-island transportation complicated and subjecting Okinawa to significant environmental degradation.[25]

Although most Japanese people wanted a reduction in the base presence, the idea of eliminating them altogether raised serious questions. "Without the Americans, we'll go back to the prewar Okinawa, where people were barefoot and ate nothing but potatoes," said one elderly man.[26] While the bases were responsible for the lack of economic development on Okinawa, their removal would not immediately bring an economic boom—rather, they would destroy what little economic prosperity existed. So many Okinawans were dependent on the bases and the U.S. personnel that even measures designed to minimize other problems could strike home economically. In the wake of the rape, for example, the military set a curfew for servicemembers of 12 A.M. to 6 A.M., but the start of the curfew was pushed back to 1 A.M. because bar owners protested its impact on their businesses.[27] In 1993 alone, the prefecture earned 162.0 billion yen from the bases.[28] So even if total withdrawal had been possible, which it was not, the disappearance of the bases would not have magically solved Okinawa's problems.

The U.S. forces in Asia continued to experience aftershocks of the crime. The commander of the U.S. forces in the Pacific, a naval officer, resigned from his post and took early retirement after he told reporters that the rape was stupid because "for the price they paid to rent the car they could have had a girl." Outraged critics charged that the Navy still didn't understand the dynamics of sexual exploitation, and the commander's casual acceptance of prostitution showed evidence of widespread insensitivity to the exploitation and violence of the sex trade surrounding the U.S. forces in Okinawa and throughout the world.

THE TRIAL

The closely watched trial began as scheduled on November 7. From the outset, Gill pleaded guilty to rape, while Ledet and Harp pleaded guilty to abduction and assault. According to newspaper reports of the trial, the victim said in a written statement, "I get scared when I see a foreigner on the streets now," and her parents expressed the wish for the death penalty for the three.[29] After months of often grueling testimony, the trial concluded in March 1996, and the three-judge tribunal hearing the case convicted the men of abduction and rape of the girl. In their remarks, the judges said that the crime was premeditated, so the men deserved no sympathy, but on the other hand, they had shown remorse and offered to compensate the victim. Rather than the 10 years the prosecution had asked for, Gill and Harp received seven years, while Ledet, who, the judges found, stopped before raping the girl when he realized her age, received $6^{1}/_{2}$ years.

The sentences were criticized by the families of the men, who charged that they were treated as scapegoats for generalized Okinawan opposition to the bases. The president of the Okinawa chapter of the NAACP also noted that the sentences were harsher than those given to Okinawans, commenting, "I'm not sure whether it's because they are American or African-American."[30] The average sentence for rape in Japan was three to five years in prison,[31] so they may have had a point, but the rape involved kidnapping of a child, two aggravating circumstances. Conversely, women's groups in Japan criticized the sentences as too lenient, noting that the victim's continued suffering was far greater than that of the men.[32] The sentences were served in Yokosuka prison, a maximum-security institution south of Tokyo, which had a special ward for U.S. military prisoners. Their incarceration would not be easy; they were sentenced to hard labor.[33]

After the trial ended and the men were sent to prison, opposition to the bases continued to rage. Most Okinawans could do little to remove the bases outright. But one group of Okinawans had at least some direct recourse because they leased their land to the U.S. military. The money from rents generated 67 billion yen annually, paid by the Japanese government as a part of their defense contribution. Many landlords, especially the elderly who comprised over 50 percent of the landlords, depended on the income from the rents, an average of 19 million yen per year,[34] and most of the 28,000 landowners who rented to the Americans had no plans to change the situation. But in the wake of the rape and the firestorm it ignited, a group of landlords, (estimates ranged from 100 to 3,000) holding as much as 10 percent of the land the Americans used, announced they would refuse to renew their leases when they expired, putting the U.S. forces in the awkward position of squatting, or illegally occupying land. It was, of course, unlikely that the U.S. armed forces would vacate the installations simply because the tenants balked at renewing the leases. The governor of Okinawa could, in effect, force a renewal, signing the leases in place of the owners. If he chose not to do so, then the matter would pass to the federal government.

A sign of the importance of the base issue for Okinawans could be seen in the continuing popularity of Masahide Ota, a determined and implacable anti-base governor, who supported the landlords' refusal to renew the leases. Ota had been elected in 1990—well before the rape—because of his promise to fight the U.S. bases.[35] His policy on the base issue stood near the extreme—he wished to "create a peaceful, base-free Okinawa" for the generations of the future.[36] In other words, he stood for total withdrawal, calling for all base land to be returned to Okinawa by 2015.[37] Ota's strong stance on the base issue was both a sign of Okinawan public opinion and a stimulus for further activism.

A local grocer named Shoichi Chibana emerged as one of the most colorful and outspoken opponents of the bases. He owned a tiny parcel of land, about 2,400 square feet, on which stood part of a complex electronic listening apparatus operated by the U.S. Navy, known to Okinawans as an "Elephant's Cage." He received about $2,000 a year for rent, but when his lease came up for renewal on March 31, 1996, he refused to sign over his land and demanded that the Elephant's Cage be removed.

Chibana's family had come up against the U.S. military before. In 1945, his grandfather refused to turn over his land to U.S. troops who were attempting to requisition it—in fact, the grandfather went after the soldiers with a bamboo spear and was shot and killed by one of them. Chibana, it appeared, possessed his grandfather's fiery temperament. In 1987 he publicly burned the Japanese flag during an athletic competition, an indication of the resentment many Okinawans felt toward Japan. For this his shop was vandalized and his family tormented by Japanese nationalists.[38]

In the weeks before Chibana's lease was due to expire, his case came up in court. A superior court judge in Okinawa ordered Governor Ota to sign the lease since Chibana refused. Ota replied that he agreed with Chibana and refused the order. Prime Minister Ryutaro Hashimoto could sign a temporary injunction allowing the Navy to continue using Chibana's land, but the Okinawan government needed to approve it, an uncertain and lengthy process. The timing of this protest was especially awkward, coming only a few weeks before President Clinton was scheduled to make a visit to Japan to meet with Hashimoto.[39]

Chibana's small parcel of land developed into a locus of popular protest, as radical groups urged demonstrators to "fight to rip up the Elephant's Cage" and activists and media converged on the site. The U.S. Navy put up a fence around the area to bar unauthorized access, including Chibana himself, who announced plans to bring family and friends to the site on the date of the lease's expiration to sing Okinawan folksongs, drink sake, and perform traditional dances.[40] On the day in question, he was not allowed the access he had hoped for, but his unbending stand had captured the Japanese imagination. On March 31, tens of thousands of people throughout Japan marched in demonstrations against the bases, including 26,000 people in Tokyo.[41]

Not everyone sided with Chibana. The Okinawan Prefectural Landowners' Association (PLA) opposed any plan to remove the bases from the island, because of the amount of income landowners received in rent. The secretary general of the PLA pointed out that it took about 10 years for land that was returned by the Americans (as many parcels had been over the years) to be restored to a condition where its owners could use it—it was usually not suitable for farming or housing after so many years as part of a military base.[42] A large percentage of the landowners were elderly people, long removed from farming life, and they preferred the annual checks from the government to the uncertainties of developing or using tiny parcels of land.

While Chibana's protest did not succeed in removing the Elephant's Cage or other military installations, the U.S. and Japan did respond to growing pressure against the bases on Okinawa. In April, on the eve of Clinton's visit to Japan, the two nations announced a preliminary plan to reduce the size of the bases on Okinawa by about 20 percent. They also announced that they would eliminate live fire artillery drills and reduce noise from aircraft. The plan, however, did not amount to a post–Cold War drawdown. It would not reduce overall troop levels in Japan—the 47,000 personnel there would remain, including the 27,000 troops in Okinawa. The goal was to consolidate some bases and move some installations to other locations to make the burden of defense more equitable for the Okinawans. In total, about 12,000 acres on Okinawa would revert to their owners. The Japanese government, officials added, would pay more than $1 billion for the transfers.[43]

In May after Clinton's visit was safely over, Chibana, wearing a T-shirt that read "Give us back our land!" was finally allowed to enter the Elephant's Cage, which he did with twenty-nine friends. They performed traditional Okinawan dances on the top secret site, as throngs of journalists watched and took photos.[44]

OKINAWA VS. JAPAN

A new controversy erupted in April, when details about the plans to move the bases became known. One of the main bases to be closed was Futenma air base, a Marine Corps installation. But planners suggested moving the base to the town of Yomitan, another town on Okinawa. The residents of Yomitan refused absolutely to allow the base to relocate in their city. Moreover, some of the functions of Futenma were to be moved to the huge base at Kadena, but the residents around Kadena, in the southern half of the island, already suffered from a disproportionate level of military buildup in their area—Kadena Air Base took up 80 percent of their land, and they resented the unequal proportion. They rejected any plan to allow Kadena to absorb additional personnel or functions.

Although the level of dissatisfaction in Okinawa spurred demands for total removal of the bases, on the mainland islands the debate did not result in any widespread call for reform of the security arrangements between Japan and the United States. The Japanese did not want to forego the military protection the Americans provided because most Japanese viewed the Chinese and North Koreans as a real threat. On the other hand, they did not wish to remilitarize Japan—and could not, under the pacifist constitution given to them by the Americans. So the necessity for extensive defense of Japan continued to be widely understood and embraced.

The announcement of the reform plan in April, however, exposed divisions in the anti-base movement. While opponents wanted to reduce the burden of hosting the American forces for the towns and regions most affected, no one wanted to assume a portion of that burden themselves. Polls showed that 78 percent of Japanese thought that Okinawa should not have to bear most of the burden of the bases, but 84 percent opposed stationing bases in their own hometowns.[45] At the same time, most believed that the heavy military presence was necessary. These incompatible positions presented a formidable difficulty for the protest movement, which could present few acceptable proposals for change.

Events during the summer of 1996 emphasized the divergent interests of Okinawa and Japan, always in the background but temporarily invisible in the aftermath of the rape. In June, the Okinawa prefectural assembly voted to conduct a non-binding referendum on the consolidation of the U.S. bases. Ota said that it would make clear the will of the Okinawan people and help them determine their future. Japanese and American advocates of the military presence believed that the vote would overwhelmingly demand reduction or outright removal of the bases but emphasized the non-binding nature of the referendum. In August, the Supreme Court ruled that Ota's refusal to renew the leases of landowners objecting to the U.S. bases was unconstitutional, and it ordered him to sign the leases. A week later, on the first anniversary of the rape, Ota accused the Japanese government of sacrificing Okinawa to the interests of mainland Japan and allowing the small island to bear most of the burden of defense for the entire nation. "I'm afraid they don't care," he said of the Japanese government. Denying that he was anti-American, he blamed the central government for creating the problems of Okinawa, saying that the Americans were willing to shift installations and military facilities but the Japanese government was not.[46]

The base controversy in Okinawa widened a rift between Okinawan and Japanese members of the two main political parties in Japan, the conservative LDP and the liberal SDP. While the Okinawans, who wanted at very least an adjustment in the basing system, or better yet, the bases out of Okinawa, expected the parties to support these goals, the LDP and SDP leadership in Tokyo supported the Japan–U.S. Security Treaty and did not make the Okinawan situation a priority except for the short time that it grabbed public attention. Unfortunately, there were few political alternatives for the Okinawans. An Okinawan party called Shadaito, founded in 1950, advocated immediate removal of the bases, but from its peak in the late 1970s it had fallen in popularity through the following decades.

Likewise, communism held little attraction. The Okinawan problem would not be a priority in party politics.[47]

REFORM IN THE MILITARY

Meanwhile, the lease controversy continued to elicit protest. As a tactic to force the Americans and the Japanese government to improve the situation, individuals or groups opposed to the U.S. presence bought tiny parcels of land used by the bases, in some cases just a few square meters. Many of the "antiwar hitosubo (3.3 square meters)" landowners, as they were called, did not live on the island but used their ownership as a way to have some input on the issue. An association of these landowners, large in number if tiny in owned acreage, made it clear that as the leases expired they would fight efforts to renew them.

On September 8, 1996, the promised referendum was held. The wording was vague and it carried no official weight, but when the votes were counted, more than 90 percent voted for a consolidation and reduction of the bases. The number of voters, however, at just below 60 percent of the adult population, was surprisingly and disappointingly low. Turnout was especially low in areas around the bases, where large numbers of people depended on the military for their jobs.[48]

Meanwhile, the Americans continued to take steps to minimize the impact of the troops. Commanders honed in on difficulties caused by troop misbehavior, a particularly sensitive issue since the rape. To curb the drinking, fighting, and prostitution rampant in Okinawa important changes were instituted. The drinking age was raised from 18 to 20; alcohol was no longer sold in base stores after 9 P.M.; the military police intensified their patrols; areas where soldiers congregated and caused trouble were placed off-limits; and all personnel received extensive instruction on what was and was not acceptable behavior in Okinawa. But Okinawans continued to be suspicious, arguing that military personnel were trained to be aggressive and therefore constituted a danger regardless of the measures taken to control their behavior. Many Okinawans wanted the Marines in particular expelled because they viewed them as the most dangerous and troublesome force. The Marine Corps constituted about 17,000 of the 28,000 American personnel on Okinawa, so removing them would have been a huge step, with repercussions both positive and negative.

But the changes did pay off in lower crime rates—a year after the rape, the number of crimes committed by U.S. forces fell to thirty-four, from 130 a year before, and 160 a year before that.[49] The military continued to work on minimizing other irritants as well, such as noise and traffic problems. Parachute drops and other intrusive training, for example, were relocated to areas where fewer people lived, and noise barriers were built around bases. Takeoffs, landings, and night flights, some of the most exasperating side effects of living next to any Air Force base, were limited as well. Army commanders prohibited units from marching with weapons along streets or highways, compelling them to take long detours through wooded areas to avoid being seen by the public. Ironically, measures to minimize the impact of training exercises also decreased the effectiveness of the training itself, and thus, the overall military utility of the island.[50] Some Americans began questioning rationale for remaining in Okinawa if they could not get the training they needed there, especially since, with the development of longer-range aircraft and weapons, the central location of the island no longer mattered as much. Bases in remote areas of Hokkaido (northern Japan), Australia, or Thailand were often mentioned. as possible alternatives. Still, the Pentagon viewed Okinawa as a vital strategic hub, and perhaps more importantly, one with already established installations, and they resisted calls to reduce the number of forces there.

In September 1996, Governor Ota finally gave up his fight against renewing the leases, after the Supreme Court called his actions unconstitutional and the prime minister offered an aid package of $46 million. Some thought Ota should have pushed for even more concessions, such as removing the Marines altogether, but most Okinawans saw him as their champion in the long fight against the bases.[51] The activism of the antiwar hitosubo, however, continued to move forward. In February 1997, the Okinawa Prefectural Land Expropriation Committee held hearings about the leases. At issue were 3,085 landowners including Shoichi Chibana, who refused to renew their leases. Aside from Chibana's already expired lease, the remaining 3,084 leases were due to end in May, and most of these were antiwar hitosubo.[52] In April, as the expirations loomed, Prime Minister Hashimoto sought parliamentary approval to extend the leases through government fiat.

In the wake of protests against moving Futenma Marine Corps Air Station from the city of Ginowan to the northern Okinawan city of Yomitan, the United States and Japan agreed to build a floating heliport to replace Futenma. It was not immediately clear whether the heliport was technologically feasible. Three proposals for building the heliport were being considered—a "pole-supported pier type" with steel columns planted in the seabed; a "pontoon type" supported by pontoons protected by a breakwater; and a "semi-submersible type" with a lower structure. Both Japanese and American companies put together bids for the project. [53]

The heliport was proposed for a site adjacent to Camp Schwab, a Marine base with about 3,000 personnel, in central Okinawa. The village of Henoko, part of the municipal area of Nago, would be the immediate neighbor of the heliport. The village of 1,400 residents maintained an economic relationship with Camp Schwab stretching back to its heyday in the Vietnam era and did not participate in the anti-base activity of the 1960s and 1970s. But in the aftermath of the rape, the dollars which had flowed into the economy, mostly from shops, bars, and nightclubs, dried up and previously good relations became strained. While about 10 percent of the population worked at the bases, and an additional 10 percent received rental income from their land, the town was no longer so dependent on the base.

When the heliport plan was announced, Henoko immediately joined the protest against the bases in Okinawa. A citizens' group formed to fight the plan said that the heliport would destroy the environment of the seaside village and bring noise and increased danger to the area. The root problem, activists claimed with some justification, was that the mainland government had made a superficial adjustment, leaving Okinawa with just as many bases as before. Okinawa's plight, activists pointed out, had only gotten worse; before reversion to Japan in 1972, Okinawa hosted 50 percent of the U.S. bases in Japan. By 1997, the percentage increased to 75, mostly because some of the bases on mainland Japan had closed. In fact, the activists blamed the Japanese government rather than the Americans for the problem because the Japanese government had come up with the heliport plan in the first place.

Not everyone in the village opposed the idea. The fishermen's union would receive compensation from the U.S. government for the loss of fishing grounds, and the municipal authorities anticipated the government funding that would flow in with the plan. Business groups said that Henoko needed the funds that the expanded base would bring—unemployment in Okinawa in general reached almost 9 percent, nearly twice that of mainland Japan. Still, more than 800 people signed a petition opposing the heliport, and the particular issue merged with the larger anti-basing movement on the island.[54] In 1996, the Nago city assembly resolved to oppose the plan in two separate resolutions, and in December 1997, a majority (54 percent) of citizens voted to reject the heliport plan in a referendum.

In October 1998, a women's group from Japan known as the Women's Peace Caravan traveled to the United States to bring attention to the problems of the U.S. military presence in Japan and especially Okinawa. Suzuyo Takazato, a spokeswoman for the group, described the unfair burden placed on Okinawa by the bases. Using Kadena Air Base as an example, she noted that in addition to the large amount of physical space taken up by the base—more than 80 percent of the area of Kadena—babies born near the air base suffered the lowest birth weight in all of Japan. According to the delegation, children living near the bases suffered other physical problems such as more sickness, mental problems like poor concentration in school, and emotional problems. The women visited schools, churches, and other U.S. venues to publicize the issue.[55]

The anti-base movement seemed to be gaining in popularity throughout Japan. In April 1999, a long-time anti-base activist was elected prefectural governor of Tokyo. Shintaro Ishihara, known for his book "The Japan that Can Say No," promised to fight to close the Yokota AFB near Tokyo. While a regional official like the prefectural governor did not have any direct influence over the basing issue, the publicity surrounding Ishihara's promise brought more attention to the basing issue.

THE DECLINE OF THE ANTI-BASE MOVEMENT

In spite of some evidence that mainland Japan was embracing the base issue, three years after the rape that spawned the wave of anti-base activity fervor began to ebb. In November 1998, Ota was defeated in an election by Keiichi Inamine, a moderate conservative more friendly to the bases, and Tokyo began to withhold vital funding from Okinawa in response to continued base opposition.[56] Inamine's election boded well for the heliport plan and freed up the frozen funding from Tokyo. However, activists found another issue in the nomination of Nago for the 2000 economic summit meeting of the Group of Eight industrial nations, which would include a visit by President Clinton. Rejecting the bribery implicit in the choice of their island for the summit meeting, the activists saw the meeting and promises of development funds as linked to acceptance of the heliport, which many continued to insist was just a cosmetic change. "They treat us like animals in the cage and think if they feed us, we will shut up," said one activist.[57]

However, the anti-base activists were losing the battle of public opinion. In December 1999, the municipal assembly of Nago voted to accept the plan to relocate Futenma to their area, a sign that public opinion had changed from three years earlier when the assembly had voted twice to reject the plan. Inamine had made it clear that he was more interested in economic stimulus than asserting Okinawan sovereignty as Ota had done. While more than twenty hours of debate raged over the issue and opponents staged a lively protest against the measure, it finally passed, and the mayor of Nago, Tateo Kishimoto, announced the city's acceptance. In exchange, the government promised a development package of almost $1 billion, and the summit of the Group of Eight would take place in Nago as planned.

Base opponents were livid and vowed to continue the fight against the heliport. They felt especially betrayed because the results of several referenda over the years had vindicated their position, and with the end of the Cold War the need for extensive bases seemed less pressing. Activists blamed the Japanese government for refusing to locate the bases elsewhere in Japan.

Four years after the rape, American officials believed that while anti-basing sentiment was still used as a political tool, actual relations between the bases and the host communities had significantly improved. Each summer Kadena held a huge three-day "America Fest," an open house for local residents who viewed the aircraft, observed demonstrations of military skills like rappelling from helicopters, and ate "typical" American food. Several hundred thousand people showed up for the festival each year, and while many visitors did actually oppose the presence of the bases, they still could see that the Americans were trying to improve their image. Even some of the bases' fiercest critics said that they showed up to the festival as a way to assert sovereignty, to stand, even for a short time, in a space that was off-limits to them the rest of the year.[58]

CONTINUED PROBLEMS

On July 3, 2000, on the eve of the Group of Eight summit in Nago, police arrested a U.S. Marine on suspicion of sexually assaulting a 14-year-old girl. Apparently, after a drunken binge, the 19-year-old marine crept into the girl's home and into her bed and was found there the next morning.

The Okinawa police demanded that the U.S. forces impose a curfew prohibiting soldiers from leaving the bases at night and also provide stricter "moral education" for the soldiers. The police were especially worried that events such as sexual assaults or crimes by U.S. servicemen might inflame anti-base sentiment and lead to unrest during the summit meeting, to take place July 21–23. A few days later an Air Force sergeant was arrested for running a red light and hitting a pedestrian, who escaped with minor injuries. With the two episodes, almost all the efforts of officials over the past few years to improve the reputation of the U.S. forces was undone.

Military officials announced that the marines would be restricted to the bases during the summit, and in the days preceding it, there would be a midnight curfew. The U.S. ambassador to Japan publicly apologized for the incidents. But opponents of the bases were re-energized and planned demonstrations during the summit. "As long as the bases are here, such incidents will happen," said one leader of the opposition. The activists stressed that the only solution was to get rid of the bases altogether.[59] Even Inamine, who initially had indicated more toleration of the bases than his predecessor Ota, expressed his outrage and said that he would consider attending a rally being planned for the weekend. The rally took place, drawing about 7,000 people—a large crowd but not nearly as large as the rallies after the 1995 rape. The mood overall remained calm.[60] The following day, the day before Clinton arrived in Okinawa, thousands of people joined hands to form a human chain around Kadena Air Base, an 11-mile stretch involving up to 25,000 people. In some places people were standing three or four deep.[61] "Bases are places where they practice killing every day," read a typical sign. Many Okinawans recalled that their island was the only place in Japan to suffer ground combat, and they had a special duty to make sure it never happened again. The summit passed without serious incident, however, and the issue faded once more.

The U.S. presence in Okinawa has not diminished. However, public opinion continues to change and develop in response to new situations. In May 2001, a survey conducted by the Japanese government revealed that the U.S. military presence was seen as "necessary" or "unavoidable" by 45.7 percent of the respondents, while 44.4 percent thought that the military was "unnecessary" or "posed a danger." The favorable rating was higher than unfavorable for the first time since the question was asked, in 1985. The percentage of respondents choosing the two unfavorable responses went down while those choosing the two favorable responses rose since the previous poll in 1994. Thus, while the opposition to the bases, which was fueled by the 1995 rape, certainly had its effect on public opinion, six years later attitudes toward the military had actually improved since the year before the rape. One reason for the improvement in public opinion toward the bases has been that Japan and the United States are making greater efforts to explain the reasons for the stationing of the military in Japan and in Okinawa. A second reason concerns the efforts of the military to be a less intrusive neighbor in many ways, from holding a strict line on crime committed by servicemen to limiting flight hours and maneuvers. A third reason is that the high unemployment rate in Okinawa and poor economic outlook in Japan in general has forced Okinawans to turn to the bases for employment. In the survey conducted by the government, the percentage of people who approved of the social and economic progress of Okinawa since the island's reversion to Japan in 1972 decreased 13.2 points from the previous survey in 1994. But overall, few Okinawans wished or planned to relocate to another prefecture in mainland Japan. [62]

In July 2001, an Air Force sergeant was arrested for the rape of a Japanese woman. The same controversies arose again—the issue of U.S. personnel being treated favorably by the authorities versus concerns about the rights of the accused, and in general, the question of the impact of the huge military presence in Okinawa. Japanese and U.S. authorities agreed that the suspect, Timothy Woodland, would be interrogated only 10 hours a day (instead of up to 18). American officials tried to ensure that Woodland would have access to interpreters and legal counsel not guaranteed under Japanese law until an indictment was handed down, up to 22 days after arrest, but finally allowed the prison to deny him an interpreter for 48 hours after his arrest and agreed that he would be denied the presence of his own lawyer during interrogation.[63]

While the rape stirred renewed anger at the U.S. presence in Okinawa, it was not the same as the rage in 1995. Woodland admitted that he had had sex with the woman, an adult rather than a 12-year-old, but claimed it was consensual while she said it was rape. The incident occurred outside a nightclub where both had gone to spend the evening. Moreover, the crime rate among American personnel had decreased drastically in the past four years. In 1995 the number of crimes reported to police in which the suspect was American totaled 12,886, while in 2000 it had declined to less than half that, at 6,226. By 2001, the U.S. military population was 4 percent of the entire Okinawan population, but made up only 0.9 percent of the suspects of crime. Military restrictions on the behavior of U.S. personnel were among the strictest in the world—marines usually were not allowed to drive, they could not go out on the town without a friend, and they were required to wear belts in taxis or private vehicles.[64]

Moreover, the anger in the rest of Japan against the U.S. forces was short-lived, as people were unwilling to consider taking on part of Okinawa's burden. Still, anti-base activists continue to hope that the large U.S. military presence in Okinawa someday will diminish, if not disappear altogether. The huge U.S. Navy and Air Force bases in the Philippines seemed at one time to be as timeless as the volcanoes at the foundation of that archipelago, but the volcanoes had their revenge, and the bases are now gone. More recently, military strategists have pointed out that with new weapons systems and strategic policies, the security needs that Okinawa allegedly fills need not be met by a large basing structure but by more mobile forces stationed in the United States and prepared for rapid deployment overseas. It remains to be seen how long Okinawa will remain a military colony, but the armed forces have done much to minimize the burdens of their presence.

9

★ ★ ★ ★ ★

The Social Effects of the Bases: South Korea

INTRODUCTION

Since the Korean War in the early 1950s, the United States has stationed tens of thousands of soldiers, mostly U.S. Army personnel, in South Korea. U.S. forces and Korean troops guard the border of the country from invasion from the north; although the Soviet Union has dissolved and the People's Republic of China has gradually grown closer to the United States, at least in economic relations, North Korea remains one of the few holdover adversaries from the Cold War.

The presence of U.S. troops in South Korea illustrates the problems that can come about when large numbers of troops are stationed without family members in a situation of semi-hostility but not actual warfare. Most of the military bases in South Korea are in relatively isolated areas in the north of the country, and several are near the Demilitarized Zone (DMZ), the border between North and South Korea. With the exception of Yongsan Garrison in Seoul, they exist far away from the attention of the civilian population. For the most part, military personnel in Korea serve 12-month tours without their families; again with the exception of Yongsan, the "Little Americas" found in other host societies do not exist. The military presence in South Korea at first glance would appear to be ideal—bases are out of the public eye and do not take up space with large housing areas.

However, since the arrival of U.S. forces in Korea after World War II, squalid camptowns (kijichon) have grown around U.S. installations, dehumanizing local South Koreans, U.S. personnel and, more recently, the Russian and Philippine women trafficked in to work in them. Prostitution is ubiquitous in the kijichon, and a high rate of alcohol abuse and violence makes them dangerous and debauched. The kijichon are a source of tragic social problems and anti-base sentiment. Ironically, their atmosphere of degradation appears to have a negative effect on military retention; soldiers are somewhat less likely to reenlist after a tour in Korea, in part, researchers say, because they feel dehumanized by what they see there.

A BRIEF HISTORY OF U.S. FORCES IN KOREA

The ancient kingdom of Korea struggled for centuries to prevent invasion and takeover by its stronger neighbors. In the tenth century, Korea united as a kingdom strongly influenced by China, but it maintained its own culture and language. Although Buddhism and Confucianism spread to Korea through China, the Korean language does not resemble other East Asian languages, but as a descendant of ancient Mongol, is closer to Finnish and Hungarian. In the nineteenth century Japan and the West began to pressure Korea to open its borders, but the Hermit Kingdom stubbornly resisted until the Japanese forced it to accept Japanese influence. In 1910 the Japanese annexed the country altogether, initiating 35 years of forced Japanese influence. Japan used Korea as a colony during its attempt to expand throughout Asia, kidnapping Koreans to work as laborers and sex slaves.

During World War II, the United States and Britain did not address the question of the liberation of Korea, as it had no strategic value and had not been either an American or a British colony. As the war in Europe wound down in early 1945, however, the Americans hoped to bring the Soviet Union into the war effort against Japan, and, to this end, Roosevelt promised Stalin at the Yalta Conference in early 1945 that the Soviet Union could consider Manchuria as part of the Soviet sphere of influence. In retrospect, it appears fairly clear that Soviet help was not needed in Northeast Asia, but U.S. military officials overestimated Japan's military strength and expected a difficult victory over Japan. Stalin did enter the Asian war, but only after the first nuclear bomb was dropped on Japan, and, contrary to the agreements made at Yalta, Stalin moved his army into North Korea. On August 15, 1945, "V–J Day," the Americans decided not to contest Stalin's move, and set the 38th parallel as the dividing line between the American and Soviet spheres in Korea.

Although Stalin quickly established a repressive communist government in North Korea, the United States, with its myriad tasks in Japan and Europe, did not pay particularly close attention to Korea during the years of occupation (1945–1949). Occupation forces, hastily sent from Okinawa simply because of their proximity to the country, had no mandate, no preparation, and no knowledge of the country. Because of their ignorance, they were forced to depend on the Japanese administrators who had so recently ruled Korea with an iron fist. The continued presence of the hated Japanese outraged Koreans, placing the U.S. Army Military Government in Korea (USAMGIK) in a difficult position. Korean exile groups complained to the State Department, and from Japan, MacArthur himself reprimanded military governor Lieutenant General John R. Hodge for the unfortunate policy.

The USAMGIK then turned to Koreans who spoke English, but they tended to be wealthy and conservative, thus opposed to any democratic or economic reform, and to make matters worse had in many cases collaborated with the Japanese; they were not significantly more popular in Korean society than the Japanese had been. Hodge was not aware of this complicated political tangle, however, and no one in the State Department thought to help him interpret the situation.[1] In August 1945, Hodge recommended that Syngman Rhee, a Korean exile with deep roots in the United States—he had moved to the United States before the First World War—be installed in Korea as its new ruler. Rhee, Hodge believed, was a reliable anti-communist and popular among the Korean people, for he was popular among the English-speaking Koreans on whom Hodge relied. Unfortunately, Rhee proved to be a right-wing extremist and a repressive leader, setting up paramilitary organizations to destroy moderate and leftist opposition groups even under the eyes of the military government. The State Department did finally recommend a shift away from Rhee and toward moderate, democratic groups, but by this time Rhee had instituted himself too deeply into the nascent political system of southern Korea, and he took decisive action against moderate organizations.

The various communist groups in Korea also vexed the American military government. The Communist Party in the North, controlled by the Soviet Union, made extreme demands on the south—for food, for political positions favoring the communists—while not promising anything substantive in return. The Communist Party in the south, made up of native Koreans and struggling for national independence at least as much as for the ideology of communism, had battled the Japanese occupation throughout the war years, but now found itself excluded from power by the Americans, while collaborationists and exiles had the ear of the military government. Moreover, Hodge viewed the political spectrum in Korea through a black and white lens; he believed, like many Americans, that any group even moderately leftist acted as a puppet of the Soviet Union.

Increasingly, the reality of the political situation did in fact resemble this polarization, and by the summer of 1946 political violence swept southern Korea. The occupation government shut down leftist organizations and supported the right-wing Rhee; as a result, Koreans blamed the Americans for fomenting or tolerating the violence and opposed the occupation all the more.

Meanwhile, the American troops became more and more unpopular. Koreans, deeply conservative and suspicious of foreigners, did not take to the GIs as had the Japanese, Germans and others (whether out of economic necessity or true interest). Women in particular who consorted with Americans found themselves ostracized from their families and shunned by friends, and the system of informal concubinage common in other occupied nations did not develop in Korea. The military had maintained the brothel system set up by the Japanese, utilizing the now-famous "comfort women" taken into sexual slavery by the Japanese forces. In the face of strenuous objections by military chaplains, however, the brothels were closed. Shutting down organized brothels did not end the sex trade, however, and GIs continued to visit prostitutes, who now walked the streets. Ironically, the incidence of venereal disease among soldiers and Korean prostitutes exploded as a result, because the system of regular health inspections for sex workers disappeared.

Soldiers in Korea, like elsewhere, found it hard to wait out the months and years until they left for home, and the troops vented their frustrations, sexual and otherwise, on the Korean populace. In 1946, GIs were implicated in increasing numbers of rapes and sexual assaults, which damaged the reputation of the U.S. forces.[2]

The 40,000 U.S. troops remaining in Korea as occupiers contributed little of strategic value to the U.S. position in Asia—they could hardly stop a massive invasion from the north—but as relations between the United States and the Soviets deteriorated, the U.S. presence in Korea was viewed by the American public and U.S. allies as symbolizing the American determination to face communism. The troops cost money, however, and the United States shouldered ever-expanding financial burdens around the world. In September 1947, the Soviets offered to withdraw their forces from Korea if the U.S. forces did likewise, an offer the Americans, although suspicious, accepted with relief.[3] On August 12, 1948, the United States recognized the creation of the Republic of Korea (ROK) and a few days later Syngman Rhee, already showing signs of messianic dementia, became the first president of the new nation. The last units of the occupation forces departed Korea on June 29, 1949, leaving the South Koreans to fend for themselves.

Having set up a faulty system in Korea, the U.S. forces now left the scene; but not, as it turned out, for long. For the United States, Cold War events moved faster than strategic decisions. The policy of containment, articulated in George Kennan's writings in 1947, led in Europe to the creation of NATO in April 1949, but in Asia containment had yet to be implemented in the form of an overall defense concept. The United States wished to avoid stationing troops in Korea, but the nation had developed into such a potent symbol of Cold War hostility that it could not be abandoned entirely, and the Americans continued to deliver military aid to the ROK. While the United States considered its options, the Chinese communists conquered mainland China in late 1949, raising the specter of a communist Asia.

The U.S.-sponsored anti-communist nationalists fled to the strategic island of Formosa, or Taiwan. In Korea, tensions between the two sides, buildup of military forces and equipment, and incursions across the border made the situation extremely dangerous. Border conflicts in the vicinity of the 38th parallel grew bloodier and more frequent. When North Korean forces invaded South Korea on June 25, 1950, the event that all sides had been expecting finally came to pass.

THE KOREAN WAR

By 1950, the United States had committed itself to a policy of containment of Communist aggression. When North Korea began its invasion, then, the United States was compelled to act, and pressed the UN Security Council to do likewise. The UN formed a multinational force, commanded by MacArthur, two days after the invasion. The first U.S. troops to land in Korea arrived from occupied Japan at the beginning of July, and the forces commanded by MacArthur enjoyed some startling successes in the early months of the war. Overall, however, the American forces from Japan were at first unready for the rigors of combat, having spent years living the soft life of occupation duty. Mistakes and failures of the Korean War, the first real Cold War engagement, obliged the armed forces to examine and reform many aspects of peacetime training. For example, the United States Military Code of Conduct, which details what a servicemember should do if he or she is captured, was developed after it was discovered that many American POWs, not having had any training in resistance methods, cooperated with their North Korean or Chinese captors.

The Korean War lasted three years, and over time the Korean armed forces, rather than the U.S. or UN troops, took over most of the fighting on the side of the ROK. Combat ended on July 27, 1953 with an armistice; as of July 2004 no peace treaty between the two sides has been signed, and the borders of North and South Korea have remained where they were before the start of the war.

In August 1953 the United States and South Korea signed a Mutual Defense Treaty, which provided for the stationing of American troops in South Korea. The bulk of U.S. Forces in Korea (USFK) were deployed along the DMZ, the 38th parallel, mostly in areas that had once been farming villages. The headquarters of the USFK, however, was located in Seoul, on Yongsan, a 699-acre base originally in the suburbs of the city. Over the years as Seoul grew, Yongsan came to be in its center,[4] but though Yongsan occupied valuable urban real estate, it continued to operate in the tradition of 1950s "Little Americas," with housing, schools, shopping, a baseball diamond, and an eighteen-hole golf course. Because the two Koreas continued in a technical state of war, the ROK has been one of the few U.S. base locations considered to be a "hardship" and "noncommand sponsored" tour, meaning that, with the exception of those stationed at Yongsan, service personnel may not bring their families at government expense, and they stay in the country for only twelve months rather than the normal three years. In retrospect, American military families would probably have been in no great danger had they accompanied the troops to Korea, but the U.S. forces did experience frequent brushfires near the DMZ. At Fort Rucker, Alabama, home of U.S. Army Aviation, a modest memorial lists the names of U.S. Army pilots killed in Korea, including dozens shot down while patrolling the DMZ after 1953. The unaccompanied policy, then, was certainly understandable from the point of view of military necessity. Unfortunately, it was to have dire consequences for the ROK and for the areas near U.S. military bases.

MILITARY PROSTITUTION IN KOREA

During the next decades, the ROK remained dependent on the Americans for defense, and while the United States paid for this defense with dollars, and the government of the ROK paid for it with loyalty, some groups in Korean society paid for it in other ways. Approximately 1 million women, in particular, supported the U.S. presence with their bodies through their work as prostitutes in the camptowns surrounding U.S. bases. Estimates during the 1980s by Korean groups suggest that one of every six Korean women age 15 to 35 worked in the sex industry.[5] Of all the elements of U.S.– Korean relations—the adoption of Korean children by Americans, the cliché of Korean immigrant grocers in large cities, the recent development of Korea's first-world economy, and large quantities of Korean products imported into the United States—Korean military prostitution is perhaps most important in the creation of impressions and attitudes of both peoples toward each other. For five decades, the U.S. bases in Korea created a culture somewhat like that of postwar Germany or Japan, where American personnel freely indulged in behavior tolerated almost nowhere else. Yet the subject, as noted historian Bruce Cumings observes, has been met with silence and denial by both Koreans and Americans.[6] "Respectable" Koreans have traditionally averted their eyes from the problem and blamed the sex workers for their participation in the business, and military personnel who have served in Korea understandably do not share stories of the club scene with their wives and families. Interestingly, military personnel often claim that soldiers are forbidden to marry Korean prostitutes, insisting that all Korean wives of servicemen have "decent" pasts. This story is a kindness to Korean wives, who deserve the chance to make a new life, but it distorts the nature of Korean–American relations in the base areas.

In the aftermath of the Korean War, millions of desperate refugees, war orphans and widows served as a pool for potential sex workers, and, as noted above, some former "comfort women" continued as sex workers for the U.S. forces. In later years, recruiters traveled into poverty stricken rural areas and purchased girls for a few hundred dollars, often telling the families that the girls would receive jobs as waitresses, maids, and the like. Prostitution also became part of a multigenerational cycle, especially among the many Amerasian children that resulted from the industry.

During the 1950s, women were trucked onto bases for the weekends, but as the base system became more stable, a relatively permanent system of clubs developed outside each installation. Although women available for hire could be found virtually anywhere,[7] registered prostitutes generally worked at clubs, where they encouraged GIs to buy them overpriced "ladies' drinks," usually soda or juice, and negotiated "short time" or "long time" (overnight) visits. The women went into debt to the club owners for their room rental, recruiting fees, furniture, clothing, cosmetics, and medical care and found it difficult to escape. In any case, after immersion in such a life, few had anywhere to escape to, since their families did not want them back.

Political scientist Katharine Moon has studied the history of military prostitution in Korea, and her findings suggest that the ROK government tolerated, even encouraged, the growth of military prostitution, for several reasons. First, it was seen as inevitable, and government officials as well as the public believed that prostitutes "protected" the rest of the female population from the depredations of soldiers. As in occupied Japan, Korean sex workers were encouraged to see themselves as sacrificing themselves for the nation. Second, the growth of the industry in Korea meant that GI dollars were not being spent on R&R visits to Japan, but rather remained in the country. In the first decades after the war, the ROK depended to an enormous extent on U.S. dollars to bolster its weak economy. By the early 1960s, the majority of Koreans living near bases earned their money from the Americans in some way or another, including employment directly on the bases, as well as prostitution and other services off base.

In 1961 the ROK passed a Prostitution Prevention Law mandating widespread reform in the treatment of prostitutes and customers as well as runaway children and orphans; most noticeably the measure punished customers more severely than women. Within a year or so, however, the government created special districts where prostitution was legalized. About 60 percent of these were located in areas near U.S. bases; in other words, the government legalized prostitution in large part for the U.S. forces.[8] Registered prostitutes in Korea were required to receive weekly VD checks and other medical tests, and to carry a "VD card" with them at all times. If they showed signs of VD, they were treated at a specially designated hospital until cured and then released. When soldiers showed signs of VD, they were required by law to report any sexual contacts, and public health officials tracked the woman or women down and treated them. VD control efforts were surprisingly austere, but they were necessary, considering the amount of sex traffic occurring on a routine basis.

THE 1970s AND THE NIXON DOCTRINE

In July 1969, President Nixon announced a new policy of gradually allowing Asian nations to assume responsibility for their own defense and pulling U.S. troops out of the region. In promulgating the Nixon Doctrine, the president addressed the crisis sparked by the Vietnam quagmire, and the policy gained the approval of the American public. The Koreans, however, at first believed that they would be an exception to the policy. It came as a shock to ROK officials when the U.S. actually began pulling army units out of Korea. The 7th Infantry Division, one of the two divisions in Korea since the 1950s, withdrew entirely, a move involving approximately 20,000 personnel. After the 7th ID left, 43,000 U.S. troops remained in the country. In addition, the responsibility for guarding the DMZ fell to the South Korean Army (ROKA), and some U.S. forces moved south, away from the border.[9]

The troop withdrawals did not, however, result in the dire consequences predicted by ROK officials. North Korea did not increase its activity along the DMZ, and eventually South Korean leaders were persuaded once again of the American commitment to the country. But the withdrawals had serious, if temporary, effects on local communities, including the withering away of some kijichon and the decline of most of the prostitution around 7th ID boomtowns. Real estate values plummeted, leading many clubs owners to simply abandon their businesses since they could not find buyers.[10] Some bar women returned home or went into other occupations, but most tried to relocate to areas where the U.S. forces still maintained a sizeable presence. With this shift, the rate of venereal disease rose drastically, as more women worked as unregistered prostitutes and received no weekly health checks. VD, previously under control, became a scourge of the sex workers and the military in the aftermath of the drawdown.[11] Rates reached the peak of 787 cases per thousand men per year in May of 1972;[12] in other words, more than three-quarters of the men were infected with venereal disease, a rate rarely seen even in the chaotic aftermath of the Second World War, when VD control was a serious concern of military authorities.

Racial tension between black and white soldiers, a problem plaguing bases throughout the world in the 1970s, also came to trouble South Korea. In the early 1970s, many black soldiers began to complain about formal and informal discrimination, both in the military institution and in the bars and clubs of the kijichon. Sex workers divided themselves into those catering to black soldiers and those catering to white. Some clubs refused to serve black soldiers, fearing that their establishments would become known as "black" and lose white customers, the majority of patrons in the kijichon. In some camptowns, the clubs catering to black clientele clustered in a different area of town, known as the DMZ—Dark Man's Zone—separate from the white clubs.[13] The Koreans, with no particular history of anti-black racism (Korean society was traditionally suspicious of all other races and ethnicities), simply mirrored American racial attitudes, having found that if a business or a sex worker associated with black clients, whites, who were more numerous, would go elsewhere. Incidents of racial violence, common throughout the global U.S. military during the early 1970s, spilled into the surrounding communities, culminating in racial riots outside Camp Humphries, an army post near Seoul, in July 1971.[14]

By 1971, both the Americans and Koreans realized that the mushrooming problems of the kijichon threatened the security relationship between the two nations and the readiness and morale of the U.S. forces. Moreover, the Koreans did not wish to see any further troop withdrawals, so they instituted policies to address the most severe irritants, in a program known as the "Base Cleanup Campaign." Measures included the creation of "Korean–American Friendship Councils," similar to those that had been operating in Germany since the 1950s. The councils, made up of local officials and businesspeople and American military commanders, met regularly to discuss issues of interest to both communities. Unlike in Germany, however, where "issues of interest" mainly involved German–American friendship activities and discussions of how to minimize aircraft noise, in Korea negotiations centered on the clubs and military prostitution. The Korean government took stringent measures to reduce the VD rate by re-registering prostitutes and compelling them to submit to regular checks and VD treatment.

The military, for its part, used its power to put clubs and bars "off-limits" to enforce cooperation among club owners. Commanders insisted that the clubs not only follow new regulations targeting VD, but also avoid racial discrimination. Sex workers and bartenders received racial awareness instruction similar to that given to soldiers and civilian employees during the early 1970s. The threat of an "off-limits" designation compelled many owners to follow the rules, because such a ruling could destroy a business.[15] Ironically, at this time in Germany military commanders fought a battle against off-limits designations set by *German* businesses who wished to keep American soldiers out, a clear illustration of how different the two overseas base systems had become.

In the Base Cleanup Campaign, other, more constructive friendship activities were emphasized, including GI visits to "normal" Korean homes, introductions to Korean culture, sports events, and so forth, activities common in Europe from the earliest days of the Cold War.[16] However, these activities did not override the prevailing trend in military–civilian relations in Korea: the flourishing sex trade.

OPPOSITION TO THE U.S. PRESENCE

Efforts to improve the camptown environment paid off, although not in the sense of diminishing the amount of prostitution around bases. The result of the cleanup was, in Katharine Moon's interpretation, to convince the USFK to lobby strongly for a continued presence in Korea, desired by the ROK and U.S. forces, but opposed by many in the United States.

In any case, pressure to bring the troops home diminished with the failure of détente and the increase in Cold War tension during the late 1970s (see Chapter 5). USFK, like American forces elsewhere in Asia, Europe, and the United States, benefited from the Reagan Administration's emphasis on a strong defense in the 1980s. The prostitution industry, which had declined during the early 1970s in the wake of the Base Cleanup Campaign, boomed once more.

The economy of the ROK also began to improve during the 1980s, and most people in the United States and the ROK believed that the stability of South Korea depended on the protection it received from the U.S. forces. However, in the 1970s and 1980s, students protested with increasing vociferousness in favor of democracy in South Korea and against the bases, linking South Korean military dictators with the U.S. presence, as activists were doing in the Philippines.

As the economy of Korea improved, the city of Seoul grew and enveloped Yongsan military base. Once on the outskirts of the city, the base now sat in the center, forcing traffic to divert in unnatural patterns around the facility. It was even said that the Seoul subway system could not expand to the farther side of the base because excavation would damage the extensive underground piping that supplied the base with water. In 1988, in the months before the Seoul Summer Olympics, American and South Korean officials agreed in principle to close Yongsan and transfer it to a less visible location. The move stalled over the question of who would pay for the move, however, as each side believed the other had the duty to fund the expensive transition.[17]

As negotiations over Yongsan dragged on without conclusion, Korean students demonstrated and protested against the bases. Initially they did not address the kijichon issue, focusing instead on the military dictatorship's repression of civil liberties. But opposition to the social degradation brought by the bases exploded in 1992 after the gruesome rape and murder of a Korean woman by Kenneth Markle, a U.S. Army private stationed at Camp Humphreys. The woman, Yum Kum-I, had been a waitress in Tongduchon, one of the most notorious of the kijichon. Her body was found naked, her legs spread wide, a Coke bottle pushed into her vagina and an umbrella 11 inches in her rectum. Powdered laundry detergent was scattered on her face and body. She had been beaten and stabbed to death.

The outrage sparked by Yum's murder and mutilation spread across the nation. In addition to the bestiality of the crime, Koreans protested the appearance of special treatment meted out to Markle by U.S. authorities. To begin with, when Korean detectives arrested him, he was delivered to American officials rather than taken to the Korean police headquarters. Korean police interrogated him on the base in the presence of U.S. Army personnel, and before his trial he was detained on the base, rather than in a Korean jail. Markle was tried by a Korean court and sentenced to 15 years in prison, which he served in a special wing of a Korean prison established for American servicemembers.

In the aftermath of the Markle crime and the anger it produced, Americans were confined to base for several days while Koreans protested in the streets.[18] Korean newspapers overflowed with criticism of the Americans for the preferential treatment they received, and Koreans of all social classes demanded that the SOFA be reformed to reflect more equity in the U.S.–ROK relationship.

The following year, another scandal involving the Americans broke in the public media, this time not involving a sex crime as so often had occurred in Korea and elsewhere in Asia, but centering on U.S. military policy. Student protesters alleged that the Americans overstated the danger of the North Korean regime in order to maintain the position of power it enjoyed in the ROK. A second criticism involved the USFK's possible role in the South Korean Army's brutal suppression of a civil uprising in Kwangju province in 1980, during which at least 250 people died and likely many more. Demonstrators believed that the commander of USFK, as supreme commander of the ROK army, would have known that Korean troops were being sent to Kwangju province and what they were to be used for. American public affairs personnel denied all knowledge of the massacre, but opponents were skeptical.[19]

The situation became increasingly sensitive for the U.S. forces in Korea during the mid-1990s, with more overt anti-Americanism expressed by Koreans. In 1995 a huge brawl occurred on a subway when an American soldier touched a Korean woman. The woman turned out to be the soldier's wife, but the scene infuriated Koreans and sparked a huge controversy.[20]

Another sensitive issue was the SOFA with Korea, concluded in 1967. Koreans demanded it be reformed, alleging that it gave special treatment to the GIs. One contested privilege was the right of U.S. servicemembers accused of crimes to be held on base until their trials, as had occurred in the Markle case. The SOFAs with Japan and West Germany allowed host nation investigators much more authority over American suspects than the South Korean SOFA, even though Okinawan protesters argued that the Japanese SOFA still gave the U.S. forces too much leeway. The Americans, for their part, said that the interrogation standards and conditions in Korean jails did not measure up to American standards.[21]

Another objectionable privilege was the tax-free status of American goods brought to the bases for consumption by American forces. The loophole, understandable from the American point of view, led to a thriving black market for American products, especially in the days when the Korean economy was weak and quality consumer goods expensive and difficult to find. While the post-WWII black markets in Germany and Japan evaporated within a decade after the end of the war, the black market in Korea continued as the Korean economy improved and standards of living increased. Even during the 1990s, South Korea had the most active U.S. forces black market in the world. Goods included not only cigarettes, alcohol, and gasoline, items heavily taxed in many countries and therefore the foundations of black market activity everywhere, but breakfast cereals, canned goods, and electronic equipment. The black market operated openly and unremarkably in Korea for decades, even though the South Korean government lost money on tax revenue. Personnel and family members sold items to their Korean acquaintances, and Korean civilians with fake military IDs shopped in base commissaries and PXs with little fear of being caught. In the late 1990s, however, the U.S. forces initiated a serious attempt to crack down on the problem by limiting the amount of beer GIs could purchase to two cases per week. The USFK itself suffered during the crackdown because it lost revenue in base shops, and U.S. Congress members in beer-producing states stepped in on the side of their home industries and, indirectly, the black marketers.[22]

In 2000, the ROK and the United States conducted negotiations on the revision of the SOFA, much desired by the Koreans. Among the most important new rules included the right of the Korean authorities to hold American suspects from the time of indictment, or, in the case of particularly brutal crimes, even earlier. With this change, the Korean SOFA moved closer to that of Japan. Other important provisions included agreements on environmental protection, labor relations, and agricultural products controls. The Americans also agreed to consult with the Korean government before undertaking any new construction on military bases.

THE FUTURE OF U.S. FORCES IN SOUTH KOREA

In the late 1990s, North Korea continued to menace the south, mostly through a nuclear weapons program. Some critics, however, wondered if the threat was exaggerated to provide a rationale for maintaining the status quo. In 2000, North and South Korea held a summit meeting, raising hopes that relations between the two nations could be normalized and the U.S. forces might go home. North Korea, moreover, was revealed to be a desperately poor nation with millions of people in danger of starvation, only surviving with the help of international assistance. The ruler of North Korea, Kim Jong Il, appeared dangerously irresponsible, spending needed funds on an enormous and costly festival attempting to compete with the

World Cup games held in South Korea and Japan. In spite of North Korea's unpredictability, fewer and fewer South Koreans believed that their northern neighbor posed a credible threat.

In 2001 President Bush declared that the world community faced an "axis of evil," consisting of the nations of Iraq, Iran, and North Korea. A final judgment on the accuracy of his assessment will be the work of future historians and international relations experts. But although attention to North Korea has highlighted the cruelty and desperation of the Kim Jong Il regime and the likelihood that he has acquired at least one nuclear weapon, the U.S. forces in Korea continue to find themselves on the defensive, criticized from all sides and increasingly unwelcome. Regardless of the danger North Korea may (or may not) pose, the Americans in South Korea are taking steps to reduce their impact on Korean society.

Several events in 2002 led to a significant transformation in the U.S. presence in Korea. The first was a plan, negotiated as early as 2001, to consolidate the many scattered bases into a smaller number of military centers far from the capital city of Seoul. As announced in March 2002, the Americans planned to close twenty-three of forty-one bases while improving conditions on those remaining. In April, the new commander of Osan Air Force Base, Brig. Gen. William L. Holland, reflected a sense of optimism when he promised to make Korea an assignment where personnel could come for two-year tours with their families, rather than the traditional unaccompanied one-year tour.

But just as plans for the consolidation were being finalized, an incident in Paju, a town north of Seoul, dangerously inflamed anti-American sentiment in Korea. On June 13, two army sergeants driving an armored vehicle ran over and killed Shim Mi-Son and Shin Hyon-Sun, two 14-year-old girls who were walking to a birthday party. Shortly after the deaths, the girls' classmates, as well as many citizens from Paju, gathered at the gate of the base to demand information and an apology. According to Korean reports, the protesters managed to get inside the gate, and a public affairs officer agreed to talk with them outside. They left the base property in good faith, whereupon the officer retreated back onto the base and South Korean police dispersed the crowd. A few days later, the commander of the base apologized for the deaths and the families of the girls received financial compensation, but the tragedy outraged many Koreans who viewed it as emblematic of the unacceptable burden the U.S. forces placed on the country.

In the months following the deaths, the angry letters, protests, and petitions subsided, although resentment of the Americans ran high. When, in November, Sergeants Fernando Nino and Mark Walker were acquitted of involuntary manslaughter by a military court, furious demonstrations erupted at the gates of many bases. Protesters charged that the men should have been tried by a Korean court and were furious when they left Korea for California on November 26. Military spokespeople countered that the outcome was fair and legal; the U.S.–South Korean SOFA prevented

American troops from being tried in civilian courts for crimes committed while they were on duty. But the SOFA had been a sore point for years, and using it as a defense only increased public hostility. Student protesters broke into several installations, burned American flags, and threw Molotov cocktails over the walls of bases during a week of demonstrations. Many of the students active in the protests were members of far-left groups, but in general public opinion strongly favored changing the SOFA which had enabled the two men to go unpunished. In December, anger turned into violence against individual personnel; a lieutenant colonel was attacked while walking home, two soldiers were harassed and spat upon by a crowd at a train station, and shops and restaurants put up signs saying "Americans not welcome." Commanders warned personnel to avoid venturing off base if possible and to be very careful when they did.

In the midst of the crisis, a third event triggered additional soul-searching among the U.S. forces in Korea. It began when a Fox television station in Ohio broadcast an investigative report that showed American soldiers socializing with women in Korean bars while "courtesy patrols," a less formal version of military police patrols, looked on. The report suggested that many of the women in the bars, who were not Korean but Russian or Filipina, had been brought to Korea by sex traffickers and held against their wills.

Unfortunately, this was not exactly breaking news. Since the mid-1990s, a rash of criticism of the U.S. forces in Korea had highlighted the problems of sex workers. Several developments influenced the growth of this protest. First, the Philippines had recently managed to eliminate their bases, and the Okinawa rape had drawn renewed attention to the problems surrounding U.S. forces in Asia. Second, reports of the sex tourism industry throughout Asia had drawn attention to the magnitude of the sex industry, especially child prostitution. Third, Korean and a few Japanese historians began to tell the long-suppressed story of Korean comfort women forced into sex slavery by the Japanese military in Korea during World War II, and new attention to the exploitation of Korean women brought awareness to postwar military prostitution. Finally, the ROK, with its booming first world economy and vibrant democracy, saw the presence of a culture of military prostitution to be an offense to the nation.

In 2001 the U.S. government criticized South Korea for failing to take measures to stop human trafficking as called for in the Victims of Trafficking and Violence Protection Act of 2000. And in September 2002, a report by the UN's International Organization for Migration (IOM) charged that more than 5,000 women from other nations, mostly Russia and the Philippines, had been trafficked into South Korea to work as prostitutes by the Korea Special Tourism Association, a group of camptown club owners. The Fox news report only stated what had been evident for several years, that most sex workers in Korea came from the Philippines, China, Thailand, and Russia.

The television broadcast, however, roused Rep. Chris Smith, a Republican congressman from New Jersey involved in anti-trafficking efforts, to demand a Pentagon investigation into the matter. Commanders in Korea, stung by accusations that they tolerated the exploitation of desperate women and girls, reacted with their own investigations. In March 2003, twenty-nine bars and clubs were placed off-limits to American servicemembers, most on a street in Itaewon known as "Hooker Hill" for its large number of red-light establishments. Commanders also stepped up educational programs designed to alert soldiers to the health risks of sex with prostitutes and added discussions on the plight of trafficked women.

In the wake of base consolidation plans, the fatal accident, and increased attention to the degradation of the camp towns, American commanders attempted to reverse the negative publicity surrounding the U.S. forces. In November 2002 a Korean–American Partnership Council was formed, in which the commander of the 2nd Infantry Division and Korean officials met each month to discuss problems and concerns. The Americans also began to focus more intently on community relations. In April 2003 a company of American soldiers "adopted" a Korean middle school; "Good Neighbor" awards were presented to Koreans and Americans involved in community efforts; Americans participated for the first time in a Korean festival held near Osan Air Base; a Korean church formed a partnership with the chaplain at Camp Carroll; and university students—among the most vocal opponents of the U.S. forces in Korea—participated in a surprisingly popular volunteer program on Army installations.

In May and June 2003, negotiations for base consolidation moved forward with plans to close Yongsan and to move troops away from the border with North Korea to south of the Han river. Planners established 2011 as a target for completion of the changes, but meanwhile, they began construction and renovation projects on the bases to be expanded. The disappearance of Yongsan will do much to improve Korean–American relations. Moreover, efforts to clean up the areas around the bases have paid off, at least in part. If commanders are successful in their efforts to allow more family members to live in Korea, the degradation of the camptowns will diminish further and opportunities for Korean–American contact of a positive sort will increase.

While public opinion in Korea has by no means turned around completely, there are signs that the greatest anger over the American presence has diminished, and attempts to foster Korean–American contact have had some limited success. In addition, troops themselves see Korea as a more desirable assignment than they did previously, especially compared with the many other unattractive assignments available to personnel. Improved morale among troops in Korea may also help to achieve more cordial relations between the U.S. armed forces and their Korean hosts.

10

★ ★ ★ ★ ★

After the Cold War

INTRODUCTION

Anyone who remembers the dramatic television images of the fall of the Berlin Wall—tiny East German autos inching through cheering crowds, young women and men balancing precariously on the graffiti-covered concrete—will remember as well the exuberant days during which it was said that a "New World Order" would come about, an order without bipolar division, with much less militarization of the world. In Europe and Asia, hopes were raised that U.S. troops would go home and many Americans expected that a "peace dividend" would accrue from the presumed savings generated after military bases in the United States and throughout the world closed their doors.

Less than a year after the Berlin Wall fell, however, a new crisis emerged in the Middle East, where, in August 1990, Iraqi forces invaded neighboring Kuwait. A coalition of forces, led by the United States, mobilized to liberate the tiny country; in the aftermath of the brief war, a small American and British military presence remained in the region to keep the peace.

Unfortunately, a true state of peace has proved as elusive as ever, and it appears that the era of the American military presence overseas is far from over. The mission of the armed forces, however, is no longer to contain the Soviet Union but rather to combat shadowy terrorist networks operating throughout the world. Even before September 11 illustrated the danger of international terrorist groups, the Pentagon was at work on a new type of armed forces—smaller, more flexible, better able to respond to sudden events. This transformation, which will not be easy, involves both reforming the leadership, training, and equipment of the troops themselves, and reconfiguring the worldwide system of installations through which military activities can be conducted. The Pentagon envisions a force of highly trained, committed men and women who can be deployed at a moment's notice to bases within striking distance of an "arc of instability" encompassing North Africa, the Middle East, and Southern Asia.

U.S. FORCES IN THE MIDDLE EAST

American interest in the Middle East as a strategically vital connection between Asia, Europe, and Africa has, as has been described, long predated current controversies. Early in the Cold War, Morocco and Libya hosted large SAC bases, but both nations expelled the U.S. forces from their soil as their ruling systems evolved. There have been American troops in Turkey for decades, coexisting more or less comfortably with their hosts. The Navy has had some success negotiating port agreements in the Gulf, and it uses Diego Garcia in the Indian Ocean as a home port. In addition, Oman has allowed the Navy to access bases since 1980.[1]

In spite of these examples, the presence of U.S. military troops in most Islamic nations has been quite problematic, and in general the region has been very ambivalent toward the United States. A large part of this is cultural—Islamic societies fear the impact of large numbers of troops, and if they have examined the baleful influence American troops have had in Asia, their concerns rest on solid ground. Another reason is nationalism— many Middle Eastern nations emerged from the European colonial experience sensitive to western incursions on their sovereignty, which any military presence unavoidably represents. Third, the Middle East has not felt especially threatened by the Soviet Union, a main reason why Asian and European nations accepted a U.S. force presence after World War II. In fact, Egyptian leader Gamel Abdel Nasser was one of the leaders of the "nonaligned" movement in the UN—developing nations that claimed to support neither the United States nor the USSR. The USSR provided aid in the 1960s and 1970s to many Middle Eastern nations, and some of the newly independent countries experimented with socialism. Thus, the Middle East, with the exceptions of Turkey and Iran along the borders of the USSR, has had little to fear from the Soviet Union. A fourth reason for suspicion has been America's support for Israel. Middle Eastern nations, even non-Arabic nations like Turkey, would not want their land turned into forward basing for assistance to Israel. In the 1973 war this issue became a crisis in many basing areas, including the Azores, Turkey, Greece, and elsewhere—the United States wished to send aircraft to help the Israelis but host nations prohibited it. Today, American support for Israel has become a major stumbling block in U.S. relations with the Middle East.

These are the traditional reasons why Middle Eastern nations have not wanted U.S. forces stationed in their countries and for the most part have resisted American efforts to achieve some kind of forward presence in the region. In August 1990 when Iraq invaded Kuwait, however, the United States pledged a military mission to expel Saddam Hussein's forces from the invaded nation, and within weeks, thousands of U.S. Army, Air Force, Navy, and Marine troops poured into hastily designated bases in Saudi Arabia and later in Bahrain. With this unexpected crisis, the United States suddenly achieved its goal of establishing a military presence in the Middle East. By December 1990, members of Congress openly discussed the likelihood that the Gulf conflict, however it ended, would enable the United States to maintain a permanent military presence in the Middle East.[2] The Pentagon officially maintained, however, that it was not looking for such a presence in the region.[3]

Within months of the first deployments, expressions of concern were already being expressed in Saudi Arabia. "We hope this will end soon and the troops will go," was a typical sentiment.[4] In response to widespread suspicion, U.S. troops were carefully monitored and controlled by their commanders. They were allowed virtually no contact with the civilian population, and interaction with local women, so ubiquitous in other parts of the world, was strictly forbidden.

Alcohol was made illegal, and all accounts suggest that temporary abstinence did nothing but good for the soldiers and officers. The disciplinary problems common to U.S. forces in other parts of the world were much less common in Saudi Arabia.[5] Approximately 10 percent of American military personnel, according to studies from the 1980s, admitted to heavy drinking on a regular basis, and military authorities feared withdrawal problems for some of them, but this did not come to pass. Commanders were able to enforce such rules in part because of the tense conditions during the buildup, when personnel expected to be fighting in a war within months or weeks, and also because alcohol was not legally available anywhere in Saudi Arabia. Commanders often compared the situation favorably to that in Vietnam, where alcohol and drugs had been commonly available and easily obtained by the troops.[6] For rest and relaxation, military personnel were sent to Bahrain, Dubai, or to cruise ships in the Gulf. Their behavior, even on leave, was carefully controlled, and no serious problems erupted.[7]

One of the biggest changes in the Gulf War deployment was the use of female personnel, not in combat, but very close to it. Women served very near the front lines in many capacities.[8] Although they were more important to the war effort than ever, in a nod to cultural sensibilities women were required to wear loose, enveloping clothes and head coverings[9] when going off base; unlike Saudi women, however, they were allowed to drive.

Although close to 500,000 U.S. troops amassed to fight what was expected to be a difficult war with Saddam Hussein, the war lasted only about 100 days. The Iraqi armies suffered tens of thousands of casualties, while the United States lost only a few hundred. The American forces demobilized quickly, but the U.S. presence in the area remained; Bahrain became the headquarters of 5th Fleet, with about 1,000 personnel on shore and 12,000 sailors on naval vessels patrolling the Gulf, and about 5,000 U.S. Army and Air Force personnel remained in Saudi Arabia. Approximately 4,500 troops remained in Kuwait; in total somewhere around 20,000 troops were stationed at any given time in the Gulf region.[10]

Troops in Saudi Arabia received an extra $150 in "imminent danger pay,"[11] but $150 did not accurately reflect the "imminent danger" they faced. On November 13, 1995, a car bomb exploded at a U.S. training facility in Riyadh, set by Islamic militants; five Americans and two Indians were killed. Several months later four extremists were beheaded by the Saudi government for that attack and the case was closed—a suspiciously quick end to the investigation, some American officials thought. Then, on June 25, 1996, a 5,000-pound truck bomb exploded outside the Khobar Towers, a high-rise housing compound at King Abdulaziz Air Base near Dhahran. Most of the 2,500 Americans at the base served in the 4404th Air Wing of the USAF, patrolling no-fly zones in Iraq from the base, but the U.S. Army also maintained some anti-aircraft units there. Nineteen Americans died in the blast, but the bombers escaped in a white Chevrolet Caprice. The second bombing brought the issue of Islamic terror attacks into the open. Not only did terrorists object to the U.S. presence, but they also opposed the Saudi government, which, they said, was corrupt, undemocratic, and depended too closely on ties to the West. One opposition leader not involved in the attacks said of the perpetrators, "I imagine that the bombers now consider themselves in a declared state of war with the Americans."[12] Statements from those with connections to terrorist groups confirmed this.

In the aftermath of the bombing, the troops in Saudi Arabia became even more isolated. For several weeks, they were not allowed to go off base at all, and a 400-foot perimeter fence went up around the compound. The few family members of military personnel, about 700 in total, were evacuated along with the families of diplomatic personnel.[13] Women were issued abayas, black costumes worn by Saudi women, required when female personnel interacted with Saudis. Later reports revealed that many security measures around the base had not been implemented because officials were trying to avoid offending the Saudis; when Saudi officials objected to a proposal, the Americans did not insist. For example, the

Americans wanted the Saudis to cut vegetation around the perimeter of the base to give guards clearer visibility, but the Saudis refused, saying they wanted the vegetation barrier to shield Saudi citizens from seeing Americans relaxing, a sight some could find offensive. "The command is imbued with a desire not to unnecessarily offend Saudi cultural and political norms," concluded investigators. Moreover, the 90-day rotation led to a lack of experience and background in dealing with the situation. The commander of the base was later denied promotion and forced to retire for his role in the fiasco.

As controversy grew over who would take the blame for the Khobar towers bombing, Saudi and American officials agreed to move the troops out of Dhahran and Riyadh to an isolated base in the desert where they would be a less visible target for terrorist attacks. About six months after the bombing, the Americans were moved to Prince Sultan Air Base, a Saudi base in the desert where they were surrounded by Saudi forces. The "Friendly Forces Housing Complex," as the American section of the base was known, offered typical American amenities, with air conditioned tents, American fast food vendors, and many recreation options. The base also had extensive security measures. "It sort of gives you the impression of a prison," commented one officer.[14]

Finally, on June 21, 2001, the United States indicted fourteen extremists on charges of bombing the Khobar Towers. All but one were members of the Saudi Hezbollah; the one exception belonged to the Lebanese Hezbollah. Most of the suspects had already been taken into custody in Saudi Arabia. The FBI also said that Iran played a role in the attacks, but without sufficient evidence, they did not charge Iranian officials. In the following days, military forces throughout the Middle East were put on alert because of threats relating to the indictment. The Saudis, however, insisted that they, not the Americans, would put the suspects on trial, a debate reminiscent of the many quarrels over jurisdiction common to U.S. overseas bases during the Cold War. The execution of the four alleged perpetrators of the November 1995 bombing attack in Riyadh, who were put to death before American investigators could interrogate them, led the Americans to suspect that the Saudis were hiding something, and Saudi attitudes about the Khobar Towers bombing incident were not reassuring. They controversy illustrates the complexity of the SOFA issue. A valuable and possibly life-saving opportunity was lost because U.S. investigators had no jurisdiction over terrorists who had perpetrated a crime against the U.S. forces in Saudi Arabia.

In the decade after the end of the first Gulf War, Middle East analysts and experts on terrorism observed anti-Americanism in the region and Saudi toleration of radical groups with growing concern, but most Americans had little notion of what was at stake. Occasionally, a spectacular event like the 1993 attempt by extremists to blow up the World Trade Center or the attack against the U.S.S. *Cole* in Yemen in October 2000 would draw attention to the problem of Islamic radicalism for a few days or weeks. But it was only after September 11 that the American public, and the world in general, realized the extent of the crisis.

The Bush administration's immediate reaction, begun within a few months of the attacks in New York and Washington, was to initiate "Operation Enduring Freedom" to overthrow the fundamentalist Taliban regime in Afghanistan, where mastermind Osama bin Laden and his al-Qaeda forces received sanctuary and support. Public opinion was mostly supportive of the effort, although some critics warned that a thoughtlessly vengeful reaction would only serve to increase the hatred for America so horrifyingly demonstrated in September. But the Taliban toppled with barely a thud, and while progress in Afghanistan must be measured by inches, not miles, opposition to the war in Afghanistan dwindled away, at least in western Europe and the United States.

Not so for the next step taken by the Bush administration in its effort to make the world safer. Having announced that Iraq posed an immediate and growing threat to the United States, the administration pushed for a showdown with Saddam Hussein, hoping to enlist the help of the UN but planning to go ahead with or without international support. In the end, the administration did not win over international opinion, and fierce protests erupted in many nations, including the United States. After a long and protracted international debate, U.S. and British forces, along with a few allies, invaded Iraq and deposed Saddam Hussein.

The war with Iraq was controversial, to say the least. A discussion of whether or not it was justified is beyond the scope of this book, but a brief mention of the impact of the war, and the Afghanistan war as well, on the armed forces overseas illustrates the challenges of balancing diverse priorities. Strategic imperatives and long-term goals, international alliances, domestic support, and the needs of military personnel have affected, and will continue to affect, the success of any overseas mission.

Even before the start of hostilities, widespread opposition throughout the world made the war effort itself more difficult. In the build-up period before the attack, several key nations refused to allow the American forces to use their bases, airspace, or ports for the war. Turkey's refusal to allow its bases to be used forced strategists to alter their plans significantly. Other nations made their opposition clear by refusing to support the war effort in any way and by hampering diplomatic efforts to achieve a wide alliance. Germany fell into this camp, as did, notoriously, France.

The roadblocks put up by some of America's allies highlighted, in the view of the Pentagon, the need to diversify its overseas installations. Bases in new locations were needed, in part to prevent a few recalcitrant nations from hindering operations, in part to provide closer access to hotspots of instability. This transformation was envisioned long before the Iraq war demonstrated the need for such a change; the Defense Department's

Quadrennial Defense Review, published on September 30, 2001, advocated spreading the U.S. military presence across the world, shifting from its 50-year focus on Europe and Northeast Asia to a variety of less stable areas where conflict was occurring or likely to occur.

Planners found an opportunity to work on the transformation process while preparing for Operation Enduring Freedom. New installations and support agreements were needed to approach Afghanistan; the old bases in Germany, Okinawa, and South Korea were of little or no use. In October 2001, for example, a former Soviet air base outside of the Uzbek city of Karshi, 200 miles from the border of Afghanistan, was reopened by troops from the 10th Mountain Division, a unit specializing in cold weather operations.[15] The president of Kyrgyzstan also offered his country as a base and in December American and French engineers began organizing a temporary base near the Manas International Airport. The tent city, known as the Peter J. Ganci Jr. Air Base after a firefighter who died in the World Trade Center, housed about 2,000 troops from France, South Korea, Spain, Denmark, Norway, Australia, and the Netherlands, in addition to Americans, and the airfield was six hours closer to Afghanistan than the next best option in Saudi Arabia. During the operations in Afghanistan, experts debated whether the United States would try to create a long-term presence in Central Asia, but it appears that if the bases in Uzbekistan and Kyrgyzstan do remain open, they will function only as depots to be reactivated in an emergency and then put back to sleep.

The Persian Gulf sheikdom of Qatar was another important staging area for the war in Afghanistan. The army and Air Force stored war material at As Sayliyah, an installation outside the capital Doha; a second base known as Al Udeid was built by the Qataris. During Operation Enduring Freedom about 3,000 U.S. troops, mostly with the 366th Aerospace Expeditionary Wing, lived in tents on the desert base. The Qatar bases proved the wisdom of the strategy of forward positioning—placing materials in strategic locations to be used in case of conflict. The United States had concluded an agreement with Qatar in 1996, and since then the U.S. forces had begun stockpiling supplies there. During the war in Iraq, Qatar also served as the headquarters for the U.S. Central Command and its commander General Tommy Frank.

Qatar is likely to be a centerpiece of the transformation plan even after operations in Afghanistan and Iraq have ended. In the longer term, however, the most significant element of the transformation will take place in Europe. In spring 2003, Marine General James L. Jones, commander of EUCOM, began to examine the idea of closing most of the remaining bases in Germany and establishing FOBs in Eastern European nations such as Romania, Bulgaria, Hungary, and Poland. Official explanations for the change include the reduced cost of bases in Eastern Europe compared with those in Germany; the more attractive training conditions in Eastern

Europe—uninhabited areas and varying terrain—and a more supportive climate for troop activities.

Other locations have been cited as possibilities as well: the Baltic states of Latvia, Lithuania, and Estonia; Georgia and Azerbaijan in the Caucasus; Djibouti and Ethiopia in the Horn of Africa; even Morocco and Algeria. It is unlikely that all these nations will become hosts to U.S. bases, but the variety of candidates mentioned in news reports illustrates the sense of change and uncertainty about the plan.

The project is not without its detractors. Many critics in Germany and elsewhere have charged that the transformation plan is merely punishment for Germany's opposition to the war in Iraq. German garrison towns are aghast at the thought of losing their bases, which have been the economic mainstay for some towns for 60 years. Others say that dismantling the defensive alliance in Germany will detach Western Europe from the United States, with serious long-term consequences.

What of the impact on military personnel and their families, those most immediately affected by reform? While the end of the Cold War brought changes in military life for thousands of personnel stationed in Western Europe, Panama, and the Philippines, the transformation envisioned by Defense Secretary Donald Rumsfeld is even more far-reaching. Families will not accompany active duty personnel to bases in Eastern Europe, the Caucasus or North Africa; rather, they will live in garrison communities in the United States, mostly in the south. Personnel will be deployed to an overseas base for six months to one year then return home for an equivalent period. This shift entails significant hardship on military families, an important consideration when the percentage of personnel with spouses and children is higher than ever before, and some will decide to leave the military. On the other hand, the traditional nomadic lifestyle of the military family has always involved hardship. The plan envisioned for the armed forces is similar to what has always been common in the navy, where personnel deploy on ships for extended periods of time. In the long run, the transformation plan could decrease the profile of the U.S. forces overseas, diminishing reaction against their impact while giving them the capability to operate efficiently.

CONCLUSION

The history of the U.S. military presence overseas is intimately connected with the growth of the United States as a world power. Military victory in two world wars enabled, or compelled, the United States to assume the controversial role of "global policeman," rebuilding war-damaged societies and containing communist expansion. The actual police officers carrying out this policy, however, were the men and women of the U.S. armed forces scattered on military bases throughout the United States and the world. While American economic power shaped the global economy and brought new (sometimes disruptive) products and ideas to societies almost everywhere, American soldiers provided millions of people with their most concrete image of the United States.

In many cases this image was a positive one; aside from the larger and somewhat abstract mission of containment, local military installations offered assistance in emergencies such as earthquakes and floods, made connections with host communities through public events, and connected more permanently through thousands of marriages and children. On the other hand, the U.S. military presence sparked nationalist reaction in many regions, furnishing a concrete symbol of "imperialism" around which nationalist groups could rally. American soldiers took advantage of the poverty and desperation of host populations to exploit women, giving rise to troubling levels of prostitution and disease in host communities. American bases took up valuable property in cities, towns, and farming villages, and U.S. officials refused to make substantive changes even as the host communities grew and pressed against military land. As a final legacy, the U.S. military has left behind horrific environmental messes on many of its most important Cold War bases.

The United States must now design a new strategy to "contain" or eliminate terrorism as a security threat, a strategy almost certain to involve the use of U.S. forces deployed to regions of the world unaccustomed to a U.S. forces presence. Perhaps the lessons derived from an examination of the U.S. military presence overseas during the Cold War can check the development of negative reaction to military deployments in the future, bolstering American security and resulting in a global presence in which Americans can take pride.

★ ★ ★ ★ ★

Notes

SERIES FOREWORD

1. Haynes Johnson, *The Best of Times: The Boom and Bust Years of America Before and After Everything Changed* (New York: A James H. Silberman Book, Harcourt, Inc., 2001), p. 3.

2. Eric Hobsbawm, *The Age of Extremes: A History of the World, 1917–1991* (New York: Pantheon, 1994).

3. Giovanni Arrighi, *The Long Twentieth Century: Money, Power, and the Origins of Our Times* (London: Verso, 1994).

INTRODUCTION

1. See James Blaker's discussion of this point in *United States Overseas Basing: An Anatomy of the Dilemma* (London: Praeger, 1990).

CHAPTER 1

1. Fred Anderson, *A People's Army: Massachusetts Soldiers and Society in the Seven Years' War* (Chapel Hill: The University of North Carolina Press, 1984).

2. John A. Logan, *The Volunteer Soldier of America* (Chicago and New York: R. S. Peale & Company Publishers, 1887), 91–92.

3. Anderson, *People's Army*, 61.

4. Allan R. Millett and Peter Maslowski, *For the Common Defense: A Military History of the United States of America*, rev. ed. (New York: The Free Press, 1994), 89–91.

5. Peter Karsten, ed., *The Military in America: From the Colonial Era to the Present*, rev. ed. (New York: The Free Press, 1986).

6. Nathan Miller, *The U.S. Navy: A History*. 3rd ed. (Annapolis, MD: Naval Institute Press, 1997), 33.

7. Millett and Maslowski, *Common Defense*, 94–95.

8. Edward M. Coffman, *The Old Army: A Portrait of the American Army in Peacetime, 1784–1898* (New York and Oxford: Oxford University Press, 1986), 6.

9. Miller, *U.S. Navy*, 111.

10. Robert M. Utley, *Frontiersmen in Blue: The United States Army and the Indian, 1848–1865* (New York: The Macmillan Company, 1967), 2.

11. Coffman, *Old Army*, 42.

12. Ibid., 58.

13. Ibid., 238.

14. Ibid., 215.

15. Millett and Maslowski, *Common Defense*, 248.

16. Ibid., 257.

17. Ibid., 362.

18. Ibid., 100.

19. Ibid., 140.

20. Ibid., 106.

21. Ibid., 144.

22. Ibid., 145.

23. Ibid., 149.

24. Ibid., 268.

25. Peter Karsten, *The Naval Aristocracy: The Golden Age of Annapolis and the Emergence of Modern American Navalism* (New York: The Free Press, 1972), 386.

26. Karsten, *Military in America*, 60.

27. Coffman, *Old Army*, 60.

28. Ibid., 46–47.

29. Ibid., 43.

30. Ibid., 227.

31. Ibid., 229.

32. Miller, *U.S. Navy*, 192.

33. Ibid., 94.

34. Coffman, *Old Army*, 69.

35. Harold D. Langley, *Social Reform in the United States Navy, 1798–1862* (Urbana: University of Illinois Press, 1967), vii.

36. Coffman, *Old Army*, 51.

37. Ibid., 72.

38. Ibid., 283.

39. Ibid., 49.

40. Ibid., 230.

41. Ibid., 232–233.

42. Ibid., 283.

43. Miller, *U.S. Navy*, 91.

44. Ibid., 90.

45. Coffman, *Old Army*, 137.

46. Miller, *U.S. Navy*, 94.

47. Coffman, *Old Army,* 139.

48. Ibid., 140.

49. Millett and Maslowski, *Common Defense,* 141.

50. Langley, *Social Reform,* 137.

51. Ibid., 141.

52. Ibid.

53. Ibid., 181.

54. Miller, *U.S. Navy,* 94.

55. Millett and Maslowski, *Common Defense,* 140.

56. Miller, *U.S. Navy,* 104.

57. Millett and Maslowski, *Common Defense,* 141.

58. Ibid., 319.

59. See Brian McAllister Linn, *Guardians of Empire: The U.S. Army and the Pacific, 1902–1940* (Chapel Hill and London: The University of North Carolina Press, 1997).

60. Albert Marrin, *The Yanks Are Coming: The United States in the First World War* (New York: Atheneum, 1986), 38.

61. Byron Farwell, *Over There: The United States in the Great War, 1917–1918* (New York: W. W. Norton & Company, 1999), 135.

62. Ibid., 136.

63. Ibid., 142.

64. Ibid., 147.

65. Marrin, *Yanks are Coming,* 104.

66. Farwell, *Over There,* 149.

67. Ibid., 160.

68. Russell F. Weigley, *History of the United States Army,* enlarged edition (Bloomington: Indiana University Press, 1967, 1984), 396.

69. Ibid., 401.

70. U.S. Army, American Military Government of Occupied Germany, 1918–1920, *Report of the Officer in Charge of Civil Affairs, Third Army and American Forces in Germany* (Washington, DC: United States GPO, 1943).

71. Keith L. Nelson, *Victors Divided: America and the Allies in Germany, 1918–1923* (Berkeley: University of California Press, 1975), 37.

72. Alfred E. Cornebise, *The Amaroc News: The Daily Newspaper of the American Forces in Germany, 1919–1923* (Carbondale and Edwardsville: Southern Illinois University Press, 1981), xix.

73. Nelson, *Victors Divided,* 212.

74. Cornebise, *Amaroc News,* 198.

75. Nelson, *Victors Divided,* 25.

76. U.S. Army, *Report of the Officer in Charge of Civil Affairs,* v.

77. Ibid., 204.

78. Ibid., 206.

79. Ibid., 217.

80. Cornebise, *Amaroc News,* 18–19.

81. Henry T. Allen, *My Rhineland Journal* (Boston and New York: Houghton Mifflin Company, 1923), 485.

82. Cornebise, *Amaroc News,* 173.

83. Ibid., 207.

84. Ibid., 197.

CHAPTER 2

1. James, D. Clayton and Anne Sharp Wells, *From Pearl Harbor to V-J Day: The American Armed Forces in World War II* (Chicago: Ivan R. Dee, 1995), 1.

2. Lee Kennett, *G.I. The American Soldier in World War II* (Norman: University of Oklahoma Press, 1997), 15.

3. Lee Kennett, *For the Duration. . . : The United States Goes to War, Pearl Harbor—1942* (New York: Charles Scribner's Sons, 1985), 5.

4. Clayton and Wells, *Pearl Harbor to V-J Day*, 2.

5. Kennett, *American Soldier*, 12.

6. Clayton and Wells, *Pearl Harbor to V-J Day*, 6.

7. Ibid., 2.

8. Ibid., 7.

9. Ibid., 11.

10. K. S. Coates and W. R. Morrison, *The Alaska Highway in World War II: The U.S. Army of Occupation in Canada's Northwest* (Norman and London: University of Oklahoma Press, 1992), 26.

11. Kennett, *For the Duration*, 8; see also Catherine Lutz, *Homefront: A Military City and the American 20th Century* (Boston: Beacon Press, 2001).

12. Kennett, *American Soldier*, 15.

13. Clayton and Wells, *Pearl Harbor to V-J Day*, 5.

14. Harry A. Gailey, *The War in the Pacific: From Pearl Harbor to Tokyo Bay* (Novato, CA: Presidio, 1995), 108.

15. Coates and Morrison, *Alaska Highway*, 29.

16. Daniel E. Potts and Annette Potts, *Yanks Down Under 1941–1945: The American Impact on Australia* (Melbourne: Oxford University Press, 1985), 6.

17. Kennett, *American Soldier*, 4.

18. Potts and Potts, *Yanks Down Under*, 30.

19. Dudley McCarthy, *South-West Pacific Area—First Year Kokoda to Wau* (Canberra: Official History of WWII, Army, Vol. 5, 1959).

20. Kennett, *American Soldier*, 56.

21. Ibid., 245.

22. Ibid., 9.

23. Potts and Potts, *Yanks Down Under*, 14–15.

24. Ibid., 88–89.

25. Kennett, *American Soldier*, 8.

26. Juliet Gardiner, "Overpaid, Oversexed, and Over Here," in *The American GI in World War II Britain* (New York: Canopy Books, 1992), 2.

27. Kennett, *American Soldier*, 45.

28. Potts and Potts, *Yanks Down Under*, 226.

29. Kennett, *American Soldier*, 19.

30. Ibid., 45.

31. Gardiner, "Overpaid, Oversexed, and Over Here," 6.

32. Kennett, *American Soldier*, 45.

33. Coates and Morrison, *Alaska Highway*, 7.

34. Yuki Tanaka, *Japan's Comfort Women: Sexual Slavery and Prostitution During World War II and the US Occupation* (London and New York: Routledge, 2002), 89–102.

35. Tanaka, *Japan's Comfort Women*, 98.

36. Gardiner, "Overpaid, Oversexed, and Over Here," 7.

37. Coates and Morrison, *Alaska Highway*, 19.

38. Potts and Potts, *Yanks Down Under*, 402.

39. Ibid., 47.

40. Potts and Potts, *Yanks Down Under*, 303–305.

41. Gardiner, "Overpaid, Oversexed, and Over Here," 8.

42. Ibid., 1.

43. Ibid., 12.

44. Kennett, *American Soldier*, 54.

45. Ibid., 37.

46. Edward N. Peterson, *The American Occupation of Germany: Retreat to Victory* (Detroit: Wayne State University Press, 1978).

47. Tanaka, *Japan's Comfort Women*, 126.

48. Ibid., 116.

49. Ibid., 144–145.

50. Ibid., 163.

51. Intelligence Report compiled by Investigator Otto Seeler, 6871st District Information Services Control Command (DISCC), September 1945, 2. (National Archives).

CHAPTER 3

1. C. T. Sandars, *America's Overseas Garrisons: The Leasehold Empire* (London and New York: Oxford University Press, 2000), 207.

2. Clifton Daniel, "U.S. Air Force in Britain Swells From Initial Wing to 20,000 Men," *New York Times,* December 6, 1951.

3. Kay Sanders, "Conflict Between the American and Australian Governments over the Introduction of Black American Servicemen into Australia during World War Two," *Australian Journal of Politics and History* 33, No. 2 (1987): 14–15.

4. Edward A. Morrow, "Army Says French Delay New Bases," *New York Times,* September 15, 1951.

5. "French Cite Steps to Cut U.S. Costs," *New York Times,* September 26, 1951.

6. Benjamin Welles, "Airmen Meet Test in European Bases," *New York Times,* July 22, 1952.

7. Edward A. Morrow, "Army Says French Delay New Bases," *New York Times,* September 15, 1951.

8. "Housing for U.S. Army in France," *New York Times,* October 6, 1951.

9. The Associated Press, "U.S. Air Force to Have Bases in French Morocco," *New York Times,* February 6, 1951.

10. "Sultan of Morocco Dissolves Cabinet," *New York Times,* February 25, 1951.

11. B. K. Thorne, "Air Bases Create Casablanca Boom," *New York Times,* October 23, 1951.

12. The United Press, "Africa Bases Found Looted of $2,000,000," *New York Times,* February 23, 1952.

13. "Air Base Job Held 'One Sordid Mess,'" *New York Times,* March 19, 1952.

14. "2 African Bases Ready," *New York Times,* July 14, 1952.

15. Sanders, "Conflict Between the American and Australian Governments."

16. Sandars, *America's Overseas Garrisons,* 70–71.

17. Ibid.

18. Austin Stevens, "U.S. Creates Huge Air Base in Far North of Greenland," *New York Times,* September 19, 1962.

19. Sandars, *America's Overseas Garrisons,* 74.

20. Ibid., 75.

21. James D. Clayton and Anne Sharp Wells, *From Pearl Harbor to V-J Day: The American Armed Forces in World War II* (Chicago: Ivan R. Dee 1995), 23–24.

22. Roland A. Paul, *American Military Commitments Abroad* (New Brunswick, NJ: Rutgers University Press, 1973).

23. "U.S. Air Depot In France," *New York Times,* June 21, 1951.

24. Benjamin Welles, "Airmen Meet Test In European Bases," *New York Times,* July 22, 1952.

25. Benjamin Welles, "Huge U.S. Air Depot Speeded in France," *New York Times,* April 26, 1952.

26. Edward A. Morrow, "U.S. Troops Object to Duty in France," *New York Times,* September 16, 1951.

27. Sanders, "Conflict Between the American and Australian Governments," 240.

28. "British Wonder if 50,000 Fliers of U.S. are Asset or Liability," *New York Times,* June 28, 1952.

29. Benjamin Welles, "Airmen Meet Test In European Bases," *New York Times,* July 22, 1952.

30. "Egypt Asks Removal of Troops from Libya," *New York Times,* January 26, 1952.

CHAPTER 4

1. Nicholas Evan Sarantakes, *The American Occupation of Okinawa and U.S.–Japanese Relations* (College Station: Texas A&M University Press, 2000), 71.

2. John Newhouse, *U.S. Troops in Europe: Issues, Costs, and Choices* (Washington, DC: The Brookings Institution, 1971), 107.

3. Ibid., 108.

4. Hubert Zimmermann, *Money and Security: Troops, Monetary Policy, and West Germany's Relations with the United States and Britain, 1950–1951* (Washington, DC: German Historical Institute and Cambridge University Press, 2002).

5. Daniel Nelson, *A History of U.S. Military Forces in Germany* (Boulder, CO: Westview, 1987), 76.

6. Nelson, *Military Forces,* 77.

7. C. T. Sandars, *America's Overseas Garrisons: The Leasehold Empire* (London and New York: Oxford University Press, 2000), 12.

8. Ibid., 13.

9. "Moroccan Strike at U.S. Bases Ends: Four-Day Halt of Workers Concluded on an Accord for New Pay Scale," *New York Times,* April 13, 1956.

10. Thomas F. Brady, "Morocco Dispute Affects U.S. Bases: Naval Unit Sharing Facilities with French Is Involved in Drive to Bar Arms Cargo," *New York Times,* December 17, 1956.

11. "Moroccan Seeks U.S. Bases Accord: Premier Hopes Trip Here Will Produce Solution of Troop Evacuation," *New York Times,* October 11, 1959.

12. "Moroccans See Gain on U.S. Bases Issue," *New York Times,* November 2, 1959.

13. "Libya Wants More Aid: It Is Held Price for Continued U.S. Operation of Air Base," *New York Times,* February 19, 1959.

14. "Dependents Aided," *New York Times,* March 7, 1968.

15. "U.S. Says it Began to Close Wheelus Base, as Libya Asked," *New York Times,* December 17, 1969.

16. Thomas F. Brady, "U.S. Gives Libya a Broader Role at Wheelus Base," *New York Times,* September 26, 1969.

17. "Libya Asks U.S. to Quit Base," *New York Times,* October 31, 1969.

18. John L. Hess, "Libya Soon Gets Wheelus, Including Bowling Alleys," *New York Times,* June 8, 1970.

19. Raymond H. Anderson, "New Libyan Regime's Goals Still Unclear," *New York Times,* April 11, 1970.

20. Raymond H. Anderson, "Arab Leaders in Libya Hail Departure of U.S.," *New York Times,* June 21, 1970.

21. Carl H. Amme Jr., *NATO Without France: A Strategic Appraisal* (Stanford, CA: The Hoover Institution on War, Revolution, and Peace, 1967), 31.

22. Ibid., 33.

23. Ibid., 35.

24. Robert Trumbull, "Anti-U.S. Marches Staged in Japan: Demonstrations Follow Fall of Jet on Campus," *New York Times,* June 8, 1968.

25. "5-Day Strike by Okinawans Ends at U.S. Military Bases," *New York Times,* January 24, 1970.

26. "8,000 at Rallies in Japan Protest Against U.S. Bases," *New York Times,* June 1, 1970.

27. William Beecher, "Joint Control Plan Reported for U.S. Bases in Japan," *New York Times,* August 5, 1970.

28. Robert Trumbull, "Tokyo Upset by Report U.S. Might Remove Bases," *New York Times,* August 10, 1970.

29. Richard Halloran, "U.S. Will Consolidate its Bases in Japan," *New York Times,* January 24, 1975.

30. "Crimes by Marines on Okinawa Prompt Outcry," *New York Times,* March 20, 1983.

31. Sadi Kocas in editorial in *Ankara Daily News,* October 19, 1966, cited in Charlotte Wolf, *Garrison Community: A Study of an Overseas American Military Community* (Westport, CT: Greenwood Pub. Corp. 1969), 40.

32. Ibid., 144.

33. Ibid., 202.

34. Ibid., 196.

35. William L. Hauser, *America's Army in Crisis: A Study in Civil–Military Relations* (Baltimore and London: The Johns Hopkins University Press, 1973), 145.

36. David Cortright, *Soldiers in Revolt: The American Military Today* (Garden City, NY: Anchor Press/Doubleday, 1975), 222–223.

37. Ibid., 127–128.

38. Ibid., 102.

39. Ibid., 93.

CHAPTER 5

1. Larry Ingraham, *The Boys in the Barracks: Observations on Military Life* (Philadelphia: Institute for the Study of Human Issues, 1984).

2. Signe Seiler, *Die GIs: Amerikanische Soldaten in Deutschland* (Reinbek bei Hamburg: Rowohlt, 1985).

3. Martin Binkin, *America's Volunteer Military: Progress and Prospects* (Washington, DC: The Brookings Institution, 1984), 4.

4. Binkins, *America's Volunteer Military*, 10.

5. Ibid., 8.

6. Ibid., 14.

7. Daniel Nelson, *A History of U.S. Military Forces in Germany* (Boulder, CO: Westview, 1987), 220.

8. Hans-Henrik Holm and Nikolaj Petersen, *The European Missiles Crisis: Nuclear Weapons and Security Policy* (New York: St. Martin's Press, 1983), 10.

9. Ibid.

10. Leon V. Sigel, *Nuclear Forces in Europe: Enduring Dilemmas, Present Prospects* (Washington, DC: The Brookings Institution, 1984), 72.

11. John Vinocur, "American-Owned Cars Set Afire in West Germany," *New York Times*, September 2, 1981.

12. Alice H. Cooper, *Paradoxes of Peace: German Peace Movements since 1945* (Ann Arbor: University of Michigan Press, 1996), 106.

13. Ibid., 108.

14. Ibid., 113.

15. James M. Markham, "Quiet Protest at U.S. Base in Germany," *New York Times*, September 2, 1983.

16. James M. Markham, "Germany's Anti-Missile Movement has Lost Its Thrust," *New York Times*, March 11, 1984.

17. "Activists in Britain, W. Germany Protest Against Nuclear Missiles," *Los Angeles Times*, April 6, 1985.

18. Anna Tobforde, "Bavarian Police Hold Easter Anti-Nuclear Demonstrators/ Anti-Nuclear Protests in West Germany," *Guardian* (London), March 31, 1986.

19. Elizabeth Pond, "German Peace Movement Sagging," *Christian Science Monitor*, April 1, 1986.

20. James M. Markham, "West German Foes of Missiles See Victory Near," *New York Times*, April 21, 1987.

21. Anna Tobforde, "Bavarian Police Hold Easter Anti-Nuclear Demonstrators/ Anti-Nuclear Protests in West Germany," *Guardian* (London), March 3, 1986.

22. "Bombs Hit U.S. Bases in West Germany," *New York Times*, June 2, 1982.

23. "US–Soldaten: "Was sollen wir noch her?"" *Wiesbadener Tagblatt,* December 23, 1982.

24. "Red Army Faction Said to Target U.S. Bases," *Washington Post,* July 12, 1984.

25. John Tagliabue, "Car Bomb Kills 2 on a U.S. Air Base in West Germany," *New York Times,* August 9, 1985.

26. Hans Josef Horchem, *Die Verlorene Revolution: Terrorismus in Deutschland* (Herford: Busse Seewald, 1988), 150.

27. John Vinocur, "Qaddafi Urges Europeans to Try to Shut U.S. Bases," *New York Times,* July 27, 1982.

28. Michael Getler, "New Life Style in Britain: Pound's Drop Benefits GIs," *Washington Post,* August 15, 1984.

CHAPTER 6

1. Denison Kitchel, *The Truth About the Panama Canal* (New Rochelle, NY: Arlington House Publishers, 1978), 134.

2. G. Harvey Summ and Tom Kelly, eds., *The Good Neighbors: America, Panama, and the 1977 Canal Treaty* (Ohio University Center for International Studies, Latin American Studies Program, Monographs in International Studies, Latin American Series Number 14, Athens, OH, 1988), 60.

3. Walter LaFeber, *The Panama Canal: The Crisis in Historical Perspective,* updated edition (NY: Oxford University Press, 1989), xi.

4. "Canal Opened 1914, Brought Dream of Pacific Link to Reality," *New York Times,* January 10, 1964.

5. Alexander Burnham, "Seekers of California Gold First Steered Idea of a Panama Canal," *New York Times,* January 11, 1964.

6. Michael L. Conniff, *Panama and the United States: The Forced Alliance* (Athens and London: The University of Georgia Press, 1992), 72.

7. John Major, *Prize Possession: The United States and the Panama Canal, 1903–1979* (Cambridge: University of Cambridge Press, 1993), 78.

8. Ibid., 81.

9. "U.S. Accused of Bias in Canal Zone Jobs," *New York Times,* June 8, 1954.

10. Major, *Prize Possession,* 102.

11. Ibid., 156.

12. Ibid., 141.

13. Ibid., 188.

14. Conniff, *Forced Alliance,* 100.

15. LeFeber, *The Panama Canal,* 83.

16. Henry Giniger, "Residents of Canal Zone Fear Effects of U.S.–Panama Pact," *New York Times,* July 16, 1967.

17. Conniff, *Forced Alliance,* 111.

18. Theodore C. Sorensen, "About That Piece of the Good Old U.S. of A. in Panama," *New York Times,* May 16, 1975.

19. "Canal Called Not Vital to Navy, But Zone is a U.S. Military Hub," *New York Times,* January 11, 1964.

20. Paul P. Kennedy, "Panama's Anger at U.S. Mounting," *New York Times*, April 10, 1954.

21. Conniff, *Forced Alliance*, 104.

22. Paul P. Kennedy, "Panama's Anger at U.S. Mounting," *New York Times*, April 10, 1954.

23. Paul P. Kennedy, "Canal Zone Plans Shift of Workers," *New York Times*, April 12, 1954.

24. "Job Differences Persist in Zone Despite U.S. Equal-Pay Policy," *New York Times*, January 12, 1964.

25. Conniff, *Forced Alliance*, 109.

26. "Canal Zone Claimed," *New York Times*, May 3, 1958.

27. Conniff, *Forced Alliance*, 111.

28. Paul P. Kennedy, "36 Are Reported Injured," *New York Times*, November 4, 1959.

29. Paul P. Kennedy, "30 Hurt in Panama in Rioters' Attempt to Enter U.S. Zone," *New York Times*, November 30, 1959.

30. Conniff, *Forced Alliance*, 112.

31. "Gunfire Flares: Relations Severed Till Pacts are Altered Chiari Asserts," *New York Times*, January 11, 1964.

32. "Job Differences at Issue," *New York Times*, January 12, 1964.

33. "6 Reported Dead: O.A.S. Inquiry Asked on Student Clashes in 2-Flag Dispute," *New York Times*, January 10, 1964.

34. Richard Eder, "Violence a Shock to Panama; Radio Continues Attacks on U.S.," *New York Times*, January 13, 1964.

35. "Capital Stunned by Panama Break," *New York Times*, January 10, 1964.

36. Richard Eder, "Violence a Shock to Panama; Radio Continues Attacks on U.S.," *New York Times*, January 13, 1964.

37. Capital Stunned by Panama Break," *New York Times*, January 10, 1964.

38. Richard Eder, "Violence a Shock to Panama; Radio Continues Attacks on U.S.," *New York Times*, January 13, 1964.

39. "U.S. General Lauds Canal Zone Police For Repelling Mob," *New York Times*, January 12, 1964.

40. "U.S. Toll in Rioting 4 Dead, 85 Wounded," *New York Times*, January 12, 1964.

41. "U.S. General Lauds Canal Zone Police for Repelling Mob," *New York Times*, January 12, 1964.

42. "Text of U.S. Statement on Troops," *New York Times*, January 13, 1964.

43. "Canal Grievance Viewed as Screen," *New York Times*, January 12, 1964.

44. "Panama's Leader Warns on Canal," *New York Times*, October 12, 1971.

45. Kitchel, *The Truth about the Panama Canal*, 128.

46. Henry Giniger, "Residents of Canal Zone Fear Effects of U.S.–Panama Pact," *New York Times*, July 16, 1967.

47. Ibid.

48. Richard Severo, "Canal Zone Is in an Identity Crisis as U.S. and Panama Haggle," *New York Times*, November 23, 1973.

49. "Panama's Leader Warns on Canal," *New York Times*, October 12, 1971.

50. Kitchel, *The Truth about the Panama Canal*, 87.

51. Summ and Kelly, *The Good Neighbors*, 80.

52. "5 G.I.s Hurt in Racial Clash at Fort Davis in Canal Zone," *New York Times*, May 30, 1974.

53. LeFeber, *Panama Canal*, 169.

54. Ibid.

55. Conniff, *Forced Alliance*, 132.

56. Ibid., 143.

57. Ibid., 149–150.

58. Ibid., 152–153.

CHAPTER 7

1. Bob Drogin, "Filipinos Love the U.S. but Hate the Bases," *Los Angeles Times*, September 25, 1990.

2. Ibid.

3. Brian McAllister Linn, *Guardians of Empire: The U.S. Army and the Pacific, 1902–1940* (Chapel Hill and London: The University of North Carolina Press, 1997).

4. Harry A. Gailey, *The War in the Pacific: From Pearl Harbor to Tokyo Bay* (Novato, CA: Presidio, 1995), 114.

5. Ibid., 122.

6. H. W. Brands, *Bound to Empire: The United States and the Philippines* (New York and Oxford: Oxford University Press, 1992), 209.

7. Ibid., 222.

8. William E. Berry, Jr., *U.S. Bases in the Philippines: The Evolution of the Special Relationship* (Boulder, CO: Westview Press, 1989), 17.

9. Ibid., 25.

10. Brands, *Bound to Empire*, 271.

11. Berry, *U.S. Bases in the Philippines*, 56.

12. Ibid., 36.

13. Ibid., 96.

14. Ibid., 110.

15. Brands, *Bound to Empire*, 284.

16. Berry, *U.S. Bases in the Philippines*, 104.

17. Ibid., 237.

18. Mark Tran, "High Cost of Quitting Philippines Bases," *Guardian* (London), March 4, 1986.

19. Ibid.

20. Robert Pear, "The U.S. Stake in the Philippines," *New York Times*, December 17, 1989.

21. William Branigin, "Sex-Market Image Stings Philippines; Reports of Child Exploitation, Cabinet Misconduct, Prostitution Cause Concern," *Washington Post*, December 18, 1983.

22. "Campaign Aims to Wipe Out the Sexual Exploitation of Third World Children," *Toronto Star*, September 7, 1991.

23. Mark Fineman, "U.S. Bases, Politics Involved; Philippines Face Difficult Obstacles in AIDS Fight," *Los Angeles Times*, March 30, 1987.

24. Ibid.

25. Terry McCarthy, "The Perils of Peacetime in Thailand's 'Sodom by Sea,'" *Independent* (London), March 25, 1991.

26. Mark Fineman, "Identity Doubts Linger; Americans at Home in Philippines," *Los Angeles Times,* March 31, 1988.

27. Richard Gott, "Third World Review Column: Shots in the Sex War/Problems of Tourism and the Sex Trade in the Philippines," *Guardian* (London), March 22, 1985.

28. "Anti-Bases Rally in Manila," *Washington Post,* October 27, 1983.

29. Pat Holt, "What Price US Military Bases?" *Christian Science Monitor,* October 3, 1984.

30. Steven Butler, "Philippines Debates Future of US Bases," *Financial Times* (London), September 16, 1986.

31. Seth Mydans, "More Debate on Bases Seems Likely in Manila," *New York Times,* September 21, 1986.

32. Keith B. Richburg, "United States, Philippines to Open Talk on Bases," *Washington Post,* April 5, 1988.

33. Keith B. Richburg, "Anti-American Sentiment Flares Up in Southeast Asia," *Washington Post,* June 25, 1988.

34. "5,000 in Manila Demand U.S. Bases be Removed," *Los Angeles Times,* July 5, 1986.

35. "Shut Down U.S. Bases Philippine Rebels Urge," *Toronto Star,* December 24, 1986.

36. Gerald Utting, "Manila Pays Social Price for U.S. Bases," *Toronto Star,* September 27, 1987.

37. Clayton Jones, "Killings of Americans Follow Signs of Cooling US-Filipino Ties," *Christian Science Monitor,* October 29, 1987.

38. Mark Fineman, "U.S. Sergeant Slain Near Philippine Air Base," *Los Angeles Times,* July 26, 1988.

39. Keith B. Richburg, "United States, Philippines to Open Talk on Bases," *Washington Post,* April 5, 1988.

40. Richard Gourlay, "Philippine Opposition Attacks Bases Deal 'Sell-Out,'" *Financial Times* (London), October 19, 1998.

41. "Philippine Anti-Base Rally Foiled by Backers, Troops," *Los Angeles Times,* January 21, 1989.

42. "Philippine Mob Stones Irish Priest," *Toronto Star,* November 10, 1989.

43. "Death Spurs Warning to GIs, Kin in Manila," *St. Louis Post-Dispatch,* April 22, 1989.

44. Bob Drogin, "Fear Stalks U.S. Bases in Philippines After Killings," *Los Angeles Times,* September 28, 1989.

45. Bob Drogin and David Lauter, "Filipinos Kill 2 Americans as Quayle Arrives," *Los Angeles Times,* September 27, 1989.

46. Steven Erlanger, "Sailors Can't Paint the Town, So Sin Trade Pales," *New York Times,* July 6, 1990.

47. "Yankee Go Home? Snub of Cheney Raises Questions on U.S. Bases, Aquino's Presidency," *St. Louis Post-Dispatch,* February 25, 1990.

48. "Scores Hurt During March on U.S. Base in Philippines," *Toronto Star,* May 2, 1990.

49. Keith B. Richburg, "Rebels Press Threat Against Americans; Philippines Sets Deadline on U.S. Bases," *Washington Post,* May 16, 1990.

50. "Talks Open on U.S. Bases in Philippines; Military; Violent Protests Mark the Opening of Negotiations a Day After Guerrillas Killed Two U.S. Servicemen," *Los Angeles Times*, May 14, 1990.

51. Keith B. Richburg, "Philippines Rebels Threaten Americans; Talks on U.S. Bases Begin as Communists Vow to Stage New Attacks," *Washington Post*, May 15, 1990.

52. Keith B. Richburg, "Talks on Philippine Base Turn Rancorous; Manila Demands Payment of Past Aid Promises; U.S. Airs Security Complaints," *Washington Post*, May 17, 1990.

53. Steven Erlanger, "Where American Might is a Bit High and Mighty," *New York Times*, August 4, 1990.

54. Keith B. Richburg, "Talks on Philippine Base Turn Rancorous; Manila Demands Payment of Past Aid Promises; U.S. Airs Security Complaints," *Washington Post*, May 17, 1990.

55. Steven Erlanger, "Where American Might is a Bit High and Mighty," *New York Times*, August 4, 1990.

56. Steven Erlanger, "Sailors Can't Paint the Town, So Sin Trade Pales," *New York Times*, July 6, 1990.

57. Keith B. Richburg, "U.S. to Start Phasing Out Military Bases in Philippines," *Washington Post*, September 14, 1990.

58. Bob Drogin, "Aquino Calls for Orderly Pullout of U.S. Forces," *Los Angeles Times*, September 18, 1990.

59. Keith B. Richburg, "U.S. to Start Phasing Out Military Bases in Philippines," *Washington Post*, September 14, 1990.

60. Bob Drogin, "Filipinos Love the U.S. but Hate the Bases," *Los Angeles Times*, September 25, 1990.

61. "GI Travel Curbed as U.S.–Philippine Base Talks Near," *Los Angeles Times*, November 3, 1990.

62. 102d Congress. 1st Session, House of Representatives, *Report of the Delegation Visit to Hawaii, Kwajalein, Guam, and Alaska, June 29–July 7, 1991*, Military Installations and Facilities Subcommittee of the CASHR (Committee on Armed Services House of Representatives) and the Select Committee on Children, Youth and Families, July 1991.

63. Bob Drogin, "Wide Differences Remain on Philippine Bases; Diplomacy: U.S. Negotiator Says He Has a New Package, But the Other Side Begs to Differ," *Los Angeles Times*, April 30, 1990.

64. Bob Drogin, "Volcano Forces 15,000 to Flee Clark Air Base; Philippines: Americans are Evacuated to Subic Bay Naval Base as Eruption Throws Out Ashes and Debris," *Los Angeles Times*, June 19, 1991.

65. William Branigin, "Volcano Blows Ash 98,000 Feet Into Sky; Opponents of U.S. Bases in Philippines Take Up Allegations of Threat of Nuclear Blast," *Washington Post*, June 15, 1991.

66. William Branigin, "Experts Say Volcano May Blow Apart; Residents Flee Towns in Philippines; Last Troops Quit U.S. Base," *Washington Post*, June 16, 1991.

67. Don Oberdorfer, "U.S. Base Rejected in Philippines; Cheney Says Subic Bay Facility Will be Closed if Decision Stands," *Washington Post*, September 10, 1991.

68. "Philippines Moving to Bar U.S. Bases," *New York Times*, September 12, 1991.

69. Philip Shenon, "How Subic Bay Became a Rallying Cry for Philippine Nationalism," *New York Times*, September 15, 1991.

70. "Subic Bay-American Bases in Philippines Don't Assure Economic Nirvana," *Seattle Times*, September 27, 1991.

71. Bob Drogin, "Americans Bid Farewell to Last Philippine Base," *Los Angeles Times*, November 25, 1992.

72. Pradnya Joshi, "Subic Bay May Serve as Model for Closed Bases; Defense Conversion: The Philippines Inherited the Giant U.S. Navy Facility and is Creating a Free Port to Attract Business," *Los Angeles Times*, July 26, 1993.

73. Ibid.

74. Luz Baguioro, "U.S., Philippines Discuss Toxic Waste Clean-Up," *Straits Times* (Singapore), April 15, 2000.

75. David Armstrong, "Toxic Impact Spreads Far: Pollution at U.S. Bases Worldwide," *The Boston Globe*, November 15, 1999.

CHAPTER 8

1. Antonia Levi, "Thousand-Year Rape of an Entire People," *Seattle Times*, November 9, 1995.

2. Christopher McCooey, "Travel: Fired up by Past Passions," *Financial Times* (London), July 22, 2000.

3. Kiyotaka Shibasaki, "Politics not Driving Force Behind Okinawa Outcry," *Daily Yomiuri* (Tokyo), May 12, 1997.

4. "U.S. Offers to End Lump Sum Payment and Give Rent for Ryukyu Base Land," *New York Times*, January 31, 1958.

5. Robert Trumbull, "Tokyo Sees Easing in Need for Bases," *New York Times*, June 6, 1968.

6. Fred Greene, *Stresses in U.S.–Japanese Security Relations* (Washington, DC: The Brookings Institution, 1975), 49.

7. "Crash of a B-52 in Okinawa Stirs New Outcry on Bases," *New York Times*, November 20, 1968.

8. Takashi Oka, "Presence of B-52's Stirs Okinawan Resentment," *New York Times*, February 10, 1969.

9. Takashi Oka, "Sato Stresses Need for U.S. Bases in Okinawa Issue," *New York Times*, June 20, 1969.

10. "Okinawans Need to Understand," *Straits Times* (Singapore), April 7, 1997 and Valerie Reitman, "Okinawa Has a Love–Hate Relationship with U.S.; Asia: Military Bases on the Island Bring Jobs and Revenue, the Trade-off, Residents Say, is Crime," *Los Angeles Times*, July 19, 2000.

11. Christopher McCooey, "Fired up by Past Passions," *Financial Times* (London), July 22, 2000.

12. Howard W. French, "Despite China, Okinawans Tire of U.S. Military," *New York Times*, April 17, 2001.

13. "19 Reported Injured as Okinawan Workers Strike Against U.S. Bases," *New York Times*, January 20, 1970.

14. "Clinton Talks with Japan's Premier," *Baltimore Sun*, February 24, 1996.

15. Tadashi Toriyama, "U.S. Bases Have Impact on Fate of Okinawans," *Daily Yomiuri* (Tokyo), August 11, 2001.

16. Toyoharu Ikeda, "Okinawa Celebrates 20th Anniversary: Tourism and U.S. Military Presence Set Course for Islands' Future," *Daily Yomiuri* (Tokyo), May 9, 1992.

17. "Clinton Talks with Japan's Premier; U.S. Bases on Okinawa are Their Principal Topic," *Baltimore Sun*, February 24, 1996.

18. Teresa Watanabe, "Rape Suspect's Lawyer Gives Dark Account; Japan: Attorney of Accused Marine Says Co-defendant Admitted Assaulting 12-Year-Old Girl 'Just for Fun,'" *Los Angeles Times*, October 28, 1995.

19. Mary Jordan, "Japan to Seek Cutbacks in U.S. Military Bases; Tokyo Responds to Furor Over Okinawa Rape," *Washington Post*, October 20, 1995.

20. Mary Jordan, "U.S. Army Receives Threats After Rape; A Vicious Attack on a 12-Year-Old has Outraged Okinawa," *Guardian* (London), September 21, 1995.

21. Sam Jameson, "Huge Rally in Okinawa Denounces U.S. Bases," *Los Angeles Times*, October 22, 1995.

22. Mary Jordan, "Japan to Seek Cutbacks in U.S. Military Bases; Tokyo Responds to Furor Over Okinawa Rape," *Washington Post*, October 20, 1995.

23. Andrew Pollack, "3 U.S. Servicemen Convicted of Rape of Okinawa Girl," *New York Times*, March 7, 1996.

24. Sheryl WuDunn, "Rage Grows in Okinawa Over U.S. Military Bases," *New York Times*, November 4, 1995.

25. "Clinton Talks with Japan's Premier; U.S. Bases on Okinawa are Their Principal Topic," *Baltimore Sun*, February 24, 1996.

26. Teresa Watanabe, "3 U.S. Servicemen Found Guilty in Okinawa Rape; Japan: Defendants Sentenced to 7 and 6 1/2 Years, Case Has Fueled Opposition to American Military Presence," *Los Angeles Times*, March 7, 1996.

27. Kiyotaka Shibasaki, "Okinawa at Crossroads; Okinawa Makes Plans to Survive Without Bases," *Daily Yomiuri* (Tokyo), April 8, 1996.

28. Teresa Watanabe, "U.S., Japan Plan Return of Land to Okinawans; Asia: About 20% of Area Used by American Troops will Revert to Owners," *Los Angeles Times*, April 15, 1996.

29. Kevin Rafferty, "Raped Girl, 'Now Fears Foreigner,'" *Guardian* (London), November 8, 1995.

30. Saki Ouchi, "Okinawa at a Crossroads; Okinawans Who Benefit from Bases Anxious," *Daily Yomiuri* (Tokyo), April 7, 1996.

31. Mary Jordan and Kevin Sullivan, "3 Americans Guilty in Okinawan Rape; Jail Terms Imposed in Case that Sparked Debate on Troop Presence," *Washington Post*, March 7, 1996.

32. "Sentences Outrage Okinawa Residents," *Daily Yomiuri* (Tokyo), March 8, 1996.

33. Jingle Davis and Pete Scott, "Families: God Will Take Care of Convicted Servicemen; Lawyer Plans Appeal in Rape Trial He Calls Mishandled from Start," *Atlanta Journal and Constitution*, March 8, 1996.

34. Saki Ouchi, "Okinawa at a Crossroads; Okinawans Who Benefit from Bases Anxious," *Daily Yomiuri* (Tokyo), April 7, 1996.

35. Chalmers Johnson, ed. *Okinawa: Cold War Island* (Cardiff, CA: Japan Policy Research Institute, 1999), 205.

36. "Clinton Talks with Japan's Premier; U.S. Bases on Okinawa are Their Principal Topic," *Baltimore Sun*, February 24, 1996.

37. Teresa Watanabe, "U.S., Japan Plan Return of Land to Okinawans; Asia; About 20% of Area Used by American Troops Will Revert to Owners," *Los Angeles Times,* April 15, 1996.

38. Sheryl WuDunn, "A Pacifist Landlord Makes War on Okinawa Bases," *New York Times,* November 11, 1995.

39. Kevin Sullivan, "Okinawan Landlords Resist U.S.; Lease Renewal Issue Dogs American Bases," *Washington Post,* March 26, 1996.

40. Ibid.

41. "Japan; Thousands Protest U.S. Bases, Lease Plan," *Los Angeles Times,* April 1, 1996.

42. Saki Ouchi, "Okinawa at a Crossroads; Okinawans Who Benefit from Bases Anxious," *Daily Yomiuri* (Tokyo), April 7, 1996.

43. Teresa Watanabe, "U.S., Japan Plan Return of Land to Okinawans; Asia; About 20% of Area Used by American Troops Will Revert to Owners," *Los Angeles Times,* April 15, 1996.

44. Nicholas Kristoff, "Okinawan Landlords Seek to Evict U.S. Military Bases," *New York Times,* May 15, 1996.

45. Sonni Efron, "Governor Calls Okinawa Tokyo's Beast of Burden; Japan: Crime, Noise, Limited Economic Opportunity are Price Paid by Island for Nation's Security, Local Leader Says," *Los Angeles Times,* September 5, 1996.

46. Ibid.

47. Kiyotaka Shibasaki, "Politics not Driving Force Behind Okinawa Outcry," *Daily Yomiuri* (Tokyo), May 12, 1997.

48. "Okinawans Vote 10–1 For Reduced U.S. Bases," *Newsday,* September 9, 1996.

49. Teresa Watanabe, "Okinawan Leader Abandons Fight; Japan: Governor Ends Effort to Block Renewal of Leases for U.S. Bases. Decision is Met with Praise, Disappointment," *Los Angeles Times,* September 14, 1996.

50. Teresa Watanabe, "Sprucing up Marines' Image in Japan; Asia: Citizens Program Debunks Stereotypes About U.S. Military Personnel Based in Okinawa," *Los Angeles Times,* December 8, 1996.

51. Teresa Watanabe, "Okinawan Leader Abandons Fight; Japan: Governor Ends Effort to Block Renewal of Leases for U.S. Bases. Decision is Met with Praise, Disappointment," *Los Angeles Times,* September 14, 1996.

52. Gaku Shibata, "Countdown to the Showdown on Okinawa Bases Problem," *Daily Yomiuri* (Tokyo), February 19, 1997.

53. Teresa Watanabe, "U.S., Japan Ok Deal to Return Okinawa Land," *Los Angeles Times,* December 2, 1996.

54. Jonathan Watts, "No More Military Bases in Our Backyard," *Daily Yomiuri* (Tokyo), May 13, 1997.

55. K. Connie Kang, "Okinawans Bring Drive to L.A.; Military Delegation of Women Demands Closure or Reduction of U.S. Bases on the Island, Saying Their Presence Harms the Culture and People," *Los Angeles Times,* October 7, 1998.

56. Mike Millard, *Leaving Japan: Observations on the Dysfunctional U.S.–Japan Relationship* (Armonk, NY: M.E. Sharpe, 2001), 181.

57. Takehiko Nomura, "Okinawans Rev up Against U.S. Base," *Christian Science Monitor,* October 7, 1999.

58. Calvin Sims, "Enmity Eases Among Hot Dogs and War Machines," *New York Times*, July 5, 1999.

59. Doug Struck, "U.S. Apologizes for Incident in Okinawa; Curfew Imposed on Military in Advance of G-8 Summit," *Washington Post*, July 11, 2000.

60. Valerie Reitman, "Okinawa has a Love-Hate Relationship With the U.S.; Asia: Military Bases on the Island Bring Jobs and Revenue," *Los Angeles Times*, July 19, 2000.

61. "Japanese Protestors to Confront Clinton; Okinawans use G-8 Summit as Stage to Denounce Presence of U.S. Military Bases, Troops," *Atlanta Journal and Constitution*, July 20, 2000.

62. "Pro-U.S. Base Residents in Okinawa Top Foes," *Daily Yomiuri* (Tokyo), May 20, 2001.

63. Mark Magnier, "Airman Arrested in Okinawa After U.S. Hand-Over; Japan: The Rare Transfer Before Indictment of the Rape Suspect Came after Tokyo Gave its Word that He Would be Treated Fairly," *Los Angles Times*, July 7, 2001.

64. Alexandra Harney, "'How Can We Live if the Troops Go Home?' Tempers Flare When U.S. Soldiers Based on Okinawa Commit Crime," *Financial Times* (London), August 11, 2001.

CHAPTER 9

1. Charles M. Dobbs, *The Unwanted Symbol: American Foreign Policy, the Cold War, and Korea, 1945–1950* (Kent, OH: The Kent State University Press, 1981), 44.

2. Ibid., 72.

3. Kim Jung-Ik, *The Future of the U.S.–Republic of Korea Military Relationship* (New York: St. Martin's Press, Inc., 1996), 9.

4. Susan Chira, "In Heart of Seoul, An Unwanted U.S. Presence," *New York Times*, August 14, 1988.

5. Rita Nakashima Brock, "Japanese Didn't Invent Military Sex Industry," *The New York Times*, February 23, 1992.

6. Bruce Cumings, "Silent but Deadly: Sexual Subordination in the U.S.–Korean Relationship," in Saundra Pollock Sturdevant and Brenda Stoltzfus, *Let the Good Times Roll: Prostitution and the U.S. Military in Asia* (New York: The New Press, 1992), 170.

7. Ibid.

8. Katharine H.S. Moon, *Sex Among Allies: Military Prostitution in U.S.–Korea Relations* (New York: Columbia University Press, 1997).

9. Ibid., 59.

10. Ibid., 68.

11. Ibid., 78.

12. Ibid., 92.

13. Cumings, "Silent but Deadly," 178.

14. Moon, *Sex Among Allies*, 73.

15. Ibid., 81.

16. Ibid., 120.

17. Susan Chira, "In Heart of Seoul, An Unwanted U.S. Presence," *New York Times*, August 14, 1988.

18. Peter Goodspeed, "U.S. Soldier's Case Enrages Koreans," *The Toronto Star*, November 15, 1992.

19. Leslie Helm, "Seoul Students Stage Anti-U.S. Protest: Police Clash with Marchers Chanting, "Yankee Go Home." But Both Sides Seem Restrained," *Los Angeles Times*, May 23, 1993.

20. Nicholas D. Kristof, "Subway Brawl Inflames Issue of G.I.s in Korea," *The New York Times*, April 24, 1995.

21. "U.S. Has Variety of Status of Forces Accords," *Yomiuri Shimbun* (Tokyo) October 3, 1995.

22. Kevin Sullivan, "Seoul's Black-Market Bonanza; Duty-Free Goods from U.S. Bases Provide Huge Profits for Those with Connections," *Washington Post*, November 17, 1997.

CHAPTER 10

1. Rosalind Miles, "Our Man in Oman: The Surprising Sultan—Feminist, Democrat, and Steadfast U.S. Ally," *Washington Post*, November 19, 1995.

2. Jo Mannies and Theresa Tighe, "Senators Expect Permanent Saudi Base," *St. Louis Post-Dispatch*, December 13, 1990.

3. Lionel Barber, "U.S. Close to Setting Up Bahrain Military Base," *Financial Times* (London), March 26, 1991.

4. James LeMoyne, "Confrontation in the Gulf," *New York Times*, October 3, 1990.

5. Philip Shenon, "Troops: Some G.I.s in Gulf Vanquish An Old Foe: Drink or Drugs," *New York Times*, February 18, 1991.

6. Ibid.

7. Kathleen Evans, "U.S. Says Gulf Troops Will Relax Aboard Cruise Ships—But Stay Close at Hand," *Christian Science Monitor*, December 13, 1990.

8. Philip Shenon, "Servicewomen: At Combat's Doorstep, She Confronts Peril and Male Doubt," *New York Times*, February 24, 1991.

9. Paul Richter, "U.S. Women Bear Brunt of Saudi Culture Clash," *Los Angeles Times*, June 28, 1996.

10. Cameron W. Barr, "Gulf Legacy: U.S. Quietly Guards Oil," *Christian Science Monitor*, February 27, 2001.

11. John Lancaster, "Bombing Increases U.S. Troops' Sense of Isolation in Saudi Arabia," *Washington Post*, June 29, 1996.

12. John Daniszewski, "The Attack in Saudi Arabia: In Tightly Controlled Kingdom, Level of Discontent Hard to Gauge," *Los Angeles Times*, June 27, 1996.

13. Ruth Fremson, "Mortar New Threat in Saudi Arabia; U.S. Troops Moved, Families to Leave," *Chicago Sun-Times*, August 4, 1996.

14. Steven Lee Myers, "American Base in Saudi Arabia Hints of Long Pull; Pentagon Prepares for Protracted Stay," *Arizona Republic*, January 4, 1998.

15. Scott Schonauer, "For Operational Secrecy, There May Be No Better Place than Uzbekistan," *Stars and Stripes*, October 19, 2001.

★ ★ ★ ★ ★

Bibliography

Allen, Henry T. *My Rhineland Journal*. Boston and New York: Houghton Mifflin Company, 1923.

Amme, Carl H., Jr. *NATO Without France: A Strategic Appraisal*. Stanford, CA: The Hoover Institution on War, Revolution, and Peace, 1967.

Anderson, Fred. *A People's Army: Massachusetts Soldiers and Society in the Seven Years' War*. Chapel Hill, NC: The University of North Carolina Press, 1984.

Bach, Julian. *America's Germany: An Account of the Occupation*. New York: Random House, 1946.

Beever, Antony, and Artemis Cooper. *Paris After the Liberation, 1944–1949*. New York: Doubleday, 1994.

Berry, William E. Jr. *U.S. Bases in the Philippines: The Evolution of the Special Relationship*. Boulder, CO: Westview Press, 1989.

Binkin, Martin. *America's Volunteer Military: Progress and Prospects*. Washington, DC: The Brookings Institution, 1984.

Blaker, James. *United States Overseas Basing: An Anatomy of the Dilemma*. London: Praeger, 1990.

Bok, L. S. *The Impact of U.S. Forces in Korea*. Washington, DC: National Defense University Press, 1987.

Boutwell, Jeffrey D., Paul Doty, and Gregory F. Treverton. *The Nuclear Confrontation in Europe*. London & Sydney: Croom Helm, 1985.

Bowman, William, Roger Little, and G. Thomas Sicilia, eds. *The All-Volunteer Force After a Decade: Retrospect and Prospect*. Washington, DC: Pergamon-Brassey's International Defense Publishers, 1986.

Bozo, Frederic. *Two Strategies for Europe: De Gaulle, the United States, and the Atlantic Alliance*. Lanham, MD: Rowman & Littlefield Publishers, Inc., 2001.

Brands, H. W. *Bound to Empire: The United States and the Philippines*. New York and Oxford: Oxford University Press, 1992.

Bresnan, John, ed. *Crisis in the Philippines: The Marcos Era and Beyond*. Princeton, NJ: Princeton University Press, 1986.

Brock, Rita Nakashima and Susan Brooks Thistlethwaite. *Casting Stones: Prostitution and Liberation in Asia and the United States*. Minneapolis, MN: Fortress Press, 1996.

Browder, Dewey. *Americans in Post-World War II Germany: Teachers, Tinkers, Neighbors, Nuisances*. Lewiston, NY: Edwin Mellen Press, 1998.

Brown, James. *Delicately Poised Allies: Greece and Turkey*. London: Brassey's (UK), 1991.

Cardolis, J. *A Friendly Invasion*. Newfoundland: Breakwater, 1990.

Cha, Victor D. *Alignment Despite Antagonism: The United States—Korea—Japan Security Triangle*. Stanford, CA: Stanford University Press, 1999.

Clayton, James D. *The Years of MacArthur* (3 vols.) New York: Macmillan, 1970–1985.

Clayton, James, D., and Anne Sharp Wells. *From Pearl Harbor to V-J Day: The American Armed Forces in World War II*. Chicago: Ivan R. Dee, 1995.

Coates, K. S., and W. R. Morrison. *The Alaska Highway in World War II: The U.S. Army of Occupation in Canada's Northwest*. Norman and London: University of Oklahoma, 1992.

Coffman, Edward M. *The Old Army: A Portrait of the American Army in Peacetime, 1784–1898*. New York and Oxford: Oxford University Press, 1986.

Cohen, Theodore. *Remaking Japan: The American Occupation as New Deal*. New York: The Free Press, 1987.

Colbert, Evelyn. *The United States and the Philippine Bases*. Washington, DC: The Johns Hopkins University Press, 1987.

Cole, Wayne S. *Charles A. Lindbergh and the Battle Against American Intervention in World War II*. New York: Harcourt, Brace, Jovanovich, 1974.

Cole, Wayne S. *Roosevelt and the Isolationists*. Lincoln: University of Nebraska Press, 1983.

Conniff, Michael L. *Panama and the United States: The Forced Alliance*. Athens and London: The University of Georgia Press, 1992.

Cordesman, Anthony H. *U.S. Forces in the Middle East: Resources and Capabilities*. Boulder, CO: Westview Press, 1997.

Cornebise, Alfred E. *The Amaroc News: The Daily Newspaper of the American Forces in Germany, 1919–1923*. Carbondale and Edwardsville: Southern Illinois University Press, 1981.

Cortright, David. *Soldiers in Revolt: The American Military Today*. Garden City, NY: Anchor Press/Doubleday, 1975.

Cottrell, A. and R. J. Hanks. *The Military Utility of U.S. Bases in the Philippines*. Washington, DC: Center for Strategic and International Studies, Georgetown University, 1980.

Cottrell, A. and T. Moorer. *U.S. Overseas Bases: The Problems of Projecting American Military Power Abroad*. Washington Paper No. 47. Beverly Hills, CA: Sage, 1977.

Dastrup, Boyd. *Crusade in Nuremberg: Military Occupation, 1945–1949*. Westport, CT: Greenwood Press, 1985.

Davis, Franklin M. Jr. *Come as Conqueror: The United States Occupation of Germany*. New York: Macmillan, 1967.

Davis, Paul C., and William T. R. Fox, "American Military Representation Abroad," in *The Representation of the United States Abroad*, ed. Vincent M. Barnett, Jr. New York: Frederick A. Praeger, 1965.

Dobbs, Charles M. *The Unwanted Symbol: American Foreign Policy, the Cold War, and Korea, 1945–1950*. Kent, OH: The Kent State University Press, 1981.

Dodd, Joseph. *Criminal Jurisdiction Under the United States–Philippine Military Bases Agreement*. The Hague: Martinus Nijhoff, 1968.

Duke, Simon. *United States Military Forces and Installations in Europe*. Oxford: Oxford University Press, 1989.

Duke, Simon W. and Wolfgang Krieger, eds. *U.S. Military Forces in Europe: The Early Years, 1945–1970*. Boulder: Westview Press, 1993.

Enloe, Cynthia. *Bananas, Beaches, and Bases: Making Feminist Sense of International Politics*. Berkeley: University of California Press, 1989.

Enloe, Cynthia. *Does Khaki Become You? The Militarization of Women's Lives*. London: Pandora, 1983.

Farwell, Byron. *Over There: The United States in the Great War, 1917–1918*. New York: W.W. Norton & Company, 1999.

Foot, Michael R. D. *Men in Uniform*. London: Weidenfeld and Nicholson, 1961.

Fredericksen, Oliver J. *The American Military Occupation of Germany 1945–1949*. Heidelberg: Headquarters, United States Army, Europe, Historical Division, 1953.

Gailey, Harry A. *The War in the Pacific: From Pearl Harbor to Tokyo Bay*. Novato, CA: Presidio, 1995.

Gardiner, Juliet. *"Overpaid, Oversexed, and Over Here:" The American GI in World War II Britain*. New York: Canopy Books. 1992.

Garnham, David. *The Politics of European Defense Cooperation: Germany, France, Britain, and America*. Cambridge, MA: Ballinger Publishing Company, 1988.

Gerson, Joseph and Bruce Birchard, eds. *The Sun Never Sets. . . Confronting the Network of Foreign U.S. Military Bases*. Boston: South End Press, 1991.

Gimbel, John. *A German Community Under Occupation*. Stanford, CA: Stanford University Press, 1961.

Greene, Fred, ed. *The Philippine Bases: Negotiating for the Future*. New York: Council on Foreign Relations, 1988.

Greene, Fred. *Stresses in U.S.–Japanese Security Relations*. Washington, DC: The Brookings Institution, 1975.

Grinter, Lawrence E. *The Philippine Bases*. Washington, DC: The National Defense University Research Directorate, 1980.

Haglund, D. and O. Mager, eds. *Homeward Bound? Allied Forces in the New Germany*. Boulder, CO: Westview, 1992.

Harkavy, Robert. *Great Power Competition for Overseas Bases*. Oxford: Pergamon, 1982.

Harkavy, Robert. *Bases Abroad: The Global Foreign Military Presence*. New York and London: SIPRI, Oxford University Press, 1989.

Harris, G. *Troubled Alliance: Turkish/American Problems in Historical Perspective 1945–1971*. Washington, DC: ACE–Hoover Policy Studies, 1972.

Hauser, William L. *America's Army in Crisis: A Study in Civil–Military Relations*. Baltimore and London: The Johns Hopkins University Press, 1973.

Hillel, Marc. *Vie et moeurs des GI's en Europe 1942–1947*. Paris: Ballard, 1981.

Holm, Hans-Henrik and Nikolaj Petersen. *The European Missiles Crisis: Nuclear Weapons and Security Policy*. New York: St. Martin's Press, 1983.

Horchem, Hans Josef. *Die Verlorene Revolution: Terrorismus in Deutschland*. Herford: Busse Seewald, 1988.

Ingraham, Larry. *The Boys in the Barracks: Observations on Military Life*. Philadelphia: Institute for the Study of Human Issues, 1984.

Johnson, Chalmers, ed. *Okinawa: Cold War Island*. Cardiff, CA: Japan Policy Research Institute, 1999.

Jonsson, A. *Iceland, NATO, and the Keflavik Base*. Reykjavik: Icelandic Commission on Security Affairs, 1989.

Karnow, Stanley. *In Our Image: America's Empire in the Philippines*. New York: Random House, 1989.

Karsten, Peter. *The Naval Aristocracy: The Golden Age of Annapolis and the Emergence of Modern American Navalism*. New York: The Free Press, 1972.

Karsten, Peter, ed. *The Military in America: From the Colonial Era to the Present*, rev. ed. New York: The Free Press, 1986.

Kawai, Kazuo. *Japan's American Interlude*. Chicago, University of Chicago Press, 1960.

Kennett, Lee. *G.I.: The American Soldier in World War II*. Norman: University of Oklahoma Press, 1997.

Kennett, Lee. *For the Duration . . . : The United States Goes to War, Pearl Harbor—1942*. New York: Charles Scribner's Sons, 1985.

Kim Jung-lk. *The Future of the US–Republic of Korea Military Relationship*. New York: St. Martin's Press, Inc., 1996.

Kirchner, E. and J. Sperlin, ed. *The Federal Republic of Germany and the United States*. London: Macmillan, 1992.

Kitchel, Denison. *The Truth About the Panama Canal*. New Rochelle, NY: Arlington House Publishers, 1978.

Koshiro, Yukiko. *Trans-Pacific Racisms and the U.S. Occupation of Japan*. New York: Columbia University Press, 1999.

LaFeber, Walter. *The Panama Canal: The Crisis in Historical Perspective*, updated edition. NY: Oxford University Press, 1989.

Langley, Harold D. *Social Reform in the United States Navy, 1798–1862*. Urbana, IL: University of Illinois Press, 1967.

Lee, Ulysses Grant. *The Employment of Negro Troops: Special Studies, United States Army in World War II*. Washington, D.C.: Office of the Chief of Military History, 1966.

Linn, Brian McAllister. *Guardians of Empire: The U.S. Army and the Pacific, 1902–1940*. Chapel Hill & London: The University of North Carolina Press, 1997.

Logan, John A. *The Volunteer Soldier of America*. Chicago and New York: R. S. Peale & Company, Publishers, 1887.

Long, D. *The United States and Saudi Arabia: Ambivalent Allies*. Boulder, CO: Westview, 1985.

Longmate, Norman. *The G.I.s: The Americans in Britain 1942–1945*. London: Hutchinson, 1975.

Loveday, Douglas F. *The Role of U.S. Military Bases in the Philippine Economy.* Santa Monica: Rand Corporation, 1971.

Lutz, Catherine. *Homefront: A Military City and the American 20th Century.* Boston: Beacon Press, 2001.

MacGregor, Morris J., Jr. *Integration of the Armed Forces 1940–1945.* Washington, DC: Center for Military History, 1981.

Maddox, Robert James. *The United States and World War II.* Boulder: Westview Press, 1992.

Major, John. *Prize Possession: The United States and the Panama Canal, 1903–1979.* Cambridge: University of Cambridge Press, 1993.

Mako, W. *U.S. Ground Forces and the Defense of Central Europe.* Washington, DC: Brookings Institution, 1983.

Marrin, Albert. *The Yanks Are Coming: The United States in the First World War.* New York: Atheneum, 1986.

May, E. *The Federal Republic of Germany and the United States.* Boulder, CO: Westview, 1984.

McCarthy, Dudley. *South–West Pacific Area–First Year.* Canberra: Australian War Memorial, 1959.

McDonald, J. W. and D. Bendahmane, eds. *U.S. Bases Overseas: Negotiations with Spain, Greece, and the Philippines.* Boulder, CO: Westview, 1990.

McGuire, Phillip, ed. *Taps for a Jim Crow Army: Letters from Black Soldiers in World War II.* Lexington: University Press of Kentucky, 1993.

Melendez, E. and E. Melendez, eds. *The Colonial Dilemma.* Boston: South End Press, 1993.

Mendl, Wolf. *Western Europe and Japan: Between the Superpowers.* New York: St. Martin's Press, 1984.

Merritt, Richard L. *Democracy Imposed: U.S. Occupation Policy and the German Public, 1945–1949.* New Haven and London: Yale University Press, 1995.

Mershon, Sherie, and Steven Schlossman. *Foxholes and Color Lines: Desegregating the U.S. Armed Forces.* Baltimore: The Johns Hopkins University Press, 1998.

Millard, Mike. *Leaving Japan: Observations on the Dysfunctional U.S.–Japan Relationship.* Armonk, NY: M. E. Sharpe, 2001.

Miller, David. *The Cold War: A Military History.* New York: St. Martin's Press, 1998.

Miller, Nathan. *The U.S. Navy: A History.* 3rd ed. Annapolis, MD: Naval Institute Press, 1997.

Millett, Allan R. and Peter Maslowski. *For the Common Defense: A Military History of the United States of America,* rev. ed. New York: The Free Press, 1994.

Molasky, Michael S. *The American Occupation of Japan and Okinawa.* London: Routledge, 1999.

Moon, Katharine H. S. *Sex Among Allies: Military Prostitution in U.S.–Korea Relations.* New York: Columbia University Press, 1997.

Moore, John Hammond. *Over-Sexed, Over-Paid, and Over Here: Americans in Australia 1941–1945.* St. Lucia, Queensland, 1981.

Motley, Mary Penich, ed. *The Invisible Soldier: The Experience of the Black Soldier.* Detroit, MI: Wayne State University, 1975.

Nalty, Bernard and Morris J. MacGregor, Jr., eds. *Blacks in the Military: Essential Documents.* Wilmington, DE: Scholarly Resources, Inc., 1981.

Nelson, Daniel. *A History of U.S. Military Forces in Germany*. Boulder, CO: Westview, 1987.

Nelson, Daniel. *Defenders or Intruders?: The Dilemmas of U.S. Forces in Germany*. Boulder, CO: Westview, 1987.

Nelson, Keith L. *Victors Divided: America and the Allies in Germany, 1918–1923*. Berkeley: University of California Press, 1975.

Newhouse, John. *U.S. Troops in Europe: Issues, Costs, and Choices*. Washington, DC: The Brookings Institution, 1971.

Palmer, M. A. *Guardians of the Gulf: A History of America's Expanding Role in the Persian Gulf 1833–1992*. New York: The Free Press, 1992.

Paul, R. *American Military Commitments Abroad*. New Brunswick, NJ: Rutgers University Press, 1973.

Perry, John Curtis. *Beneath the Eagle's Wings: Americans in Occupied Japan*. New York: Book Sales, 1980.

Peterson, Edward N. *The American Occupation of Germany: Retreat to Victory*. Detroit, MI: Wayne State University, 1977.

Petillo, Carol Morris. *Douglas MacArthur: The Philippine Years*. Bloomington: Indiana University Press, 1981.

Potts, E. Daniel, and Annette Potts. *Yanks Down Under 1941–1945: The American Impact on Australia*. Melbourne: Oxford University Press, 1985.

Raymond, Jack, *Power at the Pentagon*. New York: Harper & Row, 1964. Chapter VI, "America's Military Outposts."

Reynolds, David. *Rich Relations: The American Occupation of Britain, 1942–1945*. New York: Random House, 1995.

Rustow, D. A. *Turkey—America's Forgotten Ally*. New York: Council on Foreign Relations, 1987.

Ryan, Paul B. *The Panama Canal Controversy: U.S. Diplomacy and Defense Interests*. Stanford, CA: Hoover Institution Press, 1977.

Sandars, C. T. *America's Overseas Garrisons: The Leasehold Empire*. Oxford: Oxford University Press, 2000.

Sarantakes, Nicholas Evan. *The American Occupation of Okinawa and U.S.–Japanese Relations*. College Station, TX: Texas A&M University Press, 2000.

Schaller, Michael. *The American Occupation of Japan: The Origins of the Cold War in Asia*. New York: Oxford University Press, 1985.

Schirmer, Daniel B. and Stephen Rosskamm Shalom. *The Philippines Reader: A History of Colonialism, Neocolonialism, Dictatorship, and Resistance*. Boston: South End Press, 1987.

Schonberger, Howard B. *Aftermath of War: Americans and the Remaking of Japan, 1945–1952*. Kent, OH: Ohio State University Press, 1989.

Seiler, Signe. *Die GIs: Amerikanische Soldaten in Deutschland*. Reinbek bei Hamburg: Rowohlt, 1985.

Shiels, F. *America, Okinawa, and Japan*. Washington, DC: University Press of America, 1980.

Sigal, Leon V. *Nuclear Forces in Europe: Enduring Dilemmas, Present Prospects*. Washington, DC: The Brookings Institution, 1984.

Smith, Sheila. *Local Voices, National Issues: The Impact of Local Initiative in Japanese Policy-Making*. Ann Arbor: Center for Japanese Studies, the University of Michigan, 2000.

Snee, Joseph M. and Kenneth A. Pye. *Status of Forces Agreements and Criminal Jurisdiction.* New York: Oceana Publications, Inc., 1957.

Snyder, J. C. *Defending the Fringe: NATO, the Mediterranean, and the Persian Gulf.* Boulder, CO: Westview, 1987.

Spector, Ronald. *Eagle Against the Sun: The American War with Japan.* New York: Vintage Books, 1985.

Stallings, Laurence. *The Doughboys: The Story of the AEF, 1917–1918.* New York: Harper & Row, Publishers, 1963.

Stivers, Reuben Elmore. *Privateers and Volunteers: The Men and Women of Our Reserve Naval Forces: 1766 to 1866.* Annapolis, MD: Naval Institute Press, 1975.

Sturdevant, Saundra Pollock and Brenda Stoltzfus. *Let the Good Times Roll: Prostitution and the U.S. Military in Asia.* New York: The New Press, 1992.

Summ, G. Harvey and Tom Kelly, eds. *The Good Neighbors: America, Panama, and the 1977 Canal Treaties.* Athens: Ohio University Center for International Studies, Latin American Studies Program, Monographs in International Studies, Latin American Series No. 14, 1988.

Tanaka, Yuki. *Japan's Comfort Women: Sexual Slavery and Prostitution During World War II and the U.S. Occupation.* London and New York: Routledge, 2002.

Tolley, Kemp. *Yangtze Patrol: The U.S. Navy in China.* Annapolis, MD: Naval Institute Press, 1971 (republished by Blue Jacket Books, 2000).

U.S. Army. *American Military Government of Occupied Germany, 1918–1920.* Report of the Officer in Charge of Civil Affairs, Third Army, and American Forces in Germany. Washington, DC: United States GPO, 1943.

Utley, Jonathan. *Going to War with Japan.* Knoxville: University of Tennessee Press, 1985.

Utley, Robert M. *Frontiersmen in Blue: The United States Army and the Indian, 1848–1865.* New York: The Macmillan Company, 1967.

Utley, Robert M. *Frontier Regulars: The United States Army and the Indian, 1866–1891.* New York: The Macmillan Company, 1973.

Van Staaveren, Jacob. *An American in Japan, 1945–1948: A Civilian View of the Occupation.* Seattle and London: University of Washington Press, 1994.

Weigley, Russell F. *History of the United States Army*, enlarged edition. Bloomington: Indiana University Press, 1967, 1984.

Weller, George. *Bases Overseas: An American Trusteeship in Power.* New York: Harcourt, Brace and Company, 1944.

Whitnah, Donald R., and Edgar L. Erickson. *The American Occupation of Austria: Planning and Early Years.* Westport, CT: Greenwood Press, 1985.

Willoughby, John. *Remaking the Conquering Heroes: The Social and Geopolitical Impact of the Post-War American Occupation of Germany.* New York: Palgrave, 2001.

Wolf, Charlotte. *Garrison Community: A Study of an Overseas American Military Community.* Westport, CT: Greenwood Pub. Corp. 1969.

Wolfe, Robert, ed. *Americans as Proconsuls: United States Military Government in Germany and Japan, 1944–1952.* Carbondale: Southern Illinois Press, 1984.

Woodliffe, J. *The Peacetime Use of Foreign Military Bases.* Dordrecht: Martinus Nijhoff, 1992.

Wynn, Neil A. *The Afro-American and the Second World War.* New York: Holmes and Meier, 1993.

Yarmolinsky, Adam. *The Military Establishment.* New York: Harper and Row, 1971.

Ziemke, Earl F. *The U.S. Army in the Occupation of Germany, 1944–1946.* Washington, DC: Center for Military History, 1985.

Zimmermann, Hubert. *Money and Security: Troops, Monetary Policy, and West Germany's Relations with the United States and Britain, 1950–1971.* Washington, DC and Cambridge: German Historical Institute and Cambridge University Press, 2002.

Zink, Harold. *American Military Government in Germany.* New York: Macmillan, 1947.

Index

About the Author

ANNI P. BAKER is Assistant Professor of History at Wheaton College. She has also taught at Boston College. Her other publications include *Wiesbaden and the Americans, 1945–2003: A History* (2003). She is currently working on a study of U.S. Army officers' wives in the late 19th and early 20th centuries.